Sustainably Investing in Digital Assets Globally

Sustainably Investing in Digital Assets Globally

Selva Ozelli

WILEY

Published by John Wiley & Sons, Inc., Hoboken, New Jersey.
Published simultaneously in Canada.

For general information on our other products and services or for technical support,
please contact our Customer Care Department within the United States at (800)
762-2974, outside the United States at (317) 572-3993 or fax (317) 572-4002.

Wiley also publishes its books in a variety of electronic formats. Some content that
appears in print may not be available in electronic formats. For more information
about Wiley products, visit our web site at www.wiley.com.

Library of Congress Cataloging-in-Publication Data is Available:

ISBN 9781119885627 (Hardback)
ISBN 9781119885641 (ePDF)
ISBN 9781119885634 (ePub)

Cover Design: Wiley
Cover Images: © J0v43/Shutterstock;
Visual Generation/Shutterstock;
Cristian Baitg/iStockphoto

SKY10035746_081822

Contents

Foreword   ix
Preface   xiii
Acknowledgments   xix
About the Author   xxi

Introduction   1

PART 1: DIGITAL ASSET UTILIZATION AND
            REGULATION IN THE UNITED STATES   7

Chapter 1: About Bitcoin   9

Chapter 2: Ethereum   21

Chapter 3: Initial Coin Offering   27

Chapter 4: New Financial Alternatives   33

Chapter 5: Hedging Bitcoins with Options on the World
              Wide Web   37

Chapter 6: Cryptocurrency Spreads   45

Chapter 7: Altcoin, Stablecoin Utility Coins, and CBDC   51

Chapter 8: Cryptocurrency Tumblers and Mixing Services   59

Chapter 9: The Darknet   63

Chapter 10: Illicit Use of Cryptocurrencies   69

Chapter 11: Cybercrime Task Force   75

Chapter 12: Money Laundering   81

Chapter 13: Theft Hacking and Ransom Payments   93

Chapter 14: Cryptocurrency Bribes   97

Chapter 15: Corruption   101

Chapter 16: US Tax Evasion   103

Chapter 17: Intellectual Property Espionage and
               Cryptocurrency   107

Chapter 18: The US Government Implements Blockchain
               Programs to Improve Transparency and Efficiency 111

Chapter 19: Supply Chain Management with Blockchain Amid
               the COVID Pandemic   117

Chapter 20: Are NFTs Here to Stay?   135

Chapter 21: Regulation of Digital Assets   151

PART 2:   DIGITAL ASSET UTILIZATION AND
            REGULATION AROUND THE WORLD   153

Chapter 22: Portugal   155

Contents vii

Chapter 23: Netherlands   159

Chapter 24: South Africa   165

Chapter 25: Switzerland   169

Chapter 26: Israel   175

Chapter 27: South Korea   181

Chapter 28: Brazil   185

Chapter 29: Canada   191

Chapter 30: Malta   197

Chapter 31: Germany   201

Chapter 32: The United Arab Emirates   209

Chapter 33: Turkey   215

Chapter 34: Singapore   223

Chapter 35: Puerto Rico   229

PART 3:   SOLARIZED AROUND THE WORLD   235

Chapter 36: Is US Environmental Tax Policy Hindering
            Solar Power to Fuel Digital Technologies?   237

Chapter 37: Japan to Solarize Its Burgeoning Digital
            Economy   245

Chapter 38: Green Policy and Crypto Energy Consumption
            in the EU   259

Chapter 39: Chinese Blockchain-Based Mobile Payment
            Revolution   271

Chapter 40: India Is Fostering a Solarized Digital Future   287

Chapter 41: Russia Leads Multinational Stablecoin Initiative   295

Chapter 42: Africa's Solarized Digitalization Agenda in the
Time of Coronavirus 307

Chapter 43: The Need to Report Carbon Emissions Amid
the Coronavirus Pandemic 315

Chapter 44: The Pandemic Year Ends with a Tokenized
Carbon Cap-and-Trade Solution 327

Chapter 45: The UN's COP26 Climate Change Goals Include
Emerging Tech and Carbon Taxes 337

Index 345

Foreword

I recall very clearly the first time I met Selva Ozelli. It was 2017, in New York at an American Bar Association event focused on legal developments in blockchain. At the time, I was a Department of Justice attorney working on illicit finance involving cryptocurrency and I spoke on a panel covering recent US government enforcement actions. Selva asked me a probing question about the department's position on something, and my broad and vetted answer to her in a room full of private practice and defense lawyers taking notes ended up spilling over into a more direct and granular one-on-one conversation after the panel finished. It was the beginning of a lovely friendship.

I was very fortunate that in 2018, Selva wrote an article in the online news publication *Cointelegraph* about my early career prosecuting cryptocurrency-related criminal activity and called me "DOJ's Crypto Czar." Although the role was certainly accurately described, such a title did not technically exist within the federal government. It did, however, quickly attach to me and spread like wildfire, with friends and colleagues using the title to tease me relentlessly. But my experience with Selva in navigating that piece and the countless articles she wrote on cryptocurrency and blockchain topics revealed that she is an author to be trusted, writing with precision, purpose, and always with the goal of educating and truth seeking.

One of the most interesting things about Selva is her unique mix of talents. Although introduced to me initially as a writer, she is trained as an accountant and international tax lawyer and has worked for many years in the corporate world as a tax expert. During the pandemic, I discovered her love and aptitude for art and the environment through her series of paintings entitled "Art in the Time of Corona—Recovery Roses." I found the paintings she created and exhibited virtually to be emotionally inspired and expressive representations of pandemic pain and optimism that explored whether climate change caused by carbon emissions might be one reason for such a terrible global COVID-19 pandemic scenario. This creative side of Selva peppers everything that she does, and in my opinion, makes her accomplished at breathing life into any topic she writes about. In addition, the tax attorney side of her means that you also get a data-driven and carefully researched truth when she speaks and writes.

This is why in writing *Sustainably Investing in Digital Assets Globally*, Selva Ozelli is well-suited to explain in an understandable way how blockchain activity has evolved and where it is going and to lay out the risks of digital assets such as cryptocurrencies. There's much hype in the blockchain space, both on the detractor and supporter sides, and many simply choose to ignore this groundbreaking innovative technology because it may seem highly technical and difficult to comprehend or not a market reality which will persist. This would be a mistake, however, because the next iteration of the internet, often referred to as web3, is being built on, with, and around blockchain technology—and its effects will soon permeate everything in our daily lives. Understanding the path of this technology, from its early notorious appearances in illicit finance to its promise in digital ownership and identity, supply chain efficiency and speed, privacy, financial inclusion, building community interactions and decision-making, and solving problems like compliance and capital formation in finance is really important. It is this potential of the technology, coupled with the advantageous mechanics of how blockchains and their attendant codes and infrastructures work, that make digital assets such an exciting asset class. As with any new financial product, understanding the risks and rewards is key. Selva's tax and finance experience and mature perspective on crypto make this book a solid choice for anyone seeking to learn about the technology in order to make well-informed decisions; her coverage of its history, the rapidly developing regulatory landscape, and environmental sustainability issues also make it a fascinating read.

Michele R. Korver
Head of Regulatory, a16z crypto

Preface

In 2017, the year Bitcoin's price surged from $1,000 to $20,000 in a single year, increasing 20-fold, I received an invitation to make a presentation concerning FCPA compliance by a technology company based in Ireland—My Compliance Office.[1] While preparing my presentation for My Compliance Office, I stumbled upon three US Department of Justice (DOJ) cases that alerted me to the existence of cryptocurrencies. Via these cases, I also met two of the DOJ's first cryptocurrency experts, Michele Korver[2] and GrantRabenn,[3] who prosecuted crypto money laundering and cybercrime cases, and who were instrumental in shaping the cryptocurrency seizure and forfeiture policy and legislation and now work in the industry, focusing on keeping emerging blockchain technologies safe from illicit use.

Hansa and AlphaBay

July 20, 2017, saw the concurrent shuttering of the Netherlands-based Hansa and Thailand-based AlphaBay, two dark-web markets known for laundering illicit cryptocurrency proceeds from the sale of narcotics and weapons, along with the arrest of their operators in Thailand and Germany and the seizure of their servers in the Netherlands, Germany, Lithuania, and Canada.[4]

The synchronized crackdown on the payments made with cryptocurrencies by fraudsters around the globe involved law enforcement authorities from the United States (the DOJ, the Federal Bureau of Investigations [FBI], the Drug Enforcement Agency [DEA], and the Internal Revenue Service—Criminal Investigations [IRS CI]), Europol, and 11 other countries (the Netherlands, the UK, France, Lithuania, Canada, Germany, Thailand, Cyprus, Liechtenstein, Antigua and Barbuda, and Belgium).

A Europol press release noted the importance of the coordinated, international strategy to take down both Hansa and AlphaBay:

> [It] involved taking covert control of Hansa under Dutch judicial authority a month ago, which allowed Dutch police to monitor the activity of users without their knowledge, and then shutting down AlphaBay during the same period. It meant the Dutch police could identify and disrupt the regular criminal activity on Hansa but then also sweep up all those new users displaced from AlphaBay who were looking for a new trading platform. . . . As a law enforcement strategy, leveraging the combined operational and technical strengths of multiple agencies in the US and Europe, it has been an extraordinary success and a stark illustration of the collective power the global law enforcement community can bring to disrupt major criminal activity.[5]

Likewise, the DOJ issued a release quoting an IRS CI official who noted that his organization's unique expertise, in coordination with other domestic and international law enforcement partners, allowed them "to help shine a bright light on the accounts and customers of this shadowy, black marketplace, and we intend to continue pursuing these kinds of criminals no matter where they hide."[6]

BTC-e

On July 26, 2017, six days after the shuttering of dark-web markets AlphaBay and Hansa, came a second worldwide, synchronized law enforcement operation aimed at shutting down an illicit bitcoin market/scheme. The target was Bulgaria-based bitcoin exchange BTC-e which was one of the world's largest virtual currency exchanges by volume at the time. It was the U.S. Treasury Department Financial Crimes Enforcement Network's (FinCEN) first action in collaboration with the DOJ, IRS CI, FBI, Federal Deposit Insurance Corporation (FDIC), US Secret Service, US Immigration and Customs Enforcement, the Office of the Inspector General, and Greek law enforcement against a foreign money service business (MSB).

In a 21-count indictment alleging hundreds of millions in civil monetary penalties, FinCEN and the DOJ charged BTC-e and BTC-e's Russian head, Alexander Vinnik, with operating a purported $4 billion international money-laundering scheme. On the same day, Vinnik was arrested on vacation and jailed by Greek law enforcement in coordination with US regulators on US money laundering (AML) charges.

The DOJ's 21-count indictment painted BTC-e, operated by Vinnik, as a hub of illicit activity. FinCEN for the first time imposed civil penalties on a foreign-located MSB and its operator of more than $110 million against BTC-e for willfully violating US AML laws, and $12 million against Vinnik for his role in the AML violations.

These three cases led me to research cryptocurrencies and their underlying blockchain technology. I found out that blockchain technology's main disruptive element in the global commercial, financial, and economic ecosystem was its ability to eliminate the necessity to trust intermediaries to certify a transaction.

During 2017, I began writing articles and special reports for Bloomberg, *Tax Notes International*, *FCPA Blog*, *PV Magazine*, and a monthly column for *Cointelegraph*, a leading cryptocurrency publication published in 11 languages (Arabic, Chinese, English, French, German, Italian, Japanese, Korean, Portuguese, Spanish, and Turkish) with a focus on the tax, regulatory, and sustainability aspects of blockchain technology and cryptocurrencies hoping that I could educate the public concerning cryptocurrencies as part of "The Global Token Awareness Initiative"[7] founded by Wiley author William Mougayar. I wanted to become a voice supporting a globally coordinated approach to the regulation and sustainability of this globally and urgently booming industry so it had a chance to flourish.

G20 and OECD countries have been acting in tandem in regard to crypto sustainability and regulatory issues. As the World Economic Forum in its 2022 Global Risks Report points out, environmental and climate-change-related risks account for three of the top risks.[8] In a blog post, the International Monetary Fund (IMF) urges crypto regulation to be globally comprehensive, consistent, and coordinated.[9]

With the worldwide regulation of digital assets, more institutional investors are investing in them. In this book, I explore how to safely invest in cryptocurrencies and how they have been used by illicit operators throughout the United States and the world and how legitimate investors have sought to limit their exposure to illegal activity.

Readers will also find comprehensive treatments of US-based and global cryptocurrency regulations, as well as:

- Advice for investors concerned about the environmental sustainability of blockchain technology but who still wish to invest in cryptocurrencies
- Information about a variety of countries and governments that have explored and implemented various cryptocurrency initiatives inside their own borders
- Discussions surrounding the drive by many central banks to introduce a digital currency, in addition to the surging popularity of nonfungible tokens

Notes

1. https://mco.mycomplianceoffice.com/mco-webinar/is-this-bribe-tax-deductible
2. https://cointelegraph.com/news/meet-doj-s-crypto-czar-expert-take; https://cointelegraph.com/news/doj-s-crypto-czar-joins-fincen-in-brand-new-role-why-it-matters; https://www.linkedin.com/in/michele-korver-9774054/
3. https://www.linkedin.com/in/grant-rabenn-1081628/; https://www.justice.gov/opa/pr/alphabay-largest-online-dark-market-shut-down
4. US Department of Justice, "AlphaBay, the Largest Online 'Dark Market,' Shut Down" (July 20, 2017); and Europol release, "Massive Blow to Criminal Dark Web Activities After Globally Coordinated Operation" (July 20, 2017).
5. Europol release, "Massive Blow to Criminal Dark Web Activities after Globally Coordinated Operation," July 20, 2017.
6. US Department of Justice, "AlphaBay, the Largest Online 'Dark Market,' Shut Down," July 20, 2017.
7. http://startupmanagement.org/2017/10/10/the-global-token-awareness-initiative/
8. https://www.weforum.org/agenda/2022/01/global-risks-report-climate-change-covid19/
9. https://blogs.imf.org/2021/12/09/global-crypto-regulation-should-be-comprehensive-consistent-and-coordinated/

Acknowledgments

I thank everyone who granted me interviews, and my editors at numerous publications whose collective work is reflected in this book. And I dedicate my book to my family, my teachers and editors in life.

About the Author

Selva Ozelli, Esq., CPA, is an executive with experience dealing with highly complex issues in the field of international taxation and related matters within the banking, securities, fintech, alternative and traditional investment funds, and aerospace industries. Her first-of-its-kind legal analyses published in journals and tax treatises globally altered the transnational adjudication and disclosure of (1) corporate governance violations and (2) lobbying/bribery payments.

Her writings on the topic of digitization, sustainability, and tax/regulatory policy are translated into 34 languages and republished by over 200 publications around the world.

She is frequently quoted in mainstream media such as Thomson Reuters, the *Financial Times*, the *New York Times*, *Accounting Today*, and *Cointelegraph*. She has appeard on CBS News[1] as well as *Cointelegraph*'s documentary about crypto in the United States, Part I.[2]

Selva is also an award-winning artist whose work has been acknowledged in 18 international art contests and exhibited in over 100 art shows by the United Nations, numerous museums, ministries, and NGOs across the world.[3]

Notes

1. https://www.youtube.com/watch?v=1fCzTLFkbTE
2. https://www.youtube.com/watch?v=i6uz4MFtHIo&t=4s
3. https://www.talenthouse.com/selva-ozelli/about

Introduction

My article "Is This Bribe Deductible? Tax Implications of the U.S. Foreign Corrupt Practices Act," in *Tax Notes International* on December 17, 2007, rendered the Foreign Corrupt Practices Act (FCPA)—via tax treaties—enforceable around the world.

In 2017, the year Bitcoin's price surged from $1,000 to $20,000 in a single year, increasing 20-fold, I received an invitation to make a presentation concerning FCPA compliance by a technology company based in Ireland—My Compliance Office.[1] While preparing my presentation for My Compliance Office, I stumbled upon three U.S. Department of Justice (DOJ) cases— Hansa, AlphaBay, and BTC-e—that alerted me to the existence of cryptocurrencies.

These three cases led me to research cryptocurrencies and their underlying blockchain technology. I found out that blockchain technology's main disruptive element in the global commercial and economic ecosystem was its ability to eliminate the necessity to trust intermediaries—such as banks—to certify a financial transaction.

During 2017, I began writing articles and special reports for Bloomberg, *Tax Notes International*, *FCPA Blog*, and *PV Magazine* and a monthly column for *Cointelegraph*, a leading cryptocurrency publication published in 11 languages (Arabic, Chinese, English, French, German, Italian, Japanese, Korean, Portuguese, Spanish, and Turkish) with a focus on the tax, regulatory, and sustainability aspects of blockchain technology and cryptocurrencies, hoping that I could be a voice supporting a globally coordinated approach to the regulation and sustainability of this globally and urgently booming industry in light of the COVID-19 pandemic.

G20 and OECD countries have been acting in tandem in regard to crypto sustainability and regulation. The World Economic Forum in its 2022 Global Risks Report points out that environmental and climate-change-related risks account for three of the top risks.[2] In a blog post, the International Monetary Fund (IMF) urges crypto regulation to be globally comprehensive, consistent, and coordinated.[3]

Structure of the Book

This book is structured in three parts consisting of 45 chapters.

Part I: Chapters 1 through 21

The first part of the book provides information concerning digital asset investment risks and illicit use, as well as their regulation in the United States.

Cryptocurrency across the world

(Over 300 million crypto users worldwide)

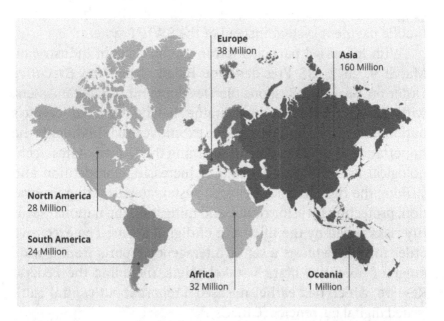

Europe
38 Million

Asia
160 Million

North America
28 Million

South America
24 Million

Africa
32 Million

Oceania
1 Million

cointelegraph.com

SOURCE: Oddup; *Cointelegraph*.

The coronavirus pandemic that began in 2020 expedited the digitization of the global economy. During the 2021 bull market, the art world embraced nonfungible tokens (NFTs), with sale volumes surging 1,000%. People began using NFTs in a multitude of areas: visual arts, videos, music, collectibles, to raise brand awareness, gaming, publishing, carbon trading, fundraising, and donations. Simultaneously, a growing number of US cities and companies began developing cryptocurrencies and NFTs (collectively, "digital assets"), with regional initiatives taking shape. At the US corporate level, Meta's "Zuck Bucks" coin is expected to function within Facebook and Instagram.[4] At the same time, local chains of US-based companies Starbucks, Subway, and McDonald's are trying out stablecoins through a pilot program launched by the People's Bank of China based on its mobile payment system instead of the SWIFT system.

With increased participation in the blockchain industry, on March 9, 2022, US President Joe Biden signed the Executive Order on Ensuring Responsible Development of Digital Assets, with Russia's invasion of Ukraine having elevated crypto's national security significance. The executive order highlights the importance of digital assets in retaining the United States' technological leadership in a world of increasing competition and striking the right balance between sustainably fostering innovation, protecting investor rights, and mitigating the national security risks posed by the illicit use of digital assets. The executive order further requests a set of interagency reports from a wide range of executive branch stakeholders, including the Federal Reserve, which had earlier released a report about central bank issued digital currencies (CBDCs).[5]

In the United States, the race to build out the metaverse and Web3 is on, despite the severe crypto market downturn during 2022.[6]

Part II: Chapters 22 through 35

The second part of the book provides information concerning digital asset investment risks and illicit use, as well as their regulation, in 14 countries around the world. According to the Atlantic Council, 87 countries out of 200 are exploring a CBDC.[7]

Venezuela issued the first state-backed digital stablecoin, the Petro, which is now mandatory for gas stations in the country to support. Other nations sanctioned by the United States, such as North Korea, Iran and Cuba, are devoting significant technical resources to develop CBDCs.

The Bank of Lithuania is slated to issue a batch of digital blockchain-based collector coins from a purpose-built e-shop that can be redeemed for physical coins. While in Senegal, Grammy-nominated singer Akon is expected to launch Akoin, a cryptocurrency that will be the local currency in Akon City, a 2,000-acre development project.

The Saudi Arabian Monetary Authority is creating a binational digital currency with the United Arab Emirates called Aber to be used for cross-border transactions, to inject liquidity into local banks via blockchain technology.

In 2021, in an unprecedented move, El Salvador gave Bitcoin (BTC) the status of legal tender, the first country in the world to do so. The second country in the world to adopt Bitcoin as official currency, in 2022, was the Central African Republic.

Countries are in a global race to emerge as the crypto-friendliest venue for investors as well as blockchain, metaverse, and Web3 developers.

Part III: Chapters 36 through 45

The third part of the book provides information concerning the sustainable development of energy-intensive blockchain technology with solar energy applications, given that the top six largest CO_2 emitters of our world have plans to roll out CBDCs as well as multinational digital currencies.

The People's Bank of China rolled out the digital yuan, distributed person to person via a mobile payment system utilizing Huawei's 5G technology, with reports saying that as of June 2022, the use had increased by 1,800% from the previous year.[8] China's vast Belt and Road Initiative and the yuan's inclusion in the Special Drawing Rights currency basket (which is based on five currencies: the dollar, the euro, the yuan, the Japanese yen, and the British pound) signifies the internationalization of the yuan, which has officially become one of the world's reserve currencies. Accordingly, China has been collaborating with many countries to develop mobile blockchain-based "cross-border payment networks." The East Asia digital currency initiative is expected to consist of the yuan, the yen, the Hong Kong dollar, and the South Korean won, with the yuan and yen accounting for about 60% and 20% of the digital currency's value, respectively. China is also collaborating with Singapore's central bank and financial regulatory authority to develop a CBDC.

Russia is leading another multinational digital currency initiative with BRICS and Eurasian Economic Union countries. During 2022, the initiative is scheduled to issue CBDCs that will be exchanged on smartphones, outside of the SWIFT and CHIPS systems.

In the eurozone, the Banque de France has become the first to successfully trial a digital euro that is operational on a blockchain, according to an announcement.[9]

Notes

1. https://mco.mycomplianceoffice.com/mco-webinar/is-this-bribe-tax-deductible
2. https://www.weforum.org/agenda/2022/01/global-risks-report-climate-change-covid19/
3. https://blogs.imf.org/2021/12/09/global-crypto-regulation-should-be-comprehensive-consistent-and-coordinated/
4. https://cryptopotato.com/meta-unveils-metaverse-monetizing-tools-for-facebook-and-instagram-creators/; https://www.ft.com/content/50fbe9ba-32c8-4caf-a34e-234031019371
5. https://cointelegraph.com/news/the-world-has-synchronized-on-russian-crypto-sanctions
6. https://cointelegraph.com/news/global-web3-metaverse-and-tax-initiatives-continue-in-the-face-of-a-market-meltdown
7. https://www.atlanticcouncil.org/cbdctracker/
8. https://beincrypto.com/digital-yuan-usage-in-china-leaps-1800-in-past-12-months/
9. https://www.banque-france.fr/en/communique-de-presse/banque-de-france-has-successfully-completed-first-tranche-its-experimentation-programme-central-bank

Part 1

Digital Asset Utilization and Regulation in the United States

Chapter 1

About Bitcoin

Computer engineer Wei Dai first described the cryptocurrency concept on the Cypherpunks mailing list in 1998. He envisioned a new form of money using cryptography, rather than a central issuing authority, to control its creation and transactions.

In 2003, Turkish-American Emin Gun Sirer, CEO of AvaLabs, professor at Cornell University, and co-director of Initiative for Cryptocurrencies and Smart Contracts (IC3), designed the first cryptocurrency, "Karma," based on a proof-of-work protocol six years earlier than the launch of Bitcoin. Since 2019 he has also developed Avalanche, an ecofriendly blockchain platform with smart contract capabilities which is one of the most promising blockchain platforms given the focus on environment and social governance investing, according to cryptocurrency billionaire Sam Bankman-Fried.[1]

In 2008, a programmer (or group of programmers) using the pseudonym Satoshi Nakamoto and purporting to be from Japan published a paper on the Bitcoin concept to launch in 2009 as a decentralized, unlicensed, worldwide cryptocurrency transfer system based on a proof-of-work protocol that allowed anyone with an internet connection to participate.

Bitcoin (BTC) is a blockchain-based peer-to-peer (P2P) system for online transactions, and, when paired with third-party services, allows users to mine, buy, sell, or accept cryptocurrencies transnationally via the internet without being tied to a particular country's identity, capital controls, currency depreciation and devaluations, currency conversions, government seizures, or environmental controls. Unlike money, BTC is not issued or regulated by any government—it can be mined by investors. It is not handled by middlemen such as the Federal Reserve Bank or represented by bank notes or any other physical note.

Strictly speaking, cryptocurrencies are nothing more than amounts associated with web addresses—unique strings of letters and numbers. For example, 1Ez69SnzzmePmZX3WpEzM KTrcBF2gpNQ55 represented nearly 30,000 BTCs, worth about $20 million, when seized by the Federal Bureau of Investigations (FBI) during the Bitcoin dark-web market shutdown of the Silk Road in October 2013. And cryptocurrencies' decentralized feature makes detecting suspicious activity, identifying users, and obtaining transaction records problematic for law enforcement.

BTC originally was used in the online gaming industry, but the increasing popularity of cryptocurrencies allows users to pay for goods, services, and even real estate in high-end Dubai real estate projects, in the same way fiat currencies do. More than 100,000 merchants worldwide accept cryptocurrencies for payment; some of the companies are Mastercard, Pavilion Hotels & Resorts, AXA Insurance, Microsoft, Starbucks, Tesla, Amazon, Visa, PayPal, AirBaltic, Sotheby's, Coca Cola, LOT Polish Airlines, Expedia, and Lush.[2]

Wallet

To possess cryptocurrency, an investor must set up a wallet. A wallet might be under the investor's exclusive control (unhosted wallets), or they might be custodial wallets hosted by a third-party service provider, such as an institutional exchange.

Unhosted/noncustodial wallets are generally software installed on a computer that can be accessed from a desktop or a smartphone, and come with two important pieces of information: a public and a private key.[3] A public key is how an investor sends and receives money to their account—like a bank account number. This is also called a "wallet address." The private key is like a bank password, allowing an investor to access their wallet.

The noncustodial wallet is controlled by the investor, who can receive, send, and exchange their cryptocurrency person-to-person (P2P) with other unhosted wallets, or on an exchange platform, without revealing their identity. In a noncustodial wallet, the investor has sole control of the password and private keys, which in turn control their cryptocurrency and prove the funds are theirs.

With a custodial wallet, a third party such as a cryptocurrency exchange controls investors passwords and private keys. Most custodial wallets are web-based exchange wallets, which are subject to the risk of hacks. Some cryptocurrency exchanges offer the investor the option of keeping their cryptocurrencies in a hot wallet in addition to letting the investor keep their cryptocurrencies in a custodial wallet. Some due diligence is required before choosing an exchange.[4]

A hot wallet is a noncustodial software wallet that is always connected to the internet, making it easy to transfer cryptocurrencies back to an exchange to make more trades or to cash out. But because of the internet connection, hot wallets are not as protected from hacks as their counterparts—cold wallets. A cold (hardware) wallet is physical, typically not connected to the internet, so while it may be more secure against hacks, it's less convenient to use.

As the Chainalysis team explains, "When it comes to crypto-currency theft, industry observers tend to focus on attacks against large organizations—namely hacks of cryptocurrency exchanges or ransomware attacks against critical infrastructure. But over the last few years, we've observed hackers using malware to steal smaller amounts of cryptocurrency from individual users."[5]

Using malware to steal or extort cryptocurrency is nothing new. In fact, nearly all ransomware strains are initially deliv-ered to victims' devices through malware, and many large-scale exchange hacks also involve malware. But these attacks take careful planning and skill to pull off, as they're typically tar-geted at deep-pocketed, professional organizations and, if suc-cessful, require hackers to launder large sums of cryptocurrency. With other types of malware, less sophisticated hackers can take a cheaper "spray-and-pray" approach, spamming millions of potential victims and stealing smaller amounts from each indi-vidual tricked into downloading the malware. Many of these malware strains are available for purchase on the darknet, mak-ing it even easier for less sophisticated hackers to deploy them against victims.

Undoubtedly, investors want to choose a digital wallet they can trust with their digital assets. Kosala Hemachandra, CEO and founder of MyEtherWallet (MEW), believes "the cryptocurrency community needs to do a better job educating investors to the risks and steps that they can take to keep their cryptocurrency funds secure. After stealing almost $15 million in Ethereum from crypto.com from custodial wallets, hackers laundered the proceeds into an 'ethereum mixer,' known as a 'Tornado Crash.' These mixers run interference on the blockchain, in this case, Ethereum, leaving investors unable to track and recover their stolen funds. MEW, a noncustodial wallet, not only practices double encryption to ensure the highest level of protection, but also prioritizes taking the right precautions to ensure investors crypto assets are safe."[6]

Investors who use noncustodial wallets for better protection can nevertheless still lose their private key to their wallet or send their digital assets cross-chain to the wrong address. In these instances, Charles Brooks, cofounder of Crypto Asset Recovery, explains, "If you provide us with a copy of your wallet and your best guesses as to what your password is, we will use your password guesses to 'brute force' your password. For example, an investor used a non-custodial wallet company called Blockchain .com, which made it possible to download a wallet backup, which is essentially an encrypted version of his private key. After the investor provided Crypto Asset Recovery with a series of password guesses, we were able to find the password that decrypted the investor's wallet backup, which allowed the investor to regain access to his Bitcoin investment. We are able to assist investors with cross-chain transaction recoveries as well."[7]

The Swiss did not want BTC to undermine the Swiss banking system, which housed around $2 trillion, or 27%, of offshore wealth, and reshape the financial landscape after the Swiss repealed their bank secrecy rules. In a landmark ruling on January 30, 2017, the Swiss Financial Market Supervisory Authority (FINMA) approved Silicon Valley–based Xapo, a Bitcoin wallet, to operate in Switzerland, marking the first regulatory step forward for companies that provide safekeeping for the cryptocurrency in their country.

Ever since, the high number of internet users who have a propensity for smartphone and mobile payments has played a key role in the explosive development of the Bitcoin-based fintech sector. A London-based innovative technology company, d.code:it, "designs first of its kind financial services applications for smartphones" while Silicon Valley–based technology company Abra develops "Bitcoin-based digital wallet applications to buy, sell, store, send, and receive Bitcoin deposits or alternatively in over 50 fiat currencies, and facilitate Bitcoin transfers between any two smartphones around the world." Abra smartphone users can even leverage up and buy Bitcoins on their smartphones with their American Express card.[8]

Bitcoin Mining

Bitcoin/cryptocurrency mining is the process by which new Bitcoins or cryptocurrencies that are based on proof-of-work protocol are entered into circulation. Mining is costly, energy intensive, and only sporadically rewarding. It is performed using sophisticated hardware that solves extremely complex computational math problems. The first computer to find the solution to the problem is awarded the next block of Bitcoins/cryptocurrencies.

Up until China's Bitcoin mining ban in May 2021, most Bitcoin mining in the world occurred in China according to IP addresses from so-called hashers that used certain Bitcoin mining pools.[9] Other top Bitcoin mining countries are Canada, Germany, Iran, Ireland, Kazakhstan, Malaysia, Russia, the United States, and Venezuela.

Mining is appealing to investors because miners are rewarded with new Bitcoins or Ethers. But this comes at a great cost to the environment, according to lawmakers in the United States and the EU since mining undermines global efforts to combat climate change in accordance with the Paris Agreement.[10]

During 2021, Elon Musk, CEO of Tesla, an electric car, solar panel, and clean energy storage company, discontinued the Bitcoin payment option at Tesla, after admitting in an interview in 2019 that Bitcoin's structure is "quite brilliant" and it is "a far better way to transfer value than pieces of paper" pointing the way to the future of money.[11] Mr. Musk cautioned that neverthe-less "one of the downsides of Bitcoin mining is that computa-tionally it is quite energy intensive" as it metabolizes electricity into money.

When the electricity used for mining Bitcoin and other proof-of-work protocoled cryptocurrencies is produced from coal or other fossil fuels that causes the most CO_2 and other green-house gas pollution, the toll cryptocurrency mining takes on the environment—with destruction manifesting in various parts of the world—is immeasurable.

A stark example of this environmental cost in the context of Bitcoin occurred on September 4, 2017—only five months after 195 countries signed on to the United Nations Framework Con-vention on Climate Change (UNFCCC), Paris Agreement—and involved events in two completely different parts of the world. These events—China's Bitcoin ban and the Caribbean's hur-ricane Irma, or "Irmageddon"—were the two most researched terms on Google during 2017, with an invisible thread connect-ing them to each other.

China's Bitcoin Ban

On September 4, 2017, China's central bank announced that it would ban initial coin offerings (ICOs) (Chapter 3, Initial Coin Offerings) and shut down all domestic Bitcoin/cryptocurrency exchanges by month-end, delivering a blow to a once-thriving industry of commercial trading and cryptocurrency mining, which began taking off four years earlier. At the time, China accounted for as much as 90% of all of world's cryptocurrency trading volume of more than 335,000 daily transactions, and 70 Selva Ozelli, "About Selva Ozelli," Talenthouse, April, 2020 of all cryptocurrency mining, as well as manufacturing of cryptocur-rency mining machines.

On March 14, 2017, Chinese President Xi Jinping announced that he was going to establish the "digital silk road of the twenty-first century" and revolutionize a blockchain-based mobile cross-border payment system, leading a global force in several areas of the blockchain-based digital economy. Encouraged by this news, investors from all over the world flocked to buy Bitcoin—which ranked as the world's best performing currency in six out of the eight years since its debut in 2009—to capture once-in-a-lifetime gains. Rumors of Bitcoin Mania, possibly surpassing Tulip Mania, spread across the World Wide Web with a mixture of fear and excitement.

Around-the-clock cryptocurrency trading and wider adoption kept pushing up Bitcoin's price, which rose 20-fold from $1,000 at the beginning of the year to $20,000 by the third week of December. This created an exponential demand for cheap coal-fueled electricity for cryptocurrency mining, which required nearly 100,000 times more computing power than the world's 500 fastest supercomputers, which in turn created more CO_2 and other greenhouse gas pollution. Chinese CO_2 and greenhouse emissions reached a new high during 2017, making China the world's largest greenhouse gas emitter, a title the country continued to hold on to during 2018.

On June 1, 2017, when then-President Donald Trump announced that the United States was pulling out of the UNFCCC Paris Agreement, which lacks an enforcement mechanism, China—both the largest consumer of coal and the largest solar technology manufacturer—clenched the mantle of world leadership on climate change.

A new paper suggests that the UNFCCC Paris Agreement's aim of limiting average global temperature increases to 1.5 degrees Celsius is likely to miss the mark since it requires substantial changes to individual countries' plans to accomplish these measures. Such measures are still vague and hard to implement within the required deadlines. Accordingly, China's choice between coal and solar energy is likely to have an impactful and lasting effect on global warming.

"Coal pollution has real consequences for our environment and public health. While the White House props up the coal industry, we've been working w/ partners like @SierraClub to retire plants & lead the transition to clean energy," explained Michael R. Bloomberg, in a tweet. Bloomberg serves as the U.N.'s Special Envoy for Climate Action. Bloomberg has given away $6.4 billion of his own money to shutter coal-fired power plants and worked across sectors and with a variety of partners globally to actuate change in existing energy systems, forcing dirty fuels out of the energy mix and lowering the policy and market barriers to renewables, efficiency, and other clean, low-carbon, solar energy solutions.

"Irmageddon" Slams the Saints

Amid levels of heat-trapping greenhouse gases in the atmosphere reaching a record high, sea levels rising, oceans acidifying, and 18 back-to-back named storms—from Tropical Storm Arlene to Tropical Storm Rina—became the "new normal" in the Caribbean during 2017. Ten of these storms transformed into hurricanes, and five of those hurricanes—Harvey, Irma, Jose, Lee, and Maria—attained hyperactive and catastrophic status.

As China banned Bitcoin transactions, in the Caribbean on September 4, 2017, Hurricane Irma—which formed on the heels of Hurricane Harvey—intensified to become a category 5 storm that was roughly 400 miles in diameter. For the next eight days, spinning counterclockwise around its eye with a force of 200-mile-per-hour winds, Irmageddon began tearing through the Caribbean, downing the operational and largely fossil fuel–powered electric grids along the way, leaving in its wake a trail of calamitous damage of $202 billion, with up to 60% of homes and 400 boats destroyed and at least 134 dead.

Irma was the strongest annular hurricane observed in the Caribbean on record and the second most intense tropical cyclone worldwide during 2017. Irmageddon hit particularly hard in the northeastern Caribbean, the Florida Keys, Antigua and Barbuda, Anguilla, the British Virgin Islands, St. Barthélemy, St. Martin, the US Virgin Islands, Puerto Rico, the Dominican Republic, Haiti, Cuba, the Bahamas, Turks and Caicos, and other islands in the Caribbean Sea—"these islands from the ocean which stood strong for centuries," as country music artist Kenny Chesney described the region in a song.

Survivors on St. John, the smallest of the three main US Virgin Islands, tackled the rebuilding efforts resiliently and creatively. After being cut off from power for six weeks, a survivor used debris from a nearby home to spell out "Send Tesla" on the ground to attract solar power installations to the island to replace fossil fuel electric grids. Chesney, who solemnly stumbled upon the wreckage of what once was his home, which served as "a huge part of my music, my creative spirit, and my soul," composed the *Song for the Saints* album. The proceeds from this album and tour are funding Chesney's Love for Love City Foundation to finance post-Irmageddon rescue and rebuilding projects in the US Virgin Islands that include solar power projects. "Join the sinner's choir singing a song for the saints by donating your cryptocurrencies," urged Kim Ledger, the foundation's administrator.[12]

Notes

1. https://markets.businessinsider.com/news/currencies/sam-bankman-fried-names-ethereum-killers-solana-avalanche-big-blockchains-2022-1
2. https://www.euronews.com/next/2021/12/04/paying-with-cryptocurrencies-these-are-the-major-companies-that-accept-cryptos-as-payment
3. https://time.com/nextadvisor/investing/cryptocurrency/best-bitcoin-cryptocurrency-wallet/
4. https://time.com/nextadvisor/investing/cryptocurrency/what-are-cryptocurrency-exchanges/
5. https://blog.chainalysis.com/reports/2022-crypto-crime-report-preview-malware/
6. https://www.myetherwallet.com
7. https://cryptoassetrecovery.com
8. Selva Ozelli, "Regulations Fall on Bitcoin Around the World," My Compliance Office, 2017.
9. https://www.statista.com/statistics/1200477/bitcoin-mining-by-country/
10. https://gizmodo.com/european-union-regulator-proof-of-work-bitcoin-ethereum-1848384679
11. https://cointelegraph.com/news/bitcoin-loses-6-in-an-hour-after-tesla-drops-payments-over-carbon-concerns
12. https://news.bloombergtax.com/daily-tax-report/insight-crypto-and-a-song-for-the-saints

Chapter 2
Ethereum

Vitalik Buterin is the cofounder of the Ethereum block-chain, a second-generation open source software platform with a general scripting language, which created a protocol for building reliable decentralized trusted networks. It extends the functionality of Satoshi Nakamoto's blockchain design, which powered decentralized peer-to-peer Bitcoin payment by adding smart contracts, also called scripting.[1]

This feature allows the platform to store and run computer programs and enables developers to build and deploy decentralized applications and create whatever operations they want with a permanent, trusted record of assets and transactions.

The first public Ethereum-backed network went live in 2015 and supports ether (ETH), currently the second-highest-valued cryptocurrency at $481 billion.[2] Ethereum's initial coin offering (ICO) has been one of the most successful, with over 778,000% in gains from 2015 to 2022. The Ethereum network is used by application developers, and ETH is used to pay for transaction fees and services on the Ethereum network.

Smart Contract Technology

The blockchain's main disruptive element in today's commercial and economic ecosystem is its ability to eliminate the need to trust intermediaries to certify a transaction. This feature lends Ethereum blockchain well to being used to create smart contracts.

Smart contracts are computer protocols, or algorithms, that can verify the negotiation process or performance of contracts—to the extent that legal relationships can be reduced neatly into code—whereby clauses are automatically enforced once the preprogrammed conditions are satisfied. These are coded instructions that execute on the occurrence of an event.

"'Smart contracts' can automatically move digital assets, including 'contracts' according to arbitrary prespecified rules, simply by writing up the logic in a few lines of code," explained Vitalik Buterin.

He added, "All transactions under blockchain come with auditable trails of cryptographic proofs. Rather than simply hoping that the parties we interact with behave honorably, we are building blockchains that inherently build the properties in the system in such a way that they will keep functioning with the guarantees that we expect, even if many of the actors involved are corrupt."[3]

Worldwide Adoption of Ethereum

The Ethereum platform has been adopted worldwide, as the platform can be utilized in multiple applications. "For the second year in a row, Ethereum is the world's most in-demand blockchain. . . . Ethereum is the foundation for a digital civilization. It is hardened, secure, and reliable. It is the bedrock necessary to support the digital cities being built on top of it. Those cities are growing fast. Because Ethereum is open to everyone, many different users have found reasons to build on it:

- Markets use it as financial infrastructure.
- Artists use it to give permanence to their work.
- Assets use it as a settlement layer.

Communities use it to govern shared resources," said Josh Stark in his 2021 Year in Ethereum report.[4]

"We are building a bridge between the human readability of cryptographic addresses and machine readability. While some others are working similar platforms that they feel may have their own advantages, the size of the development teams around Ethereum ballooned with initial spikes in interest to something larger than anything else in the space. With that, application development, innovation in scaling and other areas followed the trend, thereby creating a snowball effect," added Nick Johnson, founder of the Ethereum Name Service.[5]

Energy Efficiency of Ethereum

Proof-of-work blockchain algorithms that secure many cryptocurrencies, including BTC and ETH, are being used more and more around the world. One shared concern among world leaders is the high carbon emissions that are associated with mining these cryptocurrencies.

The US House of Representatives' Energy and Commerce Committee held a congressional hearing about cryptocurrency's carbon footprint and environmental impact, focusing on proof-of-work blockchain.[6] The hearing came one day after E&E News revealed that the Environmental Protection Agency began evaluating coal-powered power plants' use in energizing BTC mining.[7]

There are two major consensus mechanisms—algorithms used by blockchain platforms that allow the network to work together and stay secure: proof-of-work, which is high energy use, and proof-of-stake, which is energy efficient. These methods are used to secure the blockchain, verify transactions, include transactions in the history of the blockchain, and create new cryptocurrencies.

Carl Beekuizen of the Ethereum Foundation explained, "Ethereum network will be completing the transition from Proof-of-Work to Proof-of-Stake in the upcoming months." This will result in Ethereum's energy usage to decrease by ~99.95%.[8] Tim Beiko of the Ethereum Foundation added that "Ethereum's transition to proof of stake—The Merge—is designed to have minimal impact on how Ethereum operates for end users, smart contracts and dapps," in essence, Ethereum's application layer.[9]

Fee Structure of Ethereum

Ethereum network is the most used platform around the world, according to David Mihal's CryptoFees.info.[10] To make the platform available to an even wider audience, in a blog post on January 5, 2022, Vitalik Buterin proposed a new "multidimensional" Ethereum fee structure that offers users different gas prices for different resource usage to streamline the current fee structure for Ethereum network. He noted in his new fee proposal titled "Multidimensional EIP-1559"[11] that different resources in the Ethereum Virtual Machine (EVM) have different demands in terms of gas usage and cited examples of block data storage, witness data storage, and block state size changes.[12] A recent Reddit AMA with the Ethereum Foundation's Research Team (Vitalik, Danny Ryan, and others) provides greater insight into the multidimensional 1559 proposal.[13]

Notes

1. https://github.com/ethereum/wiki/wiki/White-Paper
2. https://coinmarketcap.com/currencies/ethereum/
3. https://cointelegraph.com/news/smart-contracts-are-taking-over-functions-of-lawyers-expert-blog
4. https://stark.mirror.xyz/q3OnsK7mvfGtTQ72nfoxLyEV5lfYO-qUfJIoKBx7BG1I
5. https://cointelegraph.com/news/why-canada-has-emerged-as-a-leading-blockchain-and-crypto-nation-expert-take
6. https://energycommerce.house.gov/committee-activity/hearings/hearing-on-cleaning-up-cryptocurrency-the-energy-impacts-of-blockchains
7. https://www.eenews.net/articles/epa-tackles-coal-to-crypto-industry-trend/
8. https://blog.ethereum.org/2021/05/18/country-power-no-more/
9. https://blog.ethereum.org/2021/11/29/how-the-merge-impacts-app-layer/
10. https://cryptofees.info
11. https://ethresear.ch/t/multidimensional-eip-1559/11651
12. https://cointelegraph.com/news/vitalik-proposes-new-multi-dimensional-ethereum-fee-structure
13. https://www.reddit.com/r/ethereum/comments/rwojtk/ama_we_are_the_efs_research_team_pt_7_07_january/

Chapter 3
Initial Coin Offering

An initial coin offering (ICO) is a new way of fundraising enabled by digital currencies and blockchain technology, where participants invest fiat currencies and receive "tokens" (digital assets) in return.[1]

ICOs are widely seen as an innovative fintech alternative to traditional initial public offerings of stock (IPOs) as a means for startup businesses to raise capital. A person, project, or company in need of capital creates a new kind of digital coin and sells a tranche of them for fiat currencies on a digital trading platform or exchange.

Prior to an ICO, a business would typically release a whitepaper, which provides investors with an explanation of their proposed project, the rights behind the virtual tokens they would be issuing, the risks of the investment, and details of the ICO itself.

The rights behind the digital tokens can vary considerably, and, unlike stocks, many tokens are not intended to grant the investor an ownership stake in the business.

Currently, there isn't a standardized way of preparing a whitepaper in comparison to regulated prospectuses for IPOs.

ICO Token Valuation

With the exception of hedge fund managers who indiscriminately assess ICO tokens for their long- and short-term selling prospects, the underlying motivation of an ICO investor is the expectation that the token's value will uptick after the ICO, and the investor will sell it to make a tidy profit.

A token's value is determined based on (1) the demand for the token, which may be denominated in a highly volatile cryptocurrency, and (2) the underlying company's financial performance. Currently, there isn't a standardized way of determining a token's value. ICO investors trade these tokens at a profit or loss.

ICO Technology

The Ethereum (ETH) ICO platform is public and open-source and features smart contract functionality. It is still in its early stages of development, and its application is of an experimental nature.

Vitalik Buterin, cofounder of ETH, cautioned that there are flaws in the technical intricacies of ETH blockchain networks that support ICOs arising from the centralization problem, which could take up to two to five years to solve. In 2017, the year of the ICO, Buterin expected 90% of ETH-based ICOs to fail.[2]

Despite information technology (IT) network security measures, software applications, computer hardware, the internet, and blockchain platforms supporting the ICOs are also vulnerable to computer viruses, physical or electronic break-ins, and attacks or other disruptions of a similar nature—hacks.

The revelation of the technical vulnerabilities of the ETH-based platform and the risk of hacks could add operational, technological risks for ICOs.

ICO Fraud

2017 was the year of ICOs for countries like Russia, China, and Japan. To date ICOs have raised $3 billion, averaging 20 new virtual coin offerings a month that produced an average investment return of 1,320%,[3] 293 times the S&P 500 return of 4.5% during the third quarter of 2017.

There have been many new uses for ICOs, including municipality-funding applications in Japan. But Joseph Lubin, cofounder of ETH, cautioned that some ICOs have been plain old scams.[4]

ICO Regulation

With the known ICO-related risks in mind, global regulators, legislators, and central bankers have been working on devising effective regulatory measures to mitigate concerns over security, consumer protection, and financial crime.

The first country to regulate ICOs was the US Securities and Exchange Commission (SEC), which on July 25, 2017, issued a landmark opinion concerning digital assets stating that ICOs can sometimes be considered securities—and as such are subject to strict laws and regulations.[5]

Putting the new SEC law to use: (1) the SEC brought charges against two companies and their operator for defrauding investors in a pair of fraudulent ICOs and (2) ICO token holders served Tezos with two potentially groundbreaking class action lawsuits alleging that its $232 million ICO violated U.S. securities laws and misled investors.[6] In 2020, Tezos and investors of unregistered Tezos securities settled the case out of court for $25 million.[7]

Since SEC's ICO pronouncement, many countries have proposed or enacted ICO legislation in an uncoordinated fashion. Some countries mimicked the SEC in regulating ICOs as a security. Other countries like China abruptly banned ICOs and shut down all cryptocurrency exchanges.

Other US Laws Applicable to ICOs in Addition to SEC Laws

With the enactment of ICO regulations, institutional investors have become increasingly interested in investing in them. Other US laws investors should take into consideration in addition to the SEC laws when evaluating an ICO for investment include:

- **The CFTC on ICO tokens:** The Commodity Futures Trading Commission (CFTC) regulates virtual currencies and tokens as commodities. A commissioner explained, "crypto-tokens offered in a pre-sale can transform. They may start their life as a security regulated under SEC from a capital-raising perspective but then at some point—maybe possibly quickly or even immediately—turn into a commodity." This is how many understand the simple agreement for future tokens (SAFT) concept because no bright-line rule determines which types of tokens are securities and which are not. Instead, what qualifies as a security can only be determined by a facts-and-circumstances-driven analysis of particular tokens.[8]

- **FinCEN on Foreign Cryptocurrency Businesses:** According to a spokesman for the Financial Crimes Enforcement Network (FinCEN), "A foreign cryptocurrency business may have to register with FinCEN depending on several factors. If the foreign cryptocurrency company is registered with, and functionally regulated or examined by the SEC, CFTC or if it engages in activities that, if conducted in the US would require it to register with the SEC or CFTC, then it would not have to register as an MSB with FinCEN. If it does not satisfy this condition, the answer depends on how it operates, on behalf of whom and where its customer base is located based on a facts-and-circumstances-driven analysis."[9]

- **The IRS on Foreign Cryptocurrency Businesses:** A foreign cryptocurrency business may be subject to US tax laws because virtual currencies are characterized as property according to Notice 2014-21, gains of which are subject to federal taxation and tax reporting requirements under information reporting and backup withholding, the Foreign Account Tax Compliance Act (FATCA), and Country-by-Country Reporting (CbCR). The IRS may claim jurisdiction over a foreign cryptocurrency business that lacks any physical presence in the United States, so long as the company does substantial business in the United States based on a facts-and-circumstances-driven analysis.

As regulations fall on ICOs around the world, it opens the doors for institutional investors to participate in ICOs of companies that may have a global footprint from a business, technological, and legal structure standpoint. This requires sophisticated evaluation of all ICO-related risks in all jurisdictions the company operates. "ICO companies, their executives and institutional investors should carefully take into consideration the ever-changing regulatory landscape around the world and implement a good compliance program," advised John Kearney of MyComplianceOffice.[10]

Notes

1. https://cointelegraph.com/news/icos-flow-continues-as-regulations-fall-around-the-world-expert-blog
2. https://cointelegraph.com/news/vitalik-buterin-explains-flaws-in-icos-and-scaling-issues-in-ethereum
3. https://www.businessinsider.com/ico-mangrove-capital-average-returns-crypto-icos-2017-10
4. https://www.cnbc.com/2017/11/17/many-icos-are-fraud-according-to-ethereum-co-founder-and-ripple-ceo.html
5. https://cointelegraph.com/news/in-wake-of-china-ico-ban-japan-singapore-us-give-crypto-second-look
6. https://www.sec.gov/news/press-release/2017-185-0
7. https://www.coindesk.com/policy/2020/09/01/tezos-investors-win-25m-settlement-in-court-case-over-230m-ico/
8. https://www.cftc.gov/sites/default/files/idc/groups/public/documents/file/labcftc_primercurrencies100417.pdf
9. https://cointelegraph.com/news/icos-flow-continues-as-regulations-fall-around-the-world-expert-blog
10. Ibid.

Chapter 4
New Financial Alternatives

Bitcoin's volatile upward price surge and its popularity among fintech investors since 2017 provided fertile ground for the development of cryptocurrency-based new financial alternatives for the first time in history.[1]

Virtual Currency Prediction Markets

When Bitcoin first appeared in 2009, the gambling industry was one of the industries that immediately started to adopt it due to Bitcoin's unregulated nature. Since then, hundreds of online Bitcoin prediction markets have been popping up like mushrooms, processing millions of Bitcoin trade predictions on a daily basis. If you are right, you win Bitcoins and can even open Bitcoin-denominated savings accounts that pay above-market interest rates.

Binary Bitcoin Options

A binary Bitcoin option is a simple type of option that is valued according to a true/false statement. For example, if the price of the underlying asset Bitcoin is above a certain level, the call (long) option will pay 100; if it is below, it will pay 0. For a put option the reverse is true.

Binary Bitcoin options make for simple valuation and are therefore a good way for traders to avoid complicated valuations, which often work in favor of option issuers to the detriment of buyers. There are two different ways to use Bitcoins for binary options trading:

- The first is similar to playing at a Bitcoin casino—your Bitcoin is the currency and you trade/play in the same way as someone using fiat currencies as a deposit.
- The second method is trading Bitcoin as an asset.

Both types of options brokers are often referred to as Bitcoin binary options brokers. Most Bitcoin binary options brokers only offer it as a virtual currency pair versus the US dollar.

Cryptocurrency Exchanges

Since BTC's launch in the heels of the 2007–2008 financial crisis, money began traveling via a new financial route. The first BTC exchange was established on February 6, 2010, where Bitcoin traded for the first time for 0.3 cents. Currently, 106 million people, 1% of the world population, have sent cryptocurrency payments via the internet for goods or services or have held the funds for investment. Although there are approximately 15,000 active cryptocurrencies listed, BTC is by far the most popular, comprising nearly 66% of the entire cryptocurrency market.

Traditional Banking Institutions Offer Digital Asset Management Services

On July 10, 2017, the Swiss Financial Market Supervisory Authority (FINMA) issued a breakthrough decision by approving a private Swiss bank's application to offer digital asset management services in virtual currencies, allowing customers to buy and hold Bitcoins within their Swiss bank accounts through a partnership with brokerage service Bitcoin Suisse, subjecting these accounts to tax transparency rules, the Common Reporting Standard (CRS) and the Foreign Account Tax Compliance Act (FATCA). The Swiss adored BTC so much that the municipality of Chiasso allowed residents to pay their taxes in Bitcoin.

Bitcoin Exchange-Traded Funds

There are several bitcoin exchange-traded funds (ETFs) for individual investors to choose from. ETF investing in other top cryptocurrencies could be in the future too.[2]

Notes

1. Selva Ozelli, "Regulations Fall on Bitcoin Around the World," My Compliance Office, 2017.
2. https://edition.cnn.com/2021/12/10/investing/etfs-stocks/index.html

Chapter 5

Hedging Bitcoins with Options on the World Wide Web

During 2017, Bitcoin's price rose from $1,000 at the beginning of the year to $20,000 by December, increasing 20-fold, with a few sharp drops. When the cryptocurrency markets experienced a sharp downturn during the third week of December, with leading cryptocurrencies like Bitcoin (BTC) and Ethereum (ETH) down 80% or more, skilled cryptocurrency hedge fund managers, who rushed to surf the cryptocurrency waves on the World Wide Web, were still standing on their surfboards.[1]

An altogether different story was unfolding for those who had been knocked off. "I'm not sure one can really define why some traders make it, while others do not. For myself, I can think of two important elements. First, I have the ability to imagine configurations of the world different from today and really believe it can happen. Second, I stay rational and disciplined under pressure," explained Bruce Kovner a legendary hedge fund manager in an interview with Jack Schwager for his *Market Wizards* book.[2]

"Is My Life Over?"

A college student from California, in a Reddit post, sent out SOS signals—start-of-message marks for maritime transmissions requesting help when catastrophic loss of property is imminent—"Is my life over?"[3]

Apparently, the student, encouraged by the 2017 crypto market surge—which many likened to the tulip mania—without any awareness of the tax consequences, began surfing the World Wide Web by trading cryptocurrencies. "I feel like I ruined my life by dabbling into cryptos as a clueless college kid. I first caught wind of it when a buddy of mine said he was going all in on ETH in May of last year [2017]. I said the hell with it, signed up on Coinbase, and threw $5,000 into crypto. Well, I went down the rabbit hole and struck gold a few times. I brought my 5k initial all the way up to a $880k portfolio in December 2017."

During 2018, when the cryptocurrency bear market began and the tides turned, the young crypto surfer—who did not know how to hedge his cryptocurrency portfolio—fell off his surf board and lost most of his cryptocurrency gains relating to 2017, which were declared to the IRS by Coinbase on Internal Revenue Service Form 1099.[4] "My estimated tax liability for 2017 is about $400,000.[5] I haven't paid any taxes or filed any returns for 2017," the student said—as he does not have the funds necessary to pay his 2017 taxes on his cryptocurrency gains.

Bitcoin-Invested Hedge Funds

Options are widely used to manage hedge funds' portfolio risks or "to hedge or speculate on the price of an underlying asset with a quantified risk," according to retired hedge fund manager Michael Steinhardt, whose career earnings made him a legend in the industry.

Steinhardt set up his first fund in 1967, "following a strategy created by Alfred Winslow Jones. He married (1) short sales to hedge against stock market risk; (2) leverage to boost stock trading returns; (3) and long positions in stocks, to continuously extract stock market trading profits as their prices moved up and down."

Famed hedge fund manager Michael Steinhardt, in an interview, explained to me that he expanded on Alfred Winslow Jones's hedged trading strategy "by incorporating bonds in addition to stocks, as well as new derivative hedging products that entered the markets in addition to short sales" to his portfolio, throughout his career. He began hedging with "long and short exchange-traded stock options to hedge the price of stocks when stock options debuted in 1973, at the CBOE." That same year, two professors, Fischer Black and Myron Scholes, conceived the Black–Scholes options pricing model, which standardized options pricing at options exchanges. Over a period of 28 years, using his own "Steinhardt style hedged trading strategy," he earned "hedged annual returns of 24.5%—triple the S&P 500 average," Steinhardt said.[6]

The illustrious careers of hedge fund legends have inspired contemporary Bitcoin traders to set up Bitcoin-invested hedge funds that surf Bitcoin's extreme price volatility on the World Wide Web, just like:

- Michael Steinhardt (1967–1995, 24.5%).
- George Soros, who incorporated foreign exchange in addition to stocks and bonds in his hedge fund trading strategy,

was only deemed "the man who broke the Bank of England" when he successfully shorted the British pound out of the European Exchange Rate Mechanism (ERM) mechanism. He became a billionaire overnight on Black Wednesday, September 16, 1992 (1973–2011, 20%).

- Bruce Kovner, the global macro hedge fund manager who incorporated commodities in addition to stocks, bonds, and foreign exchange to his hedge fund and combined computerized and traditional trading strategies to arbitrage world financial markets, like Mozart's piano sonatas (1983–2011, 14%).
- Professor David Shaw, the quant who developed first-of-its-kind computerized hedged-trading strategies for stocks, bonds, foreign exchange, commodities, asset-backed securities, convertible securities, and reinsurance contracts to exploit inefficiencies in world financial markets with the help of state-of-the-art high-speed computer networks (1988–2012, 14%).

Since the Commodity Futures Trading Commission's (CFTC's) approval of New York-based LedgerX in 2017, 70 additional Bitcoin-based hedge funds announced that they would be launching during 2017. Among these hedge funds was Silicon Valley–based Pantera Capital), which will launch an SEC-registered $100 million ICO -focused hedge fund. French bank BNP Paribas will add Bitcoin to one of its currency funds. In 2017 there were about 120 cryptocurrency hedge funds: (1) those that had portfolios containing exclusively virtual currencies, Bitcoin options, and ICOs; and (2) those that had added some cryptocurrency to a mix of other asset types. According to a report by PWC, Q1 2020 research shows that there are around 150 active crypto hedge funds.[7]

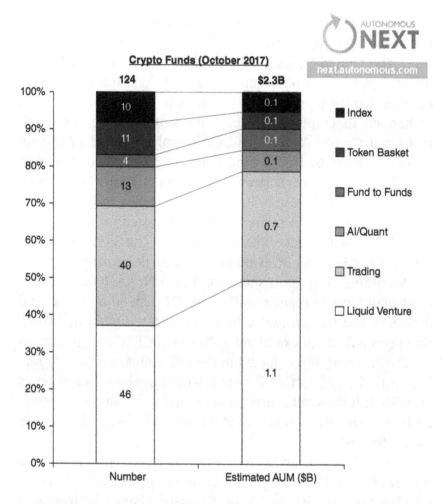

SOURCE: Autonomous Next.

In China, the Fintech Blockchain Group runs an exclusively cryptocurrency-invested hedge fund that trades virtual currencies 24 hours a day, seven days a week, using a cutting-edge computerized lightning-quick trading strategy to arbitrage tiny price discrepancies on the countless web venues on which it changes hands. Zhou Shuoji, the Fintech Blockchain Group's high-speed

Bitcoin trader, said, "It's the golden age to be in the Bitcoin market because it's imperfect."

In the United States, hedge fund manager Timothy Enneking of Crypto Asset Management said, "I don't think the world has seen but the pointy end of the spear in terms of what's going to happen in cryptocurrencies" and launched the first SEC-registered Crypto Assets Fund exclusively invested in cryptocurrency products. Hedge fund manager Mike Novogratz, who was the president of Fortress Investment Group (US), which was among early investors in virtual currencies and exchanges, admitted that "10% of my net worth is invested in Bitcoins and it has been the best investment of my life." The SoftBank Group acquired the Fortress Investment Group earlier during 2017.

According to a spokesman for FinCEN, "A foreign hedge fund may have to register with FinCEN depending on several factors. If the foreign hedge fund is registered with, and functionally regulated or examined by the SEC, CFTC or if it engages in activities that, if conducted in the US would require it to register with the SEC or CFTC, then it would not have to register as an MSB. If it does not satisfy this condition, the answer depends on how it operates, on behalf of whom and where its customer base is located."

Bitcoin-invested hedge funds can be legally structured in a variety of ways. For example, a Swedish company, XBT Provider, which is listed on the Stockholm Nasdaq exchange, is structured as an exchange-traded note (ETN) that tracks the price of Bitcoin. An unregistered cryptocurrency hedge fund managed by John Chalekson is structured as a plain vanilla, limited partnership. This hedge fund, using a "game theoretic equilibrium" trading strategy to "dominate the hedge fund indices with extraordinary numbers," delivered an astonishing "2,129% investment return to his investors through August 2017 primarily by investing in new virtual currencies, ICOs in long positions, without hedging or using any leverage—266 times the S&P 500 average." Traditional hedge funds, on average, returned 3.7% through the first half of 2017, according to data provided by HFR, and the S&P 500 gained 8% over the same period.[8]

US mutual fund giant Fidelity Investments, with $6.3 trillion under administration, joined with $10 billion Coinbase Inc, a Silicon Valley cryptocurrency exchange, "to enable Fidelity clients to track their digital assets alongside more traditional investments, like stocks, bonds and mutual funds." Fidelity did so because, a company official said, "we can see that the evolution of Bitcoin and Blockchain technology is setting the investment industry up for disruption."[9]

As virtual currencies seep into the current world's regulatory and financial infrastructure while transforming it at the same time, the good news is that there are several cryptocurrency-based financial alternatives that will satisfy both the Bitcoin bulls and the bears.[10]

Notes

1. https://cryptofundresearch.com/release-20-percent-new-hedge-funds-crypto-funds/; https://news.bloombergtax.com/daily-tax-report/insight-irs-criminal-investigations-division-issues-its-annual-report-in-midst-of-cryptocurrency-bear-market-blues
2. https://www.amazon.com/s?k=the+market+wizard&gclid=Cj0KCQjwma6TBhDIARIsAOKuANyZ1IOc8BaXGjFwspV6ruFgOzJtT16bvulfBIdjfzhKHCpFBBpLIPQaAmLZEALw_wcB&hvadid=174248687464&hvdev=c&hvlocint=9067609&hvlocphy=1012782&hvnetw=g&hvqmt=b&hvrand=8230461572944676909&hvtargid=kwd-906592142&hydadcr=24658_9648989&tag=googhydr-20&ref=pd_sl_2q8cdgwjh8_b

3. https://www.reddit.com/r/tax/comments/9tcnu8/did_i_ruin_my_life_
   by_trading_crypto/
4. https://cointelegraph.com/news/how-not-to-panic-if-coinbase-is-
   turning-over-your-info-to-the-irs-expert-take
5. https://imgur.com/a/cpPwR9u
6. https://cointelegraph.com/news/hedging-bitcoins-with-options-on-
   the-world-wide-web-expert-blog
7. https://www.pwc.com/gx/en/financial-services/pdf/pwc-elwood-
   annual-crypto-hedge-fund-report-may-2020.pdf
8. https://cointelegraph.com/news/hedging-bitcoins-with-options-on-
   the-world-wide-web-expert-blog
9. Ibid.
10. Ibid.

Chapter 6
Cryptocurrency Spreads

During December of 2017, Bitcoin prices shot up to $20,000, increasing 30-fold from the beginning of the year. This triggered rumors of Bitcoin mania possibly surpassing tulip mania, spreading across the World Wide Web with a mixture of fear and excitement.

Bitcoin's 100% price surge over the first three weeks of December agitated regulators in Asia Pacific, since Japan and Vietnam together accounted for 80% of Bitcoin trading activity. Japan's central bank chief described it as "deadly."

The central bank chiefs of the United States and Australia and the Turkish deputy prime minister were a bit more diplomatic, characterizing the surge as "highly speculative." The central bank chiefs of the United Arab Emirates and Saudi Arabia ignored it and instead kept their focus on testing a new digital currency built on blockchain technology for use in cross-border payments. Regulators in Venezuela, Zimbabwe, and Nigeria welcomed it as a savior for their highly dysfunctional economies.

The diverse reactions of investors and regulators to Bitcoin's price spike were irreconcilable.

Behavioral Economics

This phenomenon was best explained by 2017 Nobel Prize winner economist Richard H. Thaler,[1] who, by integrating economics with psychology, explored the impact of limited rationality, social preferences, and lack of self-control on individual economic decision-making. During his cameo appearance in the Oscar-winning credit crisis movie *The Big Short* (2015)—sitting at a blackjack table in Las Vegas next to beautiful pop star Selena Gomez, Thaler, encouraged by the stacks of casino tokens at his disposal, explained that a classic error investors make is the hot-hand fallacy of "thinking whatever is happening now is going to continue to happen in the future."

Therefore, when Bitcoin's price flash crashed on December 22, 2021, all the way down to $11,970, losing more than 30% of its value in a day, those investors who had developed a hot-hand fallacy regarding Bitcoin's upward price surge began selling them in a panic, all over the World Wide Web.[2] The flash crash wiped out $210 billion from the cryptocurrency markets. It bankrupted a South Korean cryptocurrency exchange after it was hacked for the second time. It halted trading at several cryptocurrency and futures exchanges, including the Chicago Mercantile Exchange (CME) and the Chicago Board Options Exchange (CBOE) due to frantic trading activity. And it brought down the prices of all other virtual currencies along the way. But panic selling was not the only investor reaction to Bitcoin's flash crash.

Limited Rationality

Thaler developed the theory of mental accounting, explaining how people simplify financial decision-making by creating separate accounts in their minds, focusing on the narrow impact of each individual economic decision on themselves rather than its overall effect.

Days before Bitcoin's price plunge, some long-term holders and founders of virtual currencies who had an aversion to losses—a phenomenon Thaler called the endowment effect—began taking their cryptocurrency profits by selling them.

For example, Emil Oldenburg, the cofounder of Bitcoin.com, one of the world's largest Bitcoin websites, divested from all of his Bitcoins with the belief that others would do the same when they realized how illiquid and high in transaction costs the Bitcoin market was.[3] And Litecoin's founder Charlie Lee sold all of his Litecoins to resolve the "conflict of interest" within himself.[4]

Social Preferences

Thaler's theoretical and experimental research on fairness was very influential and well regarded. He showed how consumers' fairness concerns may stop firms from raising prices in periods of high demand but not in times of rising costs.

Days before Bitcoin's price free fall, North American Derivatives Exchange (NADEX) CEO Timothy McDermott, in anticipation of the bearish market move in Bitcoin, launched a new trading instrument, Bitcoin Spreads.[5]

Bitcoin Spreads allows an individual trader who was bearish on Bitcoin's price to bet against it in the short term, with guaranteed limited risk and with affordable capital requirements. With these guaranteed limits, a retail trader was protected from losses outside of their risk comfort level in the volatile Bitcoin market, while still enjoying potential profit opportunities from price movements within the floor-to-ceiling range.

To trade Bitcoin Spreads on NADEX, a trader is required to make an initial deposit of at least $250, with no minimum balance required thereafter. Since Bitcoin Spreads are geared toward the retail trader, points are smaller in size with a value of $0.10 each, as opposed to the $1 or $5 per point with recently listed Bitcoin futures contracts at the CME or CBOE.

Lack of Self-Control

Thaler showed how to analyze self-control problems using a planner-doer model to describe the internal tension between an investor's long-term economic planning and short-term doing. According to Thaler, an investor could avoid succumbing to short-term temptation by nudging—a term he coined—to exercise better self-control when making economic decisions.

Too often, individual traders impulsively began trading Bitcoin binary options or spreads with little or no understanding of these products, their costs, or their risks as a knee-jerk response to Bitcoin market price movements on unregulated web-based exchanges. This resulted in material damages to these traders' financial profiles.

In response, the US Federal Bureau of Investigation (FBI) published a warning cautioning the public against unregistered binary options websites as tools to commit fraud and stated that it has these exchanges in its crosshairs.[6] The European Securities and Markets Authority (ESMA), with the backing of the UK's Financial Conduct Authority, went a step further by stating that it is considering measures to "prohibit the marketing, distribution or sale of Bitcoin binary options to retail clients," while Australia, Belgium, Canada, and Israel banned binary options marketing, distribution, or sale to retail customers.[7]

Bitcoin binary options and spreads are legal for trading by retail investors in the United States so long as they are traded on one of two Commodities Futures Trading Commission (CFTC) authorized exchanges: NADEX and Cantor Exchange.[8]

Notes

1. https://www.nobelprize.org/prizes/economic-sciences/2017/press-release/
2. https://cointelegraph.com/news/cryptocurrency-market-recovering-after-massive-correction
3. https://cointelegraph.com/news/bitcoincom-cto-denounces-bitcoin-ive-switched-to-bitcoin-cash
4. https://cointelegraph.com/news/litecoin-founder-sells-all-his-litecoin-but-promises-not-to-leave
5. https://www.nadex.com/market-news/2017/12/20/nadex-launches-bitcoin-spreads
6. https://www.financemagnates.com/binary-options/regulation/global-binary-options-regulations-overview-full-breakdown/
7. https://www.fbi.gov/news/stories/binary-options-fraud
8. https://cointelegraph.com/news/is-it-only-about-taxes-bitcoin-spreads-explained

Chapter 7
Altcoin, Stablecoin Utility Coins, and CBDC

Altcoin

Since the launch of Bitcoin, the private sector has initiated over 15,000 cryptocurrencies, whose total value exceeds $2 trillion. Coins that are not Bitcoin are also called alternative digital assets or altcoins.

Stablecoin

To stabilize the relatively large price fluctuations of cryptocurrencies, some commercial institutions launched so-called stablecoins, by pegging them to sovereign currencies or related assets. Top stablecoins include:[1]

- Tether (USDT)
- Dai (DAI)

- Binance USD (BUSD)
- TrueUSD (TUSD)
- USD Coin (USDC)
- TerraUSD (UST)
- Digix Gold Token (DGX)

The US Treasury Department issued a report assessing the risk of stablecoins.[2]

Utility Coins

Following the Swiss Financial Market Supervisory Authority (FINMA) pronouncement in 2017, six of the world's biggest banks—HSBC, Barclays, Credit Suisse, the Canadian Imperial Bank of Commerce, State Street Bank, and Mitsubishi UFJ—joined a project to create a new form of digital currency, "utility settlement coin," which was created by UBS BNY Mellon, NEX Banco Santander, and Deutsche Bank, along with blockchain startup Clearmatics in 2015. These banks aim to use the utility settlement coin that could be amplified by fiat currencies issued on the blockchain for clearing and settling financial transactions.

Others are testing their own virtual currencies across blockchain-based platforms: Citibank; the Commonwealth Bank of Australia, in partnership with Wells Fargo and Brigham Cotton; Mizuho Bank and seven other large European banks in partnership with IBM; Microsoft in partnership with Bank Hapoalim; the largest state-owned Chinese banks in partnership with prominent Chinese technology companies; and Amazon Web Services in partnership with Digital Currency Group and Mitsubishi UFJ Financial Group.

JPMorgan Chase, the largest US bank, is a member of two blockchain consortiums—the Enterprise Ethereum Alliance and the Hyperledger Project—dedicated to developing various financial services applications on blockchain technology. "Blockchain is like any other technology. If it is cheaper, effective, works, and secure, then we are going to use it and transport currency, but it will be dollars, not Bitcoins," explained the bank's CEO, Jamie Dimon.[3]

Central Bank Digital Currency (CBDC)

Many major economies are actively considering or advancing research and development of central bank digital currencies (CBDCs). According to the Atlantic Council, 87 countries out of 200 are exploring a CBDC.[4]

Not Like Before: Digital Currencies Debut Amid COVID-19

The coronavirus pandemic forced governments worldwide to focus on bringing blockchain technology to their financial services over 2020.

Famed currency speculator George Soros, who in 1992 broke the Bank of England to emerge a billionaire overnight by forcing the pound out of the European Exchange Rate Mechanism, believes, "We will not go back to where we were when the pandemic started. That is pretty certain. But that is the only thing that is certain. Everything else is up for grabs."

Giles Coghlan, the chief currency analyst at HYCM, had the following to say: "The volatile market conditions that have come about as a result of COVID-19 has investors looking for safe haven assets to protect their capital. The price of gold has risen, as has the value of the USD [which currently accounts for about 60% of all central bank foreign exchange reserves, while the next closest currency is the euro, with 20%] and JPY—some of the leading safe haven currencies. And interestingly, it looks as though market interest towards digital currencies are changing. As part of social distancing measures, there is now a preference for digital payments over traditional cash. One could argue that eventually we will become a cashless society, and COVID-19 has simply accelerated this awareness."

Elon Musk—who cofounded and leads Tesla, SpaceX, and Neuralink—pointed out that "massive currency issuance by government central banks is making Bitcoin internet money look solid by comparison," adding, "I still only own 0.25 Bitcoins, by the way."

COVID-19 Has Led to an Increased Interest in Digital Currencies Around the World

A growing number of nations, cities, and companies are looking to develop digital coins, with regional initiatives taking shape to target the US dollar's supremacy on the global stage. The Federal Reserve Bank of Philadelphia warned in a paper that with the introduction of central bank digital currencies, central banks may arise as "deposit monopolist[s]," replacing commercial banks and disrupting the existing banking system. JPMorgan Chase has also expressed agreement with the idea that the dollar is under threat due to the continued growth in CBDC traction.[5]

According to a survey by the London-based journal *Central Banking*—a specialized publication supported by the Bank for International Settlements (BIS) and the European Central Bank (ECB), among others—65% of central banks in the 46 countries surveyed were researching CBDCs, with 71% of respondents indicating their preference for a constrained form of distributed ledger technology. Yves Mersch, an ECB board member, pointed out that the number of central banks already working on a CBDC may be a bit higher, with about 80% of the 66 central banks surveyed by the BIS indicating that they were doing so.

Venezuela issued the first state-backed digital stablecoin, the Petro, which is now mandatory for gas stations in the country to support. Other nations sanctioned by the United States, such as North Korea, Iran, and Cuba, are devoting significant technical resources to develop CBDCs.

From a purpose-built e-shop, the Bank of Lithuania is slated to issue a batch of digital blockchain-based collector coins that can be redeemed for physical coins. While in Senegal, Grammy-nominated singer Akon is expected to launch Akoin, a cryptocurrency that will be the local currency in Akon City, a 2,000-acre development project. Both projects are expected to launch during July of 2020.

On the corporate stablecoin development side, 19 companies in China, including local chains of US-based companies Starbucks, Subway, and McDonald's, are trying out stablecoins through a pilot program launched by the People's Bank of China based on its mobile payment system instead of the SWIFT system.

The People's Bank of China is expected to launch a digital yuan, likely distributed person to person via a mobile payment system utilizing Huawei's 5G technology. China's vast Belt and Road initiative and the yuan's inclusion into the Special Drawing Rights currency basket (which is based on five currencies: the dollar, the euro, the yuan, the Japanese yen, and the British pound) signify the internationalization of the yuan, which has officially become one of the world's reserve currencies.

Accordingly, China has been collaborating with many countries to develop mobile blockchain-based "cross-border payment networks." The East Asia digital currency initiative is expected to consist of the yuan, the yen, the Hong Kong dollar, and the South Korean won, with the yuan and yen accounting for about 60% and 20%, respectively, of the digital currency's value. China is also collaborating with Singapore's central bank and financial regulatory authority to develop a CBDC.

Russia is testing its digital ruble and leading another multinational digital currency initiative with Brazil, Russia, India, China, and South Africa (BRICS) and Eurasian Economic Union countries.[6] Askar Zhumagaliyev—the minister of digital development, innovation, and aerospace industry for EEU member state Kazakhstan—recently stated that the country was expecting "another 300 billion tenge (US $738.4 million) in the next three years as digital investments and in general, the further development of digital mining."

Other BRICS countries India,[7] Brazil,[8] and South Africa[9] announced that they plan to launch/test CBDCs during 2022.

In the eurozone, the Banque de France has become the first to successfully trial a digital euro operational on a blockchain, according to an announcement.

The Saudi Arabian Monetary Authority, which is creating a binational digital currency with the United Arab Emirates called Aber to be used for cross-border transactions, announced that it recently injected liquidity into local banks via blockchain technology.[10]

Notes

1. https://money.usnews.com/investing/cryptocurrency/slideshows/what-is-the-best-stablecoin-list

2. https://home.treasury.gov/system/files/136/StableCoinReport_Nov1_508.pdf

3. Selva Ozelli, "Regulations Fall on Bitcoin Around the World," My Compliance Office, 2017.

4. https://www.atlanticcouncil.org/cbdctracker/
5. https://cointelegraph.com/news/not-like-before-digital-currencies-debut-amid-covid-19
6. https://blockworks.co/as-russia-tests-digital-ruble-plans-for-broader-crypto-regulation-are-uncertain/
7. https://www.cnbc.com/2022/02/01/india-digital-currency-to-launch-in-2022-2023-finance-minster-says.html
8. https://www12.senado.leg.br/noticias/materias/2021/09/01/versao-eletronica-do-real-deve-ser-lancada-ate-2024-estima-assessor-do-banco-central
9. https://www.reuters.com/business/finance/australia-singapore-south-africa-test-cross-border-cbank-digital-payments-2021-09-02/
10. https://cointelegraph.com/news/not-like-before-digital-currencies-debut-amid-covid-19

Chapter 8

Cryptocurrency Tumblers and Mixing Services

In 2018, financial investigators of more than 30 nations discussed how to combat the misuse of cryptocurrencies by criminals.

The growing concern about the rising use of cryptocurrencies in illicit activity all around the world is getting louder and louder—almost competing with stories about cryptocurrency volatility.

More than 60 financial investigators from the Interpol and Europol organizations of more than 30 countries in January of 2018 attended a cryptocurrency workshop to discuss measures that can be taken to combat the misuse of cryptocurrencies by criminals.[1]

According to Rob Wainwright, head of Europol, as much as $5.5 billion USD was being laundered through cryptocurrencies annually.[2]

While blockchain provides a public ledger of all crypto transactions, criminals are using cryptocurrency tumblers or cryptocurrency mixing services to obscure the trail back to the fund's original source.[3]

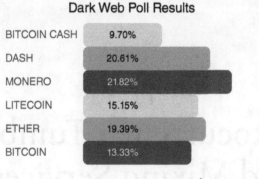

SOURCE: Recorded Future.

Newer cryptocurrencies such as Cloakcoin, Dash, PIVX, and Zcoin have built-in mixing services as a part of their blockchain network. Monero, drug dealers' favorite cryptocurrency, provides anonymity without tumbling services due to its privacy-centric blockchain design. Therefore, more effort needs to be placed on monitoring cryptocurrencies with privacy or mixing services features, crypto mixers, and tumblers, since they can impede tax collection, anti–money laundering practices, and law enforcement agencies.

In the aftermath of this workshop, many regulatory agencies around the world, including the United States, the European Union, Japan, and Australia, stepped up their fight against financial crimes utilizing cryptocurrencies.

The European Union

The 45-member committee of the European Parliament launched an investigation into money laundering and tax evasion related to the digital economy that thrives in the shadows of tax havens.

On February 7, 2018, the EU Parliament voted to create a committee, provisionally entitled Taxe 3, that investigated for the first time tax privileges established under citizenship programs or non-dom (non-domiciled) regimes offered by Portugal, Italy, Malta, the United Kingdom, and Cyprus, as well as crown dependencies and overseas territories.

Since the power to levy taxes is central to the sovereignty of the EU member states, which have assigned only limited competences to the EU in this area, Taxe 3 was confirmed by a plenary vote in order to undertake the financial crimes inquiry.

The United States

The US Department of the Treasury's Financial Crimes Enforcement Network (FinCEN) regulates cryptocurrency exchanges under existing legislation for money transmitters. It also requires US holders of a financial interest in or signatory authority over foreign financial accounts (including crypto-denominated accounts) to file a foreign bank account report, FinCEN 114, if the aggregate value of the foreign financial accounts exceeds $10,000 at any time during the calendar year. FinCEN has indicated that it is "aggressively" pursuing cryptocurrency tax evaders and platforms that lack strong internal safeguards against money laundering—even those located outside the United States.[4]

Internal Revenue Service Criminal Investigation (IRS CI) indicated that it bolstered its staff by 10 additional new investigators to make it easier to track down cross-border crypto tax evaders.[5]

US Immigration and Customs Enforcement (ICE) indicated that it uses undercover techniques to infiltrate and exploit peer-to-peer cryptocurrency exchangers who typically launder proceeds by using mixers.[6]

Japan

The Financial Services Agency (FSA) began inspecting all cryptocurrency exchanges after hackers stole $530 million worth of digital money from the Coincheck exchange in one of the biggest cyber heists on record.[7]

On December 13, 2017, the Australian Transaction Reports and Analysis Centre (AUSTRAC) amended the Anti-Money Laundering and Counter-Terrorism Financing Act 2006 to combat money laundering and terrorism financing using cryptocurrencies. Under this amendment, crypto exchanges are required to identify customers more stringently and report suspicious transactions.[8] AUSTRAC is currently consulting the industry[9] seeking feedback on the newly introduced draft rules.[10]

Notes

1. https://www.europol.europa.eu/media-press/newsroom/news/global-workshop-for-financial-investigators-detection-investigation-seizure-and-confiscation-of-cryptocurrencies
2. https://www.bbc.com/news/technology-43025787
3. https://cointelegraph.com/news/new-report-bitcoin-drug-money-laundering-is-highly-centralized
4. https://home.treasury.gov/news/press-releases/sm0251
5. https://cointelegraph.com/news/irs-forms-new-team-to-track-down-crypto-tax-evaders
6. https://www.dhs.gov/news/2018/01/25/written-testimony-ice-senate-homeland-security-and-governmental-affairs-permanent
7. https://cointelegraph.com/news/530-million-in-xem-stolen-from-coincheck-can-be-traced-nem-team-confirms
8. https://www.aph.gov.au/Parliamentary_Business/Bills_Legislation/Bills_Search_Results/Result?%20bId=r5952
9. https://www.finder.com.au/how-austrac-is-cracking-down-on-cryptocurrency-exchanges
10. https://cointelegraph.com/news/illicit-uses-of-cryptocurrency-gaining-attention-around-the-world-expert-take

Chapter 9
The Darknet

With new technologies evolving, criminals find easier ways for illicit activities—that is the dark side of anonymity and decentralization.

While the precise origin of the COVID-19 pandemic is unknown, during its first year (2020) it infected more than 30 million people, with almost 1 million confirmed to have died from it as it continues to spread across the world. According to one study, the highly contagious virus has the ability to survive up to three weeks in frozen food supplies of meat and fish.

The United States—the worst-hit country by sheer numbers—is facing two intersecting health crises: the ongoing opioid overdose epidemic and the coronavirus pandemic with more than 200,000 in 2020 and more than 900,000 in 2022 confirmed COVID-19 fatalities, which is about 15% of total global deaths. Regrettably, each has the potential to exacerbate the effects of the other. Nevertheless, in a hopeful announcement in 2020, the US Naval Research Laboratory disclosed that they found a safe way to track the spread of COVID-19 and other contagious diseases from one cell to another in the human body.

The Centers for Disease Control and Prevention reports that drug overdose deaths have been on an upward climb for several years across all demographic groups in the United States. More precisely, the catastrophic outbreaks of COVID-19 cases have been recorded in the United States' packed jails, prisons, and immigration detention centers, according to epidemiologist Dr. Chris Beyrer.

Overcrowding, poor hygiene, and inadequate access to medical care, as well as the incarcerated population suffering from a number of preexisting conditions, including substance use disorder, which is estimated at 65%, created a perfect storm for a COVID-19 outbreak. Currently, COVID-19 infection rates in prisons alone exceed the total cases of some countries.

The Darknet and the Epidemics

As the world's leader in incarceration, the United States imprisons many on drug-related offenses. These even include teenagers who run Bitcoin (BTC) drug businesses on the darknet.

A transnational task force of the United States and Europe—the Joint Criminal Opioid and Darknet Enforcement, or J-CODE—combats the complex and deadly threat of online darknet drug sales in opioids, in particular fentanyl, with assistance from the US FBI, Drug Enforcement Agency (DEA), Postal Inspection Service (USPIS), ICE of Homeland Security Investigations, the Customs and Border Protection (CBP), Department of Justice (DOJ), and Department of Defense (DOD) and Europol.

Earlier during 2020, Christopher Wray, director of the FBI, in a report to the House Judiciary Committee, noted:

> Today, international criminal enterprises run multinational, multi-billion-dollar schemes from start to finish. Modern-day criminal enterprises are flat, fluid networks with global reach.

[. . .] Transnational organized crime networks exploit legitimate institutions for critical financial and business services
that enable the storage or transfer of illicit proceeds. [. . .]
Illicit drug trafficking continues to be a growing threat. Large
amounts of high-quality, low-cost heroin and illicit fentanyl
are contributing to record numbers of overdose deaths and
life-threatening addictions nationwide. The accessibility and
convenience of the drug trade online contributes to the opioid
epidemic in the U.S.[1]

With the COVID-19 pandemic, the drug-trafficking business—
just like the rest of the economy—further shifted online to the
darknet, according to the United Nations Office on Drugs and
Crime's (UNODC's) recent World Drug Report.

Timothy J. Shea, the acting administrator of the US DEA,
highlighted:

> As technology has evolved, so too have the tactics of drug traffick-
> ers. Riding the wave of technological advances, criminals attempt
> to further hide their activities within the dark web through vir-
> tual private networks and tails, presenting new challenges to law
> enforcement in the enduring battle against illegal drugs.[2]

For a progress report regarding the work of the J-CODE,
US senators Maggie Hassan, Dianne Feinstein, and John
Cornyn asked the US attorney general's office and the FBI in a
letter whether the DOJ has a system that tracks indictments and
investigations related to crimes involving the darknet and opioids; if authorities have been able to determine which countries
opioids are coming from on the darknet; and whether there are
technology companies that provide secure or encrypted communications that don't cooperate with law enforcement with respect
to drug trafficking.

According to Chainalysis' recent Global Crypto Adoption
Index, Eastern Europe accounts for more global darknet market

activity than any other region, with most of the darknet peer-to-peer crypto and trading transaction activity occurring on Hydra Marketplace, which can only be accessed with an anonymized browser like The Onion Router (Tor).

About The Onion Router

The core principle of Tor was developed in the mid-1990s by US Naval Research Laboratory (NRL) employees, mathematician Paul Sigerson, and computer scientists Michael G. Reed and David Goldschlag, to facilitate encrypted online US intelligence communication with intelligence sources around the world. Onion routing—encrypting communications and "bouncing" them around a network of nodes so no one can ascertain where they originate—was further developed by the Defense Advanced Research Projects Agency (DARPA), a research and development agency of the US DOD in 1997.

In 2002, the alpha version of Tor was developed by Syverson and computer scientists Roger Dingledine and Nick Mathewson, with a second-generation Tor released by the NRL under a free license two years later. The Electronic Frontier Foundation began funding Dingledine, Mathewson, and others to continue Tor's development until they launched the Tor Project, a nonprofit organization to help maintain the network. Prior to 2014, the majority of funding sources for Tor came from the US government.

Tor is the most popular means by which people access darknet sites that are encrypted and hidden from traditional search engines, allowing users to interact with a high degree of confidentiality. Tor has several search engines, directories, and hidden wikis that users can easily use to navigate their way around the darknet.

The anonymity of the darknet has fostered crimes such as narcotics trafficking and money laundering with the use of cryptocurrency. By 2010, with the launch of Bitcoin and with hacktivists involved in the Arab Spring movements, sites offering almost any type of illicit service imaginable experienced an explosion of activity.

Criminals prefer using the darknet coupled with cryptocurrency tumblers or mixing services, which are transmitted person to person with no oversight by governments or central banks, to obscure the trail back to the fund's original source while paying for illicit goods and services.

Reportedly, Hydra, the largest darknet market, has been planning to expand into the English part of the darknet by launching Eternos, a new darknet called AspaNET that will be an alternative to Tor.

The DEA announced that "the Department of Justice, through the Joint Criminal Opioid and Darknet Enforcement team, joined Europol to announce the results of Operation DisrupTor, a coordinated international effort to disrupt opioid trafficking on the Darknet."[3] Law enforcement officials arrested 179 people and seized more than $6.5 million in cash and digital currency, and 500 kilograms of drugs, in a worldwide crackdown on opioid trafficking on the darknet.

The FBI's Wray noted that "with the spike in opioid-related overdose deaths during the COVID-19 pandemic, we recognize that today's announcement is important and timely." He added:

> The FBI wants to assure the American public, and the world, that we are committed to identifying Darknet drug dealers and bringing them to justice. But our work does not end with today's announcement. The FBI, through JCODE and our partnership with Europol, continues to be actively engaged in a combined effort to disrupt the borderless, worldwide trade of illicit drugs. The FBI will continue to use all investigative techniques and tools to identify and prosecute Darknet opioid dealers, wherever they may be located."[4]

Notes

1. https://cointelegraph.com/news/darknet-cryptocurrency-and-two-intersecting-health-crises
2. Ibid.
3. https://www.dea.gov/press-releases/2020/09/22/international-law-enforcement-operation-targeting-opioid-traffickers
4. https://cointelegraph.com/news/darknet-cryptocurrency-and-two-intersecting-health-crises

Chapter 10
Illicit Use
of Cryptocurrencies

First flagged by the US Federal Bureau of Investigations (FBI) in an April 2012 report that analyzed the likelihood and consequences of illegal activities involving Bitcoins, there is a dark side to Bitcoins, as they have become essential for criminal and fraudulent activity in evading the scrutiny of world law enforcement and agencies. Individuals involved in illicit activities constantly seek to exploit new ways to launder proceeds of terror financing, drug and weapons dealing, tax evasion, bribery, corruption, hacking theft ransomware, and intellectual property espionage. One of the "advantages" of Bitcoins touted by their supporters for use in illegal transactions is their independence from any government or regulation so that illicit payments made using Bitcoin go undetected and remain hidden in the deep dark web. This taints cryptocurrency's reputation.

The enactment of FinCEN's Bitcoin regulations, which imposed registration requirements on money services businesses (MSBs) in 2013, allowed US law enforcement and agencies to use the long arm of the law to work collaboratively with global law enforcement and agencies and with private technology companies in multijurisdictional investigations to shed light on criminals who laundered cryptocurrencies by using them in illicit transactions on cryptocurrency exchanges, wallets, and dark-web markets.[1]

In 2020, US agencies sought millions of dollars in new funding to bolster national and international cryptocurrency investigations.

The COVID-19 pandemic crushed businesses, crippling life all across the world. It has cost darknet drug traffickers millions as well because their methods of moving drugs and funds were compromised during the lockdown, according to a blog post by Chainalysis.

"Darknet market revenue has fallen much more than we'd expect following Bitcoin's recent major price drop," Chainalysis reported, noting that supply problems for Mexican drug cartels and dealers in China's Hubei province could be "hampering darknet market vendors' ability to do business. . . . Perhaps. darknet market customers aren't buying as many drugs given the public health crisis," Chainalysis wrote, adding, "It's also possible that vendors slowed down sales during the price drop, out of fear that the bitcoin they accept one day could be worthless the next. But it's also likely that COVID-19 itself is making it harder to sell drugs at the moment."[2]

Nevertheless, this could all be a short-lived business trend owing to the lockdown, as the opioid epidemic in the United States is predicted to get worse due to the stress, isolation, and financial devastation caused by the COVID-19 pandemic, which is spreading to every corner of society, with millions of people losing their jobs during this global recession.

To choke off the drug supply funneling into the United States and curtail the worsening of the opioid epidemic, the US Drug Enforcement Agency in multijurisdictional investigations has been cracking down on the most powerful Mexican drug cartel, known as the Cartel de Jalisco Nueva Generación (CJNG), which controls at least two-thirds of the US drug traffic of cocaine, heroin, methamphetamine, and fentanyl-laced heroin—one of the deadliest drugs in America.

In late February 2020, the US Department of Justice and the DEA charged a dual US-Mexican citizen, Jessica Johanna Oseguera Gonzalez, known as "La Negra," sister of the Mexican drug kingpin Rubén Oseguera Cervantes known as "El Mencho" of the CJNG for violating the Kingpin Act, stemming from her alleged involvement in money-laundering drug activities using five CJNG business entities. Typically, in trade-based money-laundering transactions, cartel associates who sell drugs in the United States buy American goods with the drug money and ship them to China because Mexican cartels rely on international Asian criminal organizations to launder their cash. In return, the Chinese money launderers who receive the products will then send crypto back to the cartels in Mexico. Crypto payments are widely popular in China because crypto can be used to anonymously transfer value overseas, circumventing China's capital controls.

Following La Negra's arrest on March 11, the DEA announced the arrest of more than 600 members of the CJNG cartel. As Acting Administrator Uttam Dhillon explained: "Project Python is the single largest strike by U.S. authorities against CJNG, and this is just the beginning. This strategic and coordinated project exemplifies DEA's mission: to disrupt, dismantle, and destroy drug trafficking organizations around the world and bring their leaders to justice."[3]

Assistant Attorney General Brian A. Benczkowski of the Department of Justice Criminal Division added: "When President Trump signed an Executive Order prioritizing the dismantlement of transnational criminal organizations, the Department of

Justice answered the call and took direct aim at CJNG. We deemed CJNG one of the highest-priority transnational organized crime threats we face. And with Project Python, we are delivering results in the face of that threat for the American people."[4]

Yet another assault on Mexico's deadly drug cartel arrived at the beginning of June with "Operation Blue Agave"—a joint operation between the anti–money laundering unit of Mexico's Ministry of Finance and the US DEA that targeted nearly 2,000 men, women, and companies to freeze more than $1.1 billion in assets of CJNG. Mexican President Andrés Manuel López Obrador explained: "There was a request from the government of the United States because they had information about CJNG. Following the collaboration agreements, the accounts of this group had to be frozen."[5]

However, despite the DEA's success concerning Project Python and Operation Blue Agave, an audit report released by the US Office of the Inspector General of the DOJ sounded the alarm on how the DEA failed to report millions in digital currencies, which it had earned on undercover money laundering and drug trafficking, even though in the past few years, the DEA has seen an exponential increase in cases that involve cryptocurrency, particularly investigations into dark web operations.

The 72-page, partly redacted audit of income-generating undercover operations describes the serious risks associated with DEA operations between 2015 and 2017, contending that a significant sum of the proceeds in these operations was not disclosed to designated oversight authorities and that there were even cases in which the DEA neglected to pursue the targets identified in their operations, casting the DEA as an agency whose efforts to clamp down on cryptocurrency money laundering got ahead of its own ability to monitor itself in its handling of crypto-related activities, which lacked structured procedures and oversight.

The report said that "the DEA's management of cryptocurrency-related activities was insufficient due to inadequate headquarters management, lack of policies, inadequate internal control procedures, insufficient supervisory oversight, and lack of training. This deficiency occurred more than 2 years after a former DEA Special Agent was convicted of stealing $700,000 in cryptocurrency during a joint task force investigation of the Dark Web marketplace Silk Road because DEA did not implement additional internal controls specifically related to investigations involving cryptocurrency." It also states: "Moreover, despite the unique challenges of cryptocurrency laundering schemes, such as unknown fees and spontaneous currency fluctuations [and cryptocurrency mining—which is not mentioned in the audit report] that are not present in traditional money laundering, the DEA did not create new processes and forms to conduct and document these undercover activities."[6]

To bolster their cryptocurrency oversight and enforcement efforts for 2021—which began in October of 2020—the US federal agencies sought millions of dollars in new funding and procured a cryptocurrency investigations tool called Coinbase Analytics as follows:

- The Internal Revenue Service fiscal year 2021 documentation asked for $40.54 million to "expand cyber and cryptocurrency compliance efforts" to support the hiring of 108 special agents to conduct more criminal investigations related to cyber and digital currency.
- The US Department of the Treasury's Office of Foreign Assets Control, according to documentation, demanded an additional $812,000 to recruit digital currency investigators.
- FinCEN, according to documents, asked for $819,000 to recruit three full-time employees to support building out FinCEN's cryptocurrency and cyber threat mitigation program.

- The FBI's Transnational Organized Crime office sought an additional $1.5 million to hire six analysts. The budget summary notably focused on a plan to move the US Secret Service from the Department of Homeland Security to the Treasury Department—its original home.
- The DEA asked for $3.25 million to provide analytics and data support for its transaction-centric investigations and to recruit two full-time intelligence research specialists to be assigned to trade-based money laundering (TBML) cases.

Taxpayers with crypto transactions are encouraged to comply with various US crypto regulations and US tax reporting requirements, given the enhanced investigation tools and the human resources dedicated to cryptocurrency oversight and enforcement efforts by various US agencies.[7]

Notes

1. Selva Ozelli, "Regulations Fall on Bitcoin Around the World," My Compliance Office, 2017.
2. https://cointelegraph.com/news/the-us-plan-to-monitor-illegal-crypto-activities-more-sufficiently
3. https://www.justice.gov/opa/pr/dea-led-operation-nets-more-600-arrests-targeting-c-rtel-jalisco-nueva-generaci-n
4. Ibid.
5. https://www.courier-journal.com/story/news/crime/2020/06/03/mexico-and-dea-team-freeze-billion-dollars-linked-cjng-cartel/3134761001/
6. https://cointelegraph.com/news/the-us-plan-to-monitor-illegal-crypto-activities-more-sufficiently
7. Ibid.

Chapter 11
Cybercrime Task Force

The Cryptocurrency Intelligence Program

The Immigration and Customs Enforcement, or ICE, is the principal criminal investigative agency within the US Department of Homeland Security, which developed a new technique to track unlicensed crypto activity. ICE enforces more than 400 federal statutes that target darknet markets to combat the illegal movement of crypto funds with the help of agents who have been receiving "advanced darknet training" since at least September 2019. The ICE revealed the existence of a Cryptocurrency Intelligence Program (CIP) in the agency's 2021 budget proposal.

The proposal states that the program will seek to identify unlicensed crypto capital flows taking place across peer-to-peer marketplaces, online forums, crypto exchanges, blockchain-based mobile devices, and darknet markets.

The CIP was developed by the ICE's Bulk Cash Smuggling Center, which identifies, investigates, and disrupts cryptocurrency smuggling activities around the world.[1]

Cyber Fraud Task Force

In recent years, cyber and traditional finance crimes have been intersecting at pace, particularly since the start of the COVID-19 pandemic. In an effort to address the growing issue, the US Secret Service merged its Electronic Crimes Task Force and Financial Crimes Task Force into a single unified network dubbed the Cyber Fraud Task Force, with offices in both the United States and Europe.

The Cyber Fraud Task Force, or CFTF, was created by Washington lawmakers supporting legislation that aims to move the Secret Service from within the Department of Homeland Security back to the Treasury Department in order to more effectively investigate cyber-related financial crimes.

As US Attorney General William Barr in the US Department of Justice's 83-page report titled "Cryptocurrency Enforcement Framework," explained: "Current terrorist use of cryptocurrency may represent the first raindrops of an oncoming storm of expanded use that could challenge the ability of the U.S. and its allies to disrupt financial resources that would enable terrorist organizations to more successfully execute their deadly missions or to expand their influence."

The DOJ's Cryptocurrency Enforcement Framework

The "Cryptocurrency Enforcement Framework" report is the second of its kind issued by the Attorney General's Cyber-Digital Task Force, which was established in February 2018. The report lays out the DOJ's policy formulation in a number of critical areas, including cybersecurity, cross-border data transfers and protection, emerging technologies, cryptocurrency, and encryption. It serves as a guide to shape the future vision of US authorities and regulators toward cryptocurrencies as well as details the various ways that cryptocurrency is susceptible to abuse. The report indicates a shift in the DOJ's perspective in that it recognizes digital assets' several legitimate uses—a far cry from the department's previous perception of cryptocurrency use as a red flag for money laundering and criminality. Rather, the report recognizes cryptocurrency as a legitimate instrument of commerce with law enforcement challenges like any other means of exchange.

The report is divided into three parts: an overview of the cryptocurrency space and its illicit uses, the laws and regulatory agencies that oversee the space, and the current enforcement challenges and potential strategies to address them.

In the first part of the report, the DOJ outlines both legal and illicit uses of cryptocurrency and addresses the emergence of the "next phase of the internet's evolution," known as Web 3.0, which will allow users to have greater control in protecting their digital financial information, transactions, and identity from companies and governments.

In the second part of the report, the DOJ outlines the laws and regulations that govern the use of cryptocurrency. It acknowledges that in applying existing laws to the nascent sector, the advent of decentralized finance has added an extra layer of complexity to the institution's tasks. As a result, blockchain technology has enabled crime to spread more easily across the globe, increasing the department's challenge in following the money.

In conjunction with this, the report indicates that decentralized finance applications, privacy coins, peer-to-peer exchanges, and encrypted dark markets could continue to inhibit legitimate supervision and investigation while simplifying the noncompliance of regulations for anti-money laundering and counterterrorism financing, as set by the Financial Action Task Force. The report also describes the roles and responsibilities of other agencies with oversight or enforcement power in the space, including the Financial Crimes Enforcement Network (FinCEN), the Office of Foreign Assets Control, the Office of the Comptroller of the Currency, the Securities and Exchange Commission (SEC), the Commodity Futures Trading Commission (CFTC), the

Internal Revenue Service (IRS), the Central Intelligence Agency (CIA), and the National Security Agency (NSA).

In the third part of the report, the DOJ points out that its enforcement actions are aligned with an international focus to increase anti-money laundering (AML) accountability and broad jurisdiction over cryptocurrency trading platforms.

The report explains that the DOJ's cross-border reach can be quite broad, since a jurisdictional nexus exists when the aim of a criminal activity is to cause harm inside the United States, to US citizens, or to the interests of either one, even if the individuals committing criminal activity are noncitizens acting entirely abroad. The report goes on to explain that the cross-border nature of cryptocurrency transactions—particularly those utilizing mixing, tumbling, or encryption services, which run afoul of US money-laundering restrictions—leads to compliance gaps, inconsistent regulations, and "jurisdictional arbitrage," or when participants move virtual assets to jurisdictions where authorities lack regulatory frameworks to support investigations.

In 2021, the US DOJ formed the National Cryptocurrency Enforcement Team (NCET), a team of investigators to look into the use of cryptocurrency for criminal purposes in collaboration with other federal agencies, subject matter experts, and its law enforcement partners throughout the government.[2]

Joint Cybercrime Action Taskforce

Cross-border links between terrorism and cryptocurrency-related cybercrime underscores the need for a coherent global response. Currently, the United States is part of the Joint Cybercrime Action Taskforce, which collaborates with Europol's European Cybercrime Centre, the European Commission, and the heads of the National Cybercrime Units of EU member states. The latter has also established the European Union (EU) Cybercrime Task

Force to develop and promote a harmonized approach across the EU for tackling cybercrime and the criminal misuse of information and communication technology.

According to Europol's "Internet Organized Crime Threat Assessment 2020" report, privacy-enhancing cryptocurrency wallets, coins, and open marketplaces were named as top threats for cybercrime, with Monero emerging as a favored transaction tool on the dark web.

J-CAT members and regulation status

Country	Tax/J5	AML/CFT	Additional legislation
Australia	Yes/J5	Yes	
Canada	Yes/J5	Yes	
Colombia	Yes	Proposed	
EU Member States (9): Austria, France, Germany, Italy, Romania, the Netherlands, Poland, Sweden and Spain Represented by two agencies: Policía Nacional and Guardia Civil	Yes/J5	Yes	Yes/EU level proposed
Norway	Yes	Yes	
Switzerland	Yes	Yes	
United Kingdom	Yes/J5	Yes	
United States Represented by two agencies: FBI and Secret Service	Yes/J5	Yes	Yes

cointelegraph.com

SOURCE: *Cointelegraph.*

The EU's Proposed Digital Asset Legislation

Following a policy study that outlines recent developments regarding crypto assets and addresses key regulatory risks from the increase in digital opportunities within the financial sector, the European Commission published a proposed regulation on digital operational resilience for the financial sector and a new proposed directive that amends certain pieces of existing EU financial services legislation to strengthen resilience in digital operations and provide legal clarity on crypto assets.

Published shortly before the DOJ's report was released, the proposed regulation and directive will form part of the EU's measures on digital finance for supporting innovation in the sector while mitigating risks. The commission published the EU Digital Finance Strategy, which sets out key priorities for digitally transforming the EU's financial sector over the coming years, along with a proposed regulation on a pilot regime for distributed ledger technology market infrastructure. The latter will provide detailed rules at the jurisdictional level for comprehensive and harmonized legislation governing distributed ledger technology.[3]

Notes

1. https://cointelegraph.com/news/us-takes-regulatory-steps-for-blockchain-technology-adoption
2. https://www.justice.gov/opa/pr/deputy-attorney-general-lisa-o-monaco-announces-national-cryptocurrency-enforcement-team
3. https://cointelegraph.com/news/cybercrime-task-force-monitoring-the-global-digital-financial-system

Chapter 12
Money Laundering

FinCEN's Bitcoin regulations, which imposed registration requirements on money services businesses (MSBs), were enacted in 2013. This allowed US law enforcement and agencies to use the long arm of the law to work collaboratively with global law enforcement and agencies and with private technology companies in multijurisdictional investigations to shed light on criminals who laundered cryptocurrencies by using them in drug weapons sales, cybercrime transactions on cryptocurrency exchanges, wallets, and darkweb markets.[1]

Given the financial risks of ransomware and money laundering that digital assets pose globally, participants of the G7 meeting in June 2021 committed to working together to urgently address this escalating risk effectively and expeditiously by implementing and enforcing the Financial Action Task Force's anti–money laundering (AML) standards on digital assets and virtual asset service providers.

Here are some of the important cases to date:

- **2013:** US law enforcement and agencies, with the assistance of various global law enforcement and agencies in a multijurisdictional investigation, cracked down on cyber-crime by shutting down $6 billion Costa Rica–based virtual currency exchange Liberty Reserve and popular drug trafficking dark web market $1.2 billion Silk Road for money-laundering transactions for the first time in Bitcoin's history. A person who robbed the website Sheep Marketplace of 96,000 Bitcoins—about $100 million at current prices—attempted to hide the heist by repeatedly trading it through various "tumblers," which mix up and launder old Bitcoins for new.

- **2014:** As part of "Operation Onymous," a global law enforcement effort, US federal agents and EUROPOL seized three dark web markets; the DOJ announced charges against Bitcoin exchange Silk Road's CEO and other unlicensed MSB operators and forfeited $28 million worth of Bitcoins belonging to Silk Road. 850,000 Bitcoins worth more than $450 million were stolen from the world's largest Japanese exchange, Mt. Gox, bankrupting the exchange and resulting in the arrest of the company's CEO on charges of embezzlement. A Canadian hacker stole thousands in Bitcoins from several websites.

- **2015:** Two former FBI agents were charged by the Department of Justice with stealing Bitcoins during the 2013 Silk Road probe. In another Bitcoin exit scam, administrators of the largest dark web market, Evolution, suddenly disappeared with $12 million of Bitcoins of its users' drug money. 19,000 Bitcoins worth $5 million were stolen from the world's third-largest exchange, Slovenia-based Bitcoin Bitstamp.

- **2016:** Drug dealers' favorite virtual currency, Monero, which increased 2,760% in value in 2016, made its debut at the largest and most popular darkweb market, Alphabay. US-based Bitcoin exchange Cryptsy threatened bankruptcy, claiming that millions were lost in a Bitcoin heist, while it was actually nothing more than its operator's Bitcoin exit scam.[2]

- **2017:** On July 20, 2017, the concurrent shutting down of a pair of foreign Bitcoin-based dark web markets and the arrest of their administrators all at once ranked as one of the most sophisticated takedown operations in the fight against cyber-crime. "This is likely one of the most important criminal investigations of the year taking down the largest dark net marketplace in history," said the DOJ.[3] Alpha Bay and Hansa Market were successors to the first and most famous dark web market, Silk Road, which the authorities took down in October 2013 following Liberty Reserve.

The back-to-back dark web market shutdown operation involved the teamwork of law enforcement and agencies from 12 different countries: the United States (the DOJ, FBI, DEA, and IRS-CI), the Netherlands-Europol, the UK, France, Lithuania, Canada, Germany, Thailand, Cyprus, Lichtenstein, Antigua and Barbuda, and Belgium.

The following two foreign-owned Bitcoin dark web markets operated as hidden unlicensed MSBs and were involved in laundering illicit proceeds from the sale of opioids, including fentanyl and heroin as well as weapons:

1. The Netherlands-based Hansa had 10,000 users and utilized virtual currencies to launder funds deriving from illegal transactions. Hansa's servers in the Netherlands, Germany, and Lithuania were seized.
2. Thailand-based AlphaBay had 240,000 users and utilized virtual currencies Bitcoin, Monero, and Ethereum to launder over $1 billion deriving from illegal transactions since 2014. AlphaBay's servers in Canada and the Netherlands were seized.

Law enforcement also arrested two administrators of Hansa in Germany and a Canadian man suspected of running AlphaBay in Bangkok. "Alexander Cazes was due to be extradited to the U.S.

on charges of racketeering, narcotics distribution, money laundering and related crimes" explained the DOJ. Cazes was later found hanged in a presumed suicide in his Bangkok prison cell.

As Europol explained:

> What made this operation really special was the strategy developed by the FBI, DEA, the Dutch Police and Europol to magnify the disruptive impact of the joint action to take out AlphaBay and Hansa. . . . This involved taking covert control of Hansa under Dutch judicial authority a month ago, which allowed Dutch police to monitor the activity of users without their knowledge, and then shutting down AlphaBay by U.S. law enforcement and agencies during the same period. It meant the Dutch police could identify and disrupt the regular criminal activity on Hansa but then also sweep up all those new users displaced from AlphaBay who were looking for a new trading platform. In fact they flocked to Hansa in their droves, with an eight-fold increase in the number of new members of Hansa recorded immediately following the shutdown of AlphaBay. As a law enforcement strategy, leveraging the combined operational and technical strengths of multiple agencies in the United States and Europe, it has been an extraordinary success and a stark illustration of the collective power the global law enforcement community can bring to disrupt major criminal activity.[4]

"The so-called anonymity of the dark web is illusory. . . . More to come," the DEA made clear.[5]

Shuttering of Bulgaria-Based BTC-e Bitcoin Exchange—FinCEN's First Action Against a Foreign-Located MSB and Second-Highest Penalty of $110 Million

Only six days after the shuttering of Bitcoin dark web markets AlphaBay and Hansa, on July 26, 2017, law enforcement and agencies from the United States and Greece, in a team effort, shut down Bulgarian-based Bitcoin exchange BTC-e.

This was FinCEN's first action in collaboration with the US DOJ, IRS-CI, FBI, US Secret Service (USSS), Immigration and Customs Enforcement (ICE), Federal Deposit Insurance Corporation (FDIC), Office of the Inspector General (OIG), and Greek law enforcement against a foreign MSB.

In a 21-count indictment and hundreds of millions in civil monetary penalties, FinCEN and the DOJ charged Bulgarian Bitcoin exchange BTC-e and BTC-e's Russian head, Alexander Vinnick, for operating an alleged international $4 billion money-laundering scheme. On the same day, Mr. Vinnick was arrested while on vacation in Thessaloniki and put in jail by Greek law enforcement in coordination with US regulators to face money-laundering charges in the United States.

The DOJ's 21-count indictment painted BTC-e, operated by Vinnick, as a hub of illicit activity:

- BTC-e and Vinnick were charged with one count of operating an unlicensed MSB, and one count of conspiracy to commit money laundering for processing transactions involving over 300,000 Bitcoins stolen between 2011 and 2014 from one of the world's largest Bitcoin exchanges, Japan-based Mt. Gox, valued at $840 million; for facilitating at least $3 million in Bitcoin transactions tied to ransomware attacks such as "Crypto locker" and "Locky"; for sharing customers and conducting transactions with the now-defunct virtual currency darkweb markets Silk Road, Hans Market, and Alphabay; for theft, drug trafficking, fraud, tax fraud, bribery, and public corruption.
- Vinnick, the owner and operator of BTC-e and affiliated entities, was charged with 17 counts of money laundering and two counts of engaging in unlawful monetary transactions

including laundering associated with bribery, ransomware payouts, drug trafficking, theft, fraud, tax fraud, and public corruption, together carrying a prison term of 55 years. Vinnick's numerous withdrawals from BTC-e accounts went directly to his personal bank accounts and Bitcoin wallets, which included proceeds from well-known hacks and thefts from now-defunct Bitcoin exchanges, including Mt. Gox, Bitcoinica, and Bitfloor.

BTC-e, the Bulgarian virtual currency exchange, was one of the world's biggest virtual currency exchanges by volume at the time. Founded in 2011, BTC-e served approximately 700,000 customers worldwide, processing over 9.4 million cyber currency transactions in US dollars, Russian rubles, Euros, Bitcoin, Litecoin, Namecoin, Novacoin, Peercoin, Ethereum, and Dash. Bitcoin exchanges, like BTC-e, which converted Bitcoins in and out of other fiat currencies, functioned similarly to brokerages, and offered a variety of financial services similar to banks or other financial institutions. Customers located within the United States used BTC-e to conduct at least 21,000 Bitcoin transactions worth over $296 million. BTC-e was the "go-to Bitcoin exchange for cybercriminals with suspicious usernames like "ISIS," "Cocaine-Cowboys," "blackhathackers," "dzkiller-hacker," and "hacker-4hire," who desired to conceal proceeds from illicit activities.

BTC-e maintained a sketchy multijurisdictional legal ownership and control structure spanning at least seven different countries to hide in the shadows of the web by violating disclosure and registration laws. It was located in Bulgaria but organized or otherwise subject to the laws of Cyprus. The exchange allegedly maintained a base of operations in the Seychelles Islands and its web domains were registered to shell companies in, among other places, Singapore, the British Virgin Islands, France, and New Zealand. Its shell company-infused corporate structure, buried under complex layers of offshore companies with undisclosed ownership spanning across the world, made it hard to gauge where BTC-e was located or controlled. But one thing was clear to the team of law enforcement officers and government agents: the charges that brought down BTC-e and Vinnick were straightforward because "BTC-e lacked adequate procedures for conducting due diligence, monitoring transactions, and refusing to consummate transactions that facilitated money laundering or other illicit activity."

- BTC-e and Vinnick failed to register with FinCEN as a foreign MSB. MSB registration is mandatory for all foreign-located MSBs dealing with US customers.
- BTC-e and Vinnick failed to maintain an effective AML program. Complying with US AML laws and regulations and implementing an effective AML program is mandatory for all foreign-located MSBs.
- BTC-e and Vinnick failed to detect suspicious transactions and file suspicious activity reports. Filing reports of suspicious activity is a mandatory recordkeeping requirement for all foreign-located MSBs.
- BTC-e and Vinnick failed to obtain and retain records relating to transmittals of funds in amounts of US $3,000 or more.

FinCEN has the authority under the Bank Secrecy Act (BSA) to regulate MSBs, including money transmitters. In March 2013, FinCEN issued interpretative guidance identifying "exchangers" of virtual currency—defined as persons engaged as a business in the exchange of virtual currency for real currency, funds, or other virtual currency—as money transmitters subject to regulation as MSBs under the BSA. The assessment against BTC-e alleged failure to register with FinCEN as an MSB as well as gross failures to maintain appropriate AML controls and to report suspicious transactions as required by the BSA. As a result, FinCEN for the first time imposed penalties on a foreign-located MSB and its operator as follows:

- $110 million against BTC-e for willfully violating US AML laws.
- $12 million against Alexander Vinnick for his role in the AML violations.

"Instead of acting to prevent money laundering and tax evasion, and complying with U.S. AML, BTC-e and its operator Vinnick embraced the pervasive criminal activity conducted at the exchange by failing to obtain required information from customers beyond a username, a password, and an e-mail address and concealed BTC-e's customers by using technology to enhance Bitcoin user anonymity in order to hide proceeds obtained from illicit activity without complying with applicable U.S. AML," explained FinCEN. "To dismantle BTC-e's operations, the DOJ's Criminal Division employed a multi-faceted approach by shutting down BTC-e and related entities and prosecuting Vinnick to hinder their ability to monetize their crimes through entities that facilitate money laundering," said the DOJ. "The arrest of Alexander Vinnick was the result of a multijurisdictional effort clearly displaying the benefits of global cooperation among U.S. and international law enforcement," added the FBI. "FBI agents tracked Alexander Vinnick for more than a year around the globe before his arrest in a small beachside village in northern Greece," explained the Greek police.[6]

Suex, 2021

In a first-of–its-kind case, the Office of Foreign Assets Control (OFAC) targeted Suex,[7] an over-the-counter digital currency broker, for its alleged role in laundering the proceeds of ransomware attacks.[8] The effort was part of an effort across the government to counter ransomware and disrupt criminal networks and crypto exchanges that play a part in laundering ransoms. The goal is to improve cybersecurity in the private sector and to increase reporting of incidents and ransomware payments to US government agencies. This includes both the Treasury Department and law enforcement under the Anti-Money Laundering/Countering the Financing of Terrorism (AML/CFT) framework, as digital currency is the principal means of facilitating ransomware payments and associated money-laundering activities.

BitMEX

The DOJ and the Commodity Futures Trading Commission (CFTC) brought criminal charges and concurrent civil action against directors and entities related to BitMEX,[9] a well-known trading platform for cryptocurrency derivatives that failed to register with the CFTC as a Futures Commission Merchant and implement proper AML/CFT measures. FinCEN and the CFTC reached a groundbreaking $100 million AML settlement with BitMEX in 2021.[10]

Tian Yinyin and Li Jiadong

In March 2020, the US Department of Justice charged two Chinese nationals[11] with laundering over $100 million worth of cryptocurrencies via 113 accounts. The cryptocurrencies were proceeds from a hack of a cryptocurrency exchange by North Korean actors who were trying to evade US sanctions.[12]

Helix[13]

On February 13, 2020, the DOJ announced that the darknet's go-to money launderer, who acted as a Bitcoin mixer—soliciting $300 million in cryptocurrency from criminals, slicing and dicing the coins, and then remixing them in an ultimately futile attempt to obscure their source—had been indicted.[14]

The darknet is really just the internet with a critical twist. Anyone with access to the internet can access the darknet, but must do so using Tor—The Onion Router. In its most basic form, Tor is an encrypted interconnected web of computers across the globe that allows anyone to access the internet with complete anonymity. Tor is not in and of itself illegal, but it can be used by criminals seeking to conceal their activities and evade law enforcement detection.

Darknet marketplaces also require payments to be made in cryptocurrency, stablecoins, or cryptocurrency tumblers like Monero (XMR) to add another layer of anonymity to the transactions that occur on the dark marketplace.

Laundering money through cryptocurrencies and stablecoins leaves a permanent trail on the blockchain. Criminals have repeatedly been undone because they've relied on crypto for a part of their nefarious activities. Sometimes, they've been arrested years after their alleged crimes.

To avoid detection, criminals use cryptocurrency tumblers such as Cloakcoin, Dash, PIVX, and Zcoin, which have built-in mixing services as a part of their blockchain network. Monero, drug dealers' favorite crypto, provides anonymity without tumbling services due to its privacy-centric blockchain design. Such cryptocurrency tumblers further impede tax collection and detecting AML practices by law enforcement officials.

Notes

1. Selva Ozelli, "Regulations Fall on Bitcoin Around the World," My Compliance Office, 2017.
2. Ibid.
3. Ibid.

4. https://www.europol.europa.eu/media-press/newsroom/news/massive-blow-to-criminal-dark-web-activities-after-globally-coordinated-operation

5. Selva Ozelli, "Regulations Fall on Bitcoin Around the World," My Compliance Office, 2017.

6. Ibid.

7. https://cointelegraph.com/news/crypto-in-the-crosshairs-us-regulators-eye-the-cryptocurrency-sector

8. https://cointelegraph.com/news/us-treasury-dept-sanctions-crypto-otc-broker-suex-for-alleged-role-in-facilitating-transactions-for-ransomware-attacks

9. https://cointelegraph.com/news/cybercrime-task-force-monitoring-the-global-digital-financial-system

10. https://www.moneylaunderingnews.com/2021/08/fincen-and-cftc-reach-groundbreaking-100-million-aml-settlement-with-bitmex/

11. https://cointelegraph.com/news/us-takes-regulatory-steps-for-blockchain-technology-adoption

12. https://www.justice.gov/opa/pr/two-chinese-nationals-charged-laundering-over-100-million-cryptocurrency-exchange-hack

13. https://cointelegraph.com/news/us-takes-regulatory-steps-for-blockchain-technology-adoption

14. https://www.justice.gov/opa/pr/ohio-resident-charged-operating-darknet-based-bitcoin-mixer-which-laundered-over-300-million

Chapter 13
Theft Hacking and Ransom Payments

A ccording to a report by Chainalysis,[1] North Korean hackers stole almost $400 million worth of digital assets—mainly from cryptocurrency investment firms and centralized exchanges—in at least seven attacks in 2021, which was one of the most successful years on record for cyber-criminals in the country.[2] There have been other noteworthy cryptocurrency thefts/hacks since 2013:

2013: An Australian and Czechoslovakian Bitcoin exchange were hacked, and millions in cryptocurrency were stolen. The Chinese Bitcoin exchange GBL mysteriously disappeared in a Bitcoin exit scam, taking more than $4 million of the cryptocurrency with it.[3]

2014: 850,000 Bitcoins worth more than $450 million were stolen from the world's largest Japanese exchange, Mt. Gox, bankrupt-ing the exchange and resulting in the arrest of the company's CEO on charges of embezzlement. A Canadian hacker stole thousands in Bitcoins from several websites.[4]

2015: Two former FBI agents were charged by the Department of Justice with stealing Bitcoins during the 2013 Silk Road probe. In another Bitcoin exit scam, administrators of the largest dark web market, Evolution, suddenly disappeared with $12 million of Bitcoins of its users' drug money. 19,000 Bitcoins worth $5 million were stolen from the world's third-largest exchange, Slovenia-based Bitcoin Bitstamp.[5]

2016: The DOJ convicted the fourth defendant in a scheme to defraud a Bitcoin gaming company of over $16 million worth of cryptocurrency. 120,000 Bitcoins worth $95 million were stolen from the world's largest cryptocurrency exchange, Bitfinex. North Koreans perpetrated several cybercrime attacks at banks. US-based Bitcoin exchange Cryptsy threatened bankruptcy, claiming that millions were lost in a Bitcoin heist, while it was actually nothing more than its operator's Bitcoin exit scam.[6]

2021: About 2,000 years ago, during its Han dynasty, China made peace with some of the nomadic people of Central Asia who continuously ransacked Silk Road traders for an easy payday. It did so in order to fully establish the Silk Road trade route, which stretched from China to Europe, and to secure a great source of wealth from trading in luxury goods.

As trade increasingly has shifted to the digital realm during the global COVID-19 pandemic, cyber attackers are taking advantage of organizations' lax cybersecurity measures. They are using ransomware to lock these organizations' data with encryption until a ransom payment in cryptocurrency is made. Back in 2019, 98% of ransomware payments were made in Bitcoin (BTC).

Anne Neuberger, US deputy national security adviser for cyber and emerging technology, explained: "The number and size of ransomware incidents have increased significantly. [. . .] The U.S. government is working with countries around the world to hold ransomware actors and the countries who harbor them accountable, but we cannot fight the threat posed by ransomware alone. The private sector has a distinct and key responsibility."

The administration of President Joe Biden is moving to treat cyberattacks—which are estimated to cost $1 trillion a year and often take the form of ransomware—as a national security threat. Intelligence agencies have concluded that they pose an elevated threat to the country, with gasoline, food supplies, and hospital systems at risk.

In 2021, the U.S. Department of Justice seized 63.7 BTC (worth approximately $2.3 million at the time) representing the proceeds of a ransom payment made by Colonial Pipeline to the group known as "DarkSide." It did so via a coordinated effort with the DOJ's Ransomware and Digital Extortion Task Force, which collaborates with domestic and foreign government agencies in addition to private-sector partners to combat this significant criminal threat.

Lisa Monaco, the DOJ's deputy attorney general, noted: "Following the money remains one of the most basic, yet powerful tools we have." She continued: "Ransom payments are the fuel that propels the digital extortion engine, and [. . .] the United States will use all available tools to make these attacks more costly and less profitable for criminal enterprises.

Paul Abbate, deputy director of the Federal Bureau of Investigation, added: "We will continue to use all of our available resources and leverage our domestic and international partnerships to disrupt ransomware attacks and protect our private sector partners and the American public."[7]

Notes

1. https://blog.chainalysis.com/reports/north-korean-hackers-have-prolific-year-as-their-total-unlaundered-cryptocurrency-holdings-reach-all-time-high/
2. https://www.bbc.com/news/business-59990477
3. Selva Ozelli, "Regulations Fall on Bitcoin Around the World," My Compliance Office, 2017.
4. Ibid.
5. Ibid.
6. Ibid.
7. https://cointelegraph.com/news/are-cryptocurrency-ransom-payments-tax-deductible

Chapter 14
Cryptocurrency Bribes

At the federal level in the United States, cryptocurrencies have a lot of regulators—the Financial Crimes Enforcement Network (FinCEN), the Office of Foreign Assets Control (OFAC), the Internal Revenue Service (IRS), the Commodity Futures Trading Commission (CFTC), and the Securities and Exchange Commission (SEC) among them.

These regulators characterize cryptocurrencies respectively as money, property, commodities, and a security.

The multiclassification of cryptocurrencies and their use in bribery transactions could trigger a number of questions about valuations and risks under US and other anti-corruption and tax regimes.

Here is an example: A US public company bribes a foreign official with a ZTE phone that serves as a cryptocurrency miner as well as a cryptocurrency wallet. This allows the foreign official to mine Ethereum (ETH) on an as-needed basis, sell the mined ETH on a foreign crypto exchange, and submit to the company a very large electricity bill for reimbursement for mining activities, in exchange for pursuing business in the foreign country.

This so-called new bribe eliminates the need for bankers, accountants, lawyers, consultants, and other middlemen. It also differs from traditional Foreign Corrupt Practices Act (FCPA) bribery scenarios via hidden slush funds denominated in fiat currencies. The new bribe doesn't involve nondisclosed offshore intermediary entities or bank accounts or shame consultancy contracts.

The new bribe (something of value) nevertheless creates the apparent basis of an FCPA violation. And if it is deducted for US tax purposes, it subjects the bribe-payer company to numerous fines and penalties.

But let's look deeper into questions about how to value the new bribe.

Users of ETH can obtain it by exchanging it for fiat currencies or initial coin offering tokens, or by mining, which is the process of having computers compete to solve complex mathematical problems.

The IRS said recently that when a taxpayer successfully mines virtual currency, the fair market value of the virtual currency as of the date of receipt is includible in gross income. This implies that ETH mining is akin to a service activity. Therefore, it is appropriate to treat the costs of mining virtual currency similar to expenses incurred in providing other services that are expensed as paid or incurred.[1]

A letter from the American Institute of Certified Public Accountants (AICPA) to the IRS in 2018 suggests that cryptocurrency mining should be treated as ordinary income in the year it is mined, and the expenses of mining deducted as having been incurred. AICPA argues that the matching of income and expenses is consistent with other service activities. In addition, any cryptocurrency mining equipment—like the ZTE ETH miner/wallet phone—should be capitalized and depreciated like any other property whose useful life extends beyond one year.[2]

Some cryptocurrencies like ETH are traded on centralized exchanges that operate in jurisdictions outside the United States. The exchanges are either a pure virtual currency exchange or a virtual currency exchange that allows virtual currencies to exchange into fiat currencies. These foreign virtual currency exchanges have custody of customers' virtual currencies, and an exchange failure results in the loss of customer funds.

AICPA's letter to the IRS suggests that taxpayers should report the value of cryptocurrencies and fiat currencies held at foreign exchanges for tax purposes if they meet the necessary threshold, *but not when a taxpayer holds cryptocurrency in a non-custodial wallet* (such as a ZTE ETH miner/wallet phone) that the taxpayer owns, controls, and is in possession of a private key to.

That reasoning would suggest that a ZTE phone enabled for ETH mining and wallet functions has only the intrinsic value of the phone itself, and nothing more.[3]

Notes

1. https://www.irs.gov/pub/irs-drop/n-14-21.pdf
2. https://us.aicpa.org/content/dam/aicpa/advocacy/tax/downloadabledocuments/20180530-aicpa-comment-letter-on-notice-2014-21-virtual-currency.pdf
3. https://fcpablog.com/2018/06/12/selva-ozelli-how-should-cyptocurrency-bribes-be-valued/

Chapter 15
Corruption

In 2017, a partner of an international law firm was busted by the FBI while he tried to garner Bitcoins in a corrupt transaction.

A calm lobby of Hilton Garden Hill in Cupertino, California, was transformed into a crime scene at exactly 9:55:10 a.m. on January 31, 2017, when a man shrieked "my life is over" as he was being handcuffed and arrested by FBI agent William Scanlon. The arrested man was using a fake name, Dan, and wearing an obvious wig to disguise his identity. Unfortunately, his cover was blown when Scanlon, who worked at the FBI's public corruption division, identified him in his report as none other than Jeffrey Wertkin, a partner at Akin Gump Strauss Hauer & Feld, who was an ex-US Department of Justice (DOJ) prosecutor.

Apparently, Wertkin, while still working at the DOJ in Washington, DC, stole whistleblower complaints brought against a Silicon Valley tech company, which were sealed from public view. To give the tech company a leg up in the government's ongoing investigation and to obstruct justice, Wertkin tried selling these sealed whistleblower complaints against the tech company in exchange for 310 "untraceable" Bitcoins worth $310,000, but was instead busted by the FBI.[1]

Wertkin's dreams of becoming an "undetectable" Bitcoin millionaire were shattered on November 29, 2017—when Bitcoin was trading at $7,000—and when he pleaded guilty to two charges of obstruction of justice and one count of transporting stolen goods across state lines. DOJ prosecutors said they would seek 30 to 37 months of prison time when he was sentenced on March 14, 2018. The law firm has since fired Wertkin.[2]

In President Biden's National Security Study Memorandum issued on June 3, 2021, he said, "[c]orruption, both domestic and foreign, threatens U.S. national security by eroding citizens' faith in government, distorting economies, and weakening democratic institutions." Accordingly, FinCEN declared the money-laundering risks associated with corruption to be a threat to US national security.[3]

Notes

1. https://docs.google.com/viewerng/viewer?url=http://abovethelaw
   .com/wp-content/uploads/2017/02/USA-v-Wertkin-criminal-
   complaint.pdf&hl=en_US
2. https://cointelegraph.com/news/smart-contracts-are-taking-over-
   functions-of-lawyers-expert-blog
3. https://www.whitehouse.gov/briefing-room/presidential-actions/
   2021/06/03/memorandum-on-establishing-the-fight-against-
   corruption-as-a-core-united-states-national-security-interest/

Chapter 16
US Tax Evasion

Bob Brockman

The United States faces a growing threat of transnational cyber-crime, particularly against its financial system. In what may be the largest prosecution of its kind in US history, the US Department of Justice charged Texas tech billionaire Bob Brockman in a 39-count indictment of evading $2 billion in taxes. The businessman used encrypted devices and code words to conceal his wire fraud, tax fraud, and money laundering within a network of offshore entities and bank accounts.

As the CEO of Reynolds & Reynolds Co., Brockman contributed 6.4% to the United States' current annual deficit of $3.1 trillion—more than double the previous record of $1.4 trillion set bailing out the 2007–2008 financial crisis. Aside from Brockman's tax fraud, the COVID-19 pandemic deepened the debt, as both shrinking revenues and heightened spending intensify, along with rising daily coronavirus infections, which have now hit 81 million people in the United States and 531 million worldwide as of May 1, 2022.[1]

John McAfee

Antivirus software pioneer John McAfee, the founder of McAfee Associates—the company that released the first commercial antivirus software, McAfee VirusScan, in the late 1980s, contributing to the birth of a multibillion-dollar industry—was indicted on five counts of tax evasion and five counts of willful failure to file a tax return, which could have resulted in a maximum sentence of 30 years if convicted. He could also have expected to pay US taxes and penalties, according to the US Department of Justice (DOJ). The DOJ's charges were announced shortly after the US Securities and Exchange Commission (SEC) revealed that it had brought civil charges against McAfee related to cryptocurrency offerings.

McAfee had been a controversial figure in several countries, not only in the United States. He went into "exile" after claiming he had been charged with using cryptocurrencies against the US government, foolishly tweeting from a boat, boasting about the fact that he hadn't filed any US tax returns.

According to the DOJ's indictment—which was unsealed following McAfee's arrest in Spain, where he was pending extradition to the United States—McAfee failed to file tax returns for four years, from 2014 to 2018, despite earning millions from consulting work, speaking engagements, cryptocurrencies, and selling the rights to his life story to be used in a documentary. McAfee was accused of evading tax liability by having this income paid into bank accounts and cryptocurrency exchange accounts that were in the names of nominees. He allegedly also concealed assets in the names of others, such as a yacht and real estate property.[2]

Shortly after McAFee's extradition to the United States was authorized by the Spanish National Court on June 23, 2021, he was found dead by hanging in his prison cell.[3]

Notes

1. https://coronavirus.jhu; https://cointelegraph.com/news/cybercrime-task-force-monitoring-the-global-digital-financial-system
2. https://cointelegraph.com/news/better-regulation-needed-to-stop-crypto-tax-evaders-from-running-wild
3. https://www.reuters.com/legal/government/john-mcafee-found-dead-prison-after-spanish-court-allows-extradition-2021-06-23/

Chapter 17
Intellectual Property Espionage and Cryptocurrency

In recent cases and reports from 2021, cryptocurrency was involved in intellectual property espionage.

Ethereum developer Virgil Griffith pleaded guilty to conspiring to violate the International Emergency Economic Powers Act—which is used to prevent US citizens from exporting technology and intellectual property to communist countries—when he gave a cryptocurrency and blockchain presentation at a North Korean conference in 2019. He will serve 63 months in prison and pay a $100,000 fine.[1]

Jonathan Toebbe, a US Navy nuclear engineer who held a top-secret security clearance and specialized in naval nuclear propulsion—and had access to military secrets—was charged in October 2021 with trying to pass information about the design of American nuclear-powered submarines to someone he thought was a representative of a foreign government in exchange for cryptocurrency in violation of the Atomic Energy Act, the Justice Department stated.[2]

Cybereason, a provider of operation-centric cyberattack protection, published a new report, titled "Operation GhostShell: Novel RAT Targets Global Aerospace and Telecoms Firms," that unmasks a highly focused cyber espionage operation against global aerospace and telecommunications companies.[3] The report, which follows the August publication of the firm's "DeadRinger" report, discloses a newly identified Iranian actor, dubbed MalKamak, who was behind the attacks and has been operating since at least 2018. MalKamak has been using a previously unknown, highly sophisticated remote access Trojan, known as ShellClient, that evades antivirus and other security tools and abuses cloud service provider Dropbox for command and control.[4]

According to research published by Slovak security vendor ESET, a cyberespionage group called FamousSparrow has targeted hotels, international governments, international organizations, engineering companies, and law firms since at least 2019.[5] The group used a known Microsoft Exchange vulnerability—which was also exploited by suspected Chinese hackers[6] and scammers seeking to mine cryptocurrency—to attack its victims, which include the US Republican Governors Association.[7] While ESET didn't connect FamousSparrow to a specific nation, it did find similarities between its techniques and those of SparklingGoblin,[8] an offshoot of Winnti Group—which is linked to China—and DRBControl.[9]

In July 2021, the US government blamed China for exploiting the Microsoft Exchange Server attacks[10] and—for the first time—it also accused the Chinese government of employing criminal hackers to conduct the attacks,[11] releasing a report[12] that warns of China's ongoing targeting of the defense, semiconductor, medical, and other industries in order to steal intellectual property.[13]

Notes

1. https://cointelegraph.com/news/eth-developer-pleads-guilty-for-conspiracy-to-violate-sanctions-laws; https://www.coindesk.com/business/2022/04/12/former-ethereum-developer-virgil-griffith-sentenced-to-5-years-in-prison-for-north-korea-trip/
2. https://www.justice.gov/opa/press-release/file/1440946/download; https://www.justice.gov/opa/pr/maryland-nuclear-engineer-and-spouse-arrested-espionage-related-charges
3. https://www.cybereason.com/blog/operation-ghostshell-novel-rat-targets-global-aerospace-and-telecoms-firms
4. https://www.cybereason.com/blog/deadringer-exposing-chinese-threat-actors-targeting-major-telcos
5. https://www.cyberscoop.com/famoussparrow-eset-microsoft-exchange-proxylogon/
6. https://techcrunch.com/2021/07/19/biden-china-exchange-hacks-ransomware/
7. https://www.forbes.com/sites/leemathews/2021/09/20/republican-governors-association-hit-by-exchange-server-hack/?sh=458a467b7ad9
8. https://threatpost.com/sparklinggoblin-apt/168928/
9. https://www.cyberscoop.com/trend-micro-chinese-hacking-group-new-backdoors-gambling/
10. https://www.cyberscoop.com/china-microsoft-exchange-server-indictments-us-allies/
11. https://www.whitehouse.gov/briefing-room/statements-releases/2021/07/19/the-united-states-joined-by-allies-and-partners-attributes-malicious-cyber-activity-and-irresponsible-state-behavior-to-the-peoples-republic-of-china/
12. https://www.cisa.gov/uscert/ncas/alerts/aa21-200b
13. https://cointelegraph.com/news/crypto-in-the-crosshairs-us-regulators-eye-the-cryptocurrency-sector

Chapter 18

The US Government Implements Blockchain Programs to Improve Transparency and Efficiency

US government agencies launch new projects to keep up with the economy's digital transformation. Blockchain and cryptocurrency issues were on the agenda of the World Economic Forum for 2018.

The US government has been evaluating blockchain technology since they have funded, collaborated, and partnered with businesses and other countries as well as educational institutions in fostering and continuously developing innovative technologies and science. Contracts, transactions, and the records of intellectual property (IP) are among the defining structures of the US economic, legal, and political system, and the government agencies formed to manage them need to keep up with the economy's digital transformation. Accordingly, blockchain technology is under evaluation or being implemented by several US government agencies to improve transparency, efficiency, and trust in information sharing in:[1]

- Financial management
- Procurement
- IT asset and supply chain management
- Smart contracts
- Patents, trademarks copyrights, and royalties
- Government-issued credentials like visas, passports, Social Security numbers, and birth certificates
- Federal personnel workforce data
- Appropriated funds
- Federal assistance and foreign aid delivery

The General Services Administration (GSA)

The GSA's Emerging Citizen Technology Office launched the US federal blockchain program for federal agencies and US businesses that are interested in exploring blockchain technology and its implementation within the US government.[2] So far, the GSA has used blockchain to automate and speed up contracts review for its FASt Lane program.[3]

Department of the Treasury

The Treasury Department is running a pilot program to determine whether blockchain technology can be utilized for supply chain management, which has accelerated, processing times, created efficiencies, and strengthened financial controls in the private sector.

Ex–Treasury Secretary Steven Mnuchin, who sat on a Davos blockchain panel, believed in forming public-private partnerships (PPPs) with foreign investors to stimulate economic growth, with the aim of passing on substantial risk of funding to the private sector.

PPPs typically involve a government agency identifying a potential project, determining that there is sufficient revenue potential from the project to attract investor interest, soliciting competitive bids, and then selecting one or more private sector entities to design, finance, build, operate, and maintain the project. In a PPP, the government generally owns the project but grants the private sector significant authority over its development and operation.

"Working with foreign investors is going to be a critical part of any plan we put forward and public-private partnerships are crucial to ensuring that the American taxpayer does not bear the full cost of any proposed program," Mnuchin explained.[4]

The Treasury Department has also undertaken initiatives to improve the "anti-money laundering/combating the financing of terrorism (AML/CFT)" laws for blockchain-based cryptocurrencies,[5] formed PPPs with financial institutions to share information,[6] and issued reports on stablecoins.[7]

US State Department

The US State Department underscores the importance of innovation in world economic development and encourages dialogue with the private sector partners currently using blockchain technology.

"The State Department supports public-private partnerships. For example, in maximizing the impact and accountability of foreign development/assistance, Blockchain technology by bringing transparency, may address corruption, fraud or misappropriation of funds and inefficiencies within the public procurement funding process itself," explained ex–Deputy Secretary John J. Sullivan.[8]

Government procurement accounts for a substantial part of the global economy, 20% of GDP or around $9.5 trillion of public money. According to an Organisation for Economic Co-operation and Development (OECD) study, corruption drains off between 20 and 25% or around $2 trillion annually. It accounts for a substantial portion of the taxpayers' money and remains the government activity that is most vulnerable to waste, fraud, and corruption due to the size of the financial flows involved. Corruption distorts the fair awarding of contracts, reduces the quality of basic public services, limits opportunities to develop a competitive private sector, and undermines trust in public institutions.

Countries around the world are putting technological innovation at the heart of public procurement to reshape procurement into a strategic tool for income growth, national competitiveness, and improvements in health, economic well-being, and overall quality of life. More than four dozen countries have created national innovation strategies and/or launched national innovation foundations. These countries are relaxing foreign direct investment constraints, providing funding, financing, using public-private collaborations, and tax breaks and asking the private sector from outside their borders for commitments to their countries. In maximizing the impact and accountability of foreign development/assistance, blockchain technology may address corruption, fraud, or misappropriation of funds and inefficiencies within the funding process.

Department of Defense (DOD)

As reflected in the 2018 National Defense Authorization Act (H.R. 2810) as signed into law on December 12, 2017, the US federal government and its agencies are exploring the adoption of blockchain technology in various areas, after carefully studying the risks posed by this new distributed ledger technology. This evaluation will shed light on the blockchain technology capabilities to both the federal government and Department of Defense IT environments.[9]

Department of Homeland Security (DHS)

The DHS is awarding Small Business Innovation Research (SBIR) grants to develop a use case for blockchain technology's role in border security.[10]

National Aeronautics and Space Administration (NASA)

Efficient communications systems and effective computing techniques are crucial to ensure the success of each NASA mission. Greater accessibility of digital information and cost-effective technologies of manned and unmanned space flights are expected to become much better integrated via blockchain technology. A new NASA grant to the University of Akron in Ohio will fund research to use deep-learning artificial intelligence that works over an Ethereum blockchain network to develop a resilient networking and computing paradigm in various space communication environments.[11]

Blockchain is not a silver bullet for digital government, but as this technology is more widely implemented, it could represent the future of smart, legal contracts and how entire industries in partnership with the US government conduct themselves in a transparent and streamlined manner.[12]

Notes

1. https://digital.gov/topics/emerging-tech/
2. https://digital.gov/event/2018/07/16/emerging-technology-leadership-series-brian-behlendorf-blockchain/
3. https://www.gsa.gov/technology/technology-purchasing-programs/mas-information-technology/sell-through-mas-information-technology/fast-lane-making-it-easier
4. https://thehill.com/policy/transportation/338649-white-house-says-foreign-investment-key-to-infrastructure-plan
5. https://cointelegraph.com/news/eu-amends-aml-laws-for-cryptotrading-as-us-ponders-expert-blog
6. https://home.treasury.gov/news/press-releases/sm0251
7. https://home.treasury.gov/system/files/136/StableCoinReport_Nov1_508.pdf
8. https://cointelegraph.com/news/us-government-implements-blockchain-programs-to-improve-transparency-and-efficiency-expert-blog
9. https://docs.house.gov/billsthisweek/20171113/HRPT-115-HR2810.pdf
10. https://www.dhs.gov/science-and-technology/news/2017/01/10/snapshot-blockchain-technology-explored-homeland-security
11. https://www.nasa.gov/directorates/spacetech/strg/ecf17/RNCP/
12. https://cointelegraph.com/news/us-government-implements-blockchain-programs-to-improve-transparency-and-efficiency-expert-blog

Chapter 19
Supply Chain Management with Blockchain Amid the COVID Pandemic

To gain transparency and consumer safety, the food-processing and meatpacking plants are implementing blockchain technology to their operation services.

COVID-19 continued to wreak havoc throughout 2020, with United States meat producers being victims of the pandemic in a "cascading series of events," including the shutting down of the food service sector, universities, and school lunch programs, all likely to impact millions of Americans.

Meat-processing plants around the United States, which emerged as the world's epicenter of the pandemic, saw huge outbreaks of COVID-19, as the virus spread quickly among workers crammed in close quarters, often without recommended protective gear. "After the outbreak was announced in the U.S., we never stopped working," a meatpacking employee said. He continued: "I had to keep working without any protective [equipment] in place because I have no other means of income. But we were always afraid we might be too exposed to the virus."

The outbreak interrupted work at meat processing plants, with workers, truckers, and meat inspectors expressing fears of traveling to hotspots. One hundred workers of the Food Safety and Inspection Service—part of the US Department of Agriculture—tested positive for the coronavirus as the illness ravaged the nation's meat-processing plants.

Prior to the COVID-19 pandemic's quick spread to nearly every country around the world, blockchain technology had already begun its entrance into the livestock and meat-packing industry for increased risk tracking. The worldwide production and trade of livestock is a major economic, social, and political force. Supporting around 1.3 billion people, the sector has an estimated value of $1.4 trillion, equal to 40% of agricultural gross domestic product worldwide. Along the complex multinational global livestock/meat chain supply, there are various risks to keep track of, such as possible sanitary restrictions, trade barriers, sanctions, corruption, and now, COVID-19-related risks.

Blockchain Adoption by US Federal Food and Disease Regulators

In the United States, the federal meat and disease regulators are the Department of Agriculture (USDA) and the Centers for Disease Control and Prevention (CDC), respectively. Both have been turning to blockchain technology to track food safety as well as disease, which has become a more urgent task with the spread of COVID-19 worldwide.

The US Department of Agriculture: The USDA is a federal agency responsible for overseeing meat, poultry, and egg product safety. Meat, for example, goes through three separate USDA inspections: at the slaughterhouse, at the meat-processing facility, and at the meat factory.

While digitization was identified in the USDA's report to the president in 2018, the emergence of COVID-19 in November 2019 expedited implementation of blockchain technology for tracing food safety throughout the supply chain.

At the beginning of 2020, the USDA announced that IBM was developing a blockchain proof-of-concept for the Food Safety and Inspection Service (FSIS)—the United States' food safety arm—as part of its 2020 Annual Plan to evaluate how blockchain can be optimized to track goods throughout supply chains for export certification systems. So far, the USDA has allocated $250,000 to develop this software.

Centers for Disease Control and Prevention: The CDC timeline for implementing the needed technological tools to trace the spread of COVID-19 became a "here-and-now" priority. The CDC and different organizations, including the Bloomberg School of Public Health at Johns Hopkins University, the Villanova University Department of Electrical and Computer Engineering, and the coalition network, among others, developed contact tracing platforms to contain COVID-19 by utilizing blockchain, artificial intelligence, and Internet of Things (IoT) technology to help track coronavirus cases globally.

Blockchain Adoption to Track Meat Supply Chain in Australia

The first testing of blockchain technology for supply chain management in the meatpacking industry was announced by JBS S.A., one of the world's largest animal protein companies, in November 2019 as the COVID-19 pandemic surfaced in Wuhan, China.

The company's Australian subsidiary is the nation's largest food-processing company, marketer, and exporter. It began developing a tracer that provides data "from paddock to plate" with Sydney-based startup Lumachain. The project uses Microsoft technology including Azure AI, IoT, and blockchain, and is in collaboration with Australia's national science agency, CSIRO.

According to JBS Australia CEO Brent Eastwood: "The end-to-end transparency that this trial is demonstrating has enormous potential for not only Australia's meat producers—but the entire food chain. For consumers Lumachain's solution provides the rich information that they want, giving them peace of mind about what they are feeding their family for dinner."[1]

JBS's blockchain-based food supply tracking initiative followed a $1.5 billion meat sales deal closed in November between JBS Australia and Win Chain—a supply chain e-commerce platform and subsidiary of Chinese tech behemoth Alibaba—that links upstream and downstream fresh food resources, providing integration between supplier, processing, warehousing, distribution, supply chain finance, and brand marketing to help international suppliers sell their products in China.

Operation Carne Fraca and Other Violations in the Meat Industry

Despite the meat conglomerate showing signs of a progressive stance on technology across the Pacific, JBS S.A. has demonstrated time and again its propensity for misconduct, one instance of which, the alleged sale of chemically treated rotten meat, resulted in a federal investigation by Brazilian authorities named Operation Carne Fraca. The company's path is additionally paved with legal breaches, scandals, high-level corruption schemes, unfavorable labor conditions, and environmental breaches involving the use of deforested Amazon rainforest fragments for cattle grazing. Brazil's JBS S.A. operates in over 150 countries with an annual revenue of about $50 billion, 53% of which comes from its US operations. The company has yet to test or implement blockchain technology to track the safety of its food supply chain within its parent company or subsidiaries other than JBS Australia.

JBS S.A. has been able to get away with multiple corporate governance lapses for a long time, mainly because JBS S.A. founder Joesley Batista confessed to, and served prison time for, bribing 2,000 officials in the Brazilian government (including ex-President Michel Temer) with a total of $250 million. This systemic corruption allowed the company to not only sell and export salmonella-contaminated meat, but also secure government funding from Brazil's development bank to finance its international expansion, including the purchase of its US beef-producing units of Smithfield Foods Inc. in 2008 and US poultry producer Pilgrim's Pride Corporation in 2009, among other companies. For these corporate governance violations, JBS executives were slapped with more than $3.2 billion in fines in 2017, one of the largest fines in history.

That same year, under the OECD's tax transparency rules, multinational companies were required to adhere to a new country-by-country reporting standard. Since 2017, the standard mandated that all multinational companies disclose cryptocurrency and property bribery payments for each tax jurisdiction in which they conduct business. Accordingly, the US Justice Department and the Securities and Exchange Commission had been investigating JBS S.A.'s parent company, J&F Investimentos, for potential violations of the Foreign Corrupt Practices Act for bribery payments made to foreign government officials before three US senators and one US House representative urged other US government agencies, mainly the USDA and the Treasury Department, to investigate JBS S.A. amid the widening COVID-19 outbreaks, which resulted in JBS plant closures in several states, including Minnesota, South Dakota, Pennsylvania, and Colorado. To add to this, JBS received up to $100 million of US taxpayer funds intended for struggling American farmers and instead spent it on financing JBS S.A.'s expansion spree mainly to supply the growing meat demand from China.

Senator Richard Blumenthal urged the Secretary of Agriculture, Sonny Perdue: "Immediately cease any existing or future bailout payments to foreign-owned corporations, like the Brazilian-owned meatpacker JBS, and remove them from your approved and eligible vendors list." U.S. House representative Rosa De Lauro also urged the USDA Inspector General to investigate payments made to JBS.[2]

US Senators Marco Rubio and Robert Menendez asked then–Treasury Secretary Steven Mnuchin for the Committee on Foreign Investment in the United States to review transactions by JBS S.A., which purchased several US meat companies in recent years with ill-gotten financing and to assess its implications on the national security and safety of the nation's food supply. The letter listed the meat conglomerate's ties to the sanctioned Venezuelan Maduro regime as an additional reason for the request, perhaps due to its use of cryptocurrencies in barter trades for food sales.

In December 2019, Brazilian prosecutors filed a case against JBS S.A., its holding company, and 14 people for alleged fraud in loans from Brazil's National Bank for Economic and Social Development (BNDES), which allowed the company to internationally expand and become one of the world's largest beef producers. Prosecutors are seeking compensation of 21 billion reais ($5 billion) and are seeking conviction of the company's founders, Joesley and Wesley Batista, for their wrongdoing and resulting illegal enrichment related to transactions made between the corporation and BNDES.

Following JBS's corruption investigation and lawsuit, BNDES—JBS's biggest shareholder after the Batista family— announced the sale of part of its 21.3% stake in the company as part of a plan to exit investments in private companies to replenish government coffers. The meat giant's profitability soared by 40% in 2019 compared to the year before.

Blockchain for Tracking Corruption in Government Funds and Grants

The Brazilian bank's changed focus toward the prosperity of its nation does not end at selling its stake in JBS. Since late 2018, BNDES has also been in the process of developing a stablecoin, BNDES Token, for higher transparency in public spending. Similarly, the US Treasury Department began testing a blockchain-based grants payment system in early 2020 that tokenizes electronic federal letters of credit sent out to grant recipients, ensuring their traceability and transparency. For cases such as JBS S.A.'s, the traceability of government grant money would expose the meat conglomerate's expenditure of these funds on bribery and foreign expansion. When funding provided by the US government is used to finance illegal activity (a cross-border bribe, for example), that legal violation can then be pursued in the US justice system, even if the bribe occurred outside of the country.

As for bringing food supply chains further into the next era of tech, acting FDA Commissioner Ned Sharpless explained: "We expect to see more innovation in the agriculture, food production, and food distribution systems in the next 10 years than we've seen in the past 20, which will continue to provide an even greater variety of food options and delivery conveniences to American consumers. With this ever-changing landscape, we know we must continue preparing to take advantage of new opportunities and address potential risks."[3]

The widespread COVID-19 outbreaks in at least 79 US food-processing and meatpacking plants during 2020, while most unfortunate, spurred expedited blockchain technology adoption in the meatpacking industry to bring the world closer to a point where consumer safety is a priority and corporate corruption is a reprehensible and unfavorable means of doing business for all parties concerned. To avert a food shortage, then–US President Donald Trump signed an executive order under the Defense Production Act on April 28, 2020, to compel meat-processing plants to remain open, with the government providing additional protective gear for employees as well as regulatory guidance.[4]

Tracing Fishy Risks with Blockchain Tech Amid the COVID-19 Pandemic

The COVID-19 pandemic highlighted challenges in global seafood supply chains, and blockchain tech may help improve them.

COVID-19 is the most devastating plague to ravage humankind this century. Every day, the number of patients infected with the coronavirus is rising globally and taking the highest human toll in the United States. The highly infectious virus was first contracted in November 2019 in Wuhan, the capital city of China's Hubei province, through horseshoe bat-to-human contact at the Huanan seafood market.

Many of the initial COVID-19 patients were either stall owners, market employees, or regular visitors of the market, who rapidly developed a severe respiratory illness. Despite the market being shut down on January 1, 2020, the virus rapidly spread airborne during exhalation, talking, and coughing via microdroplets small enough to remain aloft in the air, spreading to over 200 countries and regions around the world.

Seafood is a major source of nourishment, providing sustenance to billions of people as well as to fish and animals worldwide. It is considered to be one of the world's largest industries, generating a value of about $152 billion in 2017, with more than half of this trade originating in developing regions.

At present, China accounts for nearly 75% of the global seafood and aquaculture market in terms of both volume and value, while the second-largest market share is held by India, followed by Indonesia, Chile, Norway, Japan, South Korea, the United States, and the United Kingdom.

Seafood Industry-Related Malpractices

At the same time, the seafood industry is plagued by malpractices, including fraud, product mislabeling, tax evasion, price fixing, and poor management of fisheries:

- Overfishing—in 2018, almost 90% of global wild fish stocks were either exploited or overfished, and this number is estimated to grow.
- Bycatches—approximately 60% of the seafood taken from the ocean is discarded, lost, or wasted in supply chains.
- Illegal, unreported, and unregulated fishing—representing up to 26 million tons of fish caught, valued from $10 billion to $23 billion annually.

COVID-19-Related Risks in Seafood Supply Chains

The COVID-19 pandemic highlighted the challenges and inadequacies of the global seafood supply chain, according to a report prepared by the Food and Agriculture Organization of the United Nations. With the emergence of the pandemic, seafood businesses shuttered their doors overnight, processing facilities ceased or significantly curtailed operations, restaurants shut down, and markets subsequently dried up. As entire fishing fleets hung up their nets, products were left stranded across the globe, hindering the export of seafood products. Furthermore, countries imposed border and trade restrictions and ramped up seafood inspections. This added to industry problems as COVID-19 mysteriously continued to spread fishing boats and processing facilities, causing great health and financial repercussions worldwide.

China's General Administration of Customs began mass-testing seafood imports at ports and blocking shipments from fisheries that reported infections among workers, particularly after samples from the Sustainable Shrimp Partnership, a group of certified shrimp importers from Ecuador, and the Global Salmon Initiative, a group of certified salmon importers from Chile, tested positive for the novel coronavirus on both the inside and outside of packaging.

The 190,000 residents of Dalian—a fishing community with a population of 6.7 million in the Liaoning province of China—were also rescreened for COVID-19 and quarantined after a second-wave outbreak linked to a seafood processing firm was reported following the first outbreak 100 days prior. The intense testing of seafood, other products, and people for the coronavirus tripled customs clearance times at some major Chinese ports, hindering global seafood trade flows.

In Argentina, health officials struggled to piece together how the disease infected 57 of 61 healthy sailors while they were at sea for 35 days. Alejandra Alfaro, the director of primary health care in Tierra del Fuego, said: "It's hard to establish how the crew was infected, considering that for 35 days, they had no contact with dry land. Supplies were only brought in from the port of Ushuaia. [The virus] entered somewhere. We have to think that it was human contact or contact with merchandise, products, supplies."

Alfaro added: "We know that for 35 days, no one, or any new input, got on the ship. Obviously something happened, perhaps there has been some degree of contagion inside the boat that was not registered."

In the United States, the first major COVID-19 outbreak occurred aboard Seattle-based American Seafoods' *American Dynasty*. The huge fishing vessel hosts an onboard fish-processing factory and operates in the Pacific Northwest, which has the world's highest seafood production, at 25% of global landings. Similarly to the Argentinian case, nearly 75% of the onboard crew (92 out of 126) tested positive for COVID-19, even though all the fishermen tested negative when they boarded the ship. American Seafoods is one of the biggest players in the billion-dollar fishery for Alaska pollock, which goes into products like McDonald's Filet-O-Fish sandwiches.

A report stated that the prevalence of COVID-19 on ships was "likely to be significantly underestimated, and strategies are needed to assess and monitor all passengers to prevent community transmission after disembarkation."[5]

More than 120 workers at Oregon-based Pacific Seafood, a Newport seafood processing plant, also tested positive for the virus in an outbreak so large that it contributed to Oregon's highest single-day count of new cases since the start of the pandemic.

The owners of a seafood processor in Juneau, Alaska, thought they did everything right to keep their business safely running during the pandemic. However, even with mandatory COVID-19 screening and a two-week quarantine for out-of-state staff, the virus still found its way into the facility. Alaskan seafood processors are consistently seeing large outbreaks as the rise in COVID-19 infections continued, according to state officials. Dr. Joe McLaughlin, Alaska's state epidemiologist, said: "Alaska is currently experiencing three large, separate outbreaks of COVID-19 in the seafood industry. These outbreaks are reminiscent of the meat packing plant outbreaks in the Lower 48 and stress the importance of vigilant symptom screening and prompt facility-wide testing in congregate work settings when index cases are identified."

Seafood Safety in the United States

Ensuring the safety and quality of seafood products in the United States is a joint effort of the US Food and Drug Administration (FDA) and state regulatory agencies.

The FDA has the primary federal responsibility for the safety of seafood products in the United States, and adopted a regulation that requires all seafood processors to utilize a science-based system of preventive food safety controls known as Hazard Analysis Critical Control Points.

However, other federal agencies also play a role in ensuring the safety of certain seafood products.

The USDA has a regulation called Country of Origin Labeling, designed to ensure that seafood available in large retail stores is labeled to identify its country of origin.

The National Oceanic and Atmospheric Administration's Fisheries Service, part of the US Department of Commerce, is responsible for the management of the nation's fishery resources in the United States' territorial waters and also operates a voluntary seafood inspection and grading program. It requires traceability for seafood at risk of illegal fishing and seafood fraud through the US Seafood Import Monitoring Program, which currently applies to 13 species of imported fish—including blue crab, cod, and tuna—tracing them from the boat to the US border. Ninety percent of seafood consumed in the United States is imported, yet only 0.1% is inspected by federal agencies.

The CDC conducts food-borne illness investigations and provides recommendations to the medical community and "guidance for employers and workers performing seafood processing operations in onshore facilities and aboard vessels offshore." Currently, it is using the Oracle blockchain and the IBM Cloud to support its COVID-19 data collection efforts.

These federal agencies work cooperatively to provide consistent standards and regulations for seafood products and the various industry sectors that fish, farm, harvest, and deliver them to consumers. Food safety has become even more critical during the pandemic, with FDA spokesman Peter Cassell stating: "We have no evidence that COVID-19, a respiratory virus, is transmitted through food or food packaging."

Seafood Fraud in the United States

The US seafood industry's fraud-related issues were exacerbated by the pandemic. In response, the Department of Justice established a new task force and urged people to report COVID-19-related fraud. Study after study has proven the existence of fraud in the US seafood industry: The Office of the Attorney General in New York found that more than 25% of seafood at supermarkets in the state was mislabeled[6]; a study by the University of

California in Los Angeles and Loyola Marymount found that nearly half of the sushi served in Los Angeles was not what it was purported to be; in its seafood fraud investigation, the ocean-protection foundation Oceana found that 21% of fish tested—species not included under the existing federal traceability program—were mislabeled. Beth Lowell, Oceana's deputy vice president of US campaigns, explained: "It's clear that seafood fraud continues to be a problem in the U.S., and our government needs to do more to tackle this once and for all. Seafood fraud ultimately deceives consumers who fall victim to a bait and switch, disguises conservation and health risks, and hurts honest fishermen and seafood businesses. Seafood traceability—from boat to plate—is critical to ensure that all seafood sold in the U.S. is safe, legally caught and honestly labeled."[7]

Mislabeling, Fraud, and Tax Evasion

Blockchain technology authenticates the ownership of seafood, makes it traceable, and facilitates its digital transfer. However, some seafood companies found this technology to be irrelevant to their operations.

Phillip Carawan, the owner, president, and CEO of Captain Neill's Seafood Inc., is serving a jail sentence after pleading guilty to the Department of Justice in federal court on charges that his company, at his direction, fraudulently mislabeled over 179,872 pounds of foreign blue crab meat worth more than $4 million as a "Product of USA." Blue crab is a popular exported species native to the waters of the western Atlantic Ocean and the Gulf of Mexico. From at least 2012 to 2015, the company sold counterfeit crab meat to wholesale clubs such as Costco and Sam's Club as well as to major retailers.

A Virginia blue crab supplier was also accused of cutting a total of 398,000 pounds of blue crab harvested in the Chesapeake Bay with cut-rate crab meat from Indonesia and Brazil while labeling it as a product from the United States. The meat was worth about $14 million.

Roy Tuccillo, Sr., his son, Roy Tuccillo, Jr., and their food processing and distribution companies, Anchor Frozen Foods Inc. and Advanced Frozen Foods Inc., pleaded guilty to conspiracy to commit wire fraud for importing 113,000 pounds of squid and selling it as octopus to more than 10 grocery stores.

Carlos Rafael, "The Codfather," served a jail sentence for selling more than 782,000 pounds of counterfeit cod fish as well as tax evasion while he was in charge of a large portion of New England's fishing fleet.

Minh Phú Seafood Corp's US subsidiary MSeafood is being investigated by US federal authorities for violating national trade laws. The company evaded anti-dumping taxes on 57,700 tons of frozen warm water shrimp—worth $643 million—transshipped from India to the United States through Vietnam.

Price Fixing and Collusion

Blockchain technology allows the direct trading of assets by providing trust in transactions and reducing uncertainty through its use of trustworthy self-executing code. From the perspective of competition policy, this technology creates opportunities to enhance competition and efficiency, but also introduces risks of anticompetitive conduct.

The top three leaders in the North American shelf-stable seafood industry, whose canned tuna-fish product sales increase during times of economic distress, are:

- Bumble Bee—owned by Taiwan-based Fong Chun Formosa Fishery Company, one of the top three global tuna traders
- StarKist—owned by South Korea's Dongwon Group
- Chicken of the Sea—owned by Tri-Union Seafoods of Thai Union Group

These companies not only trace their tuna products via blockchain technology, but are also members of the World Economic Forum's Tuna 2020 Traceability Declaration. Nevertheless, each pleaded guilty to criminal price-fixing charges after Chicken of the Sea blew the whistle to avoid paying steep criminal fines. Earlier this year, Chris Lischewski, the former president and CEO of Bumble Bee Foods, was sentenced to 40 months in prison and charged a $100,000 fine.

With the emergence of the worldwide COVID-19 pandemic, the Food and Agriculture Organization of the United Nations published a report titled "Blockchain Application in Seafood Value Chains" to raise governmental and international awareness of the role of blockchain in tracking seafood mislabeling and fraud as well as supplying reliable data and product origin in the seafood industry in order to promote mainstream adoption of blockchain. The report has guided the seafood industry into the Global Dialogue on Seafood Traceability and issued the first-ever global standards for tracking seafood products from point of origin to point of sale in order to verify the authenticity of the food item and validate the sustainability efforts of the producer.

Product standards body MarinTrust has announced plans to mandate the recording of key data about fish by-products for traceability and outlined its vision for blockchain's role. Many seafood companies have joined blockchain initiatives, such as IBM's blockchain-based Food Trust, Envisible's Wholechain system, the VeChain Blockchain Traceability Platform, Australia-based Two Hands, and Norway-based SeafoodChain AS.

Nevertheless, according to two recent studies, there is still a need for a global network of real-time human disease surveillance systems, which can be based on the use of blockchain technology to track the spread of COVID-19 via the seafood value chain across the world.[8]

Notes

1. https://news.microsoft.com/en-au/features/ai-iot-and-blockchain-trace-meat-from-paddock-to-plate-at-nations-largest-food-processing-company-jbs-in-australian-first-trial/
2. https://delauro.house.gov/media-center/press-releases/delauro-pushes-usda-inspector-general-investigate-payments-corrupt
3. https://www.fda.gov/news-events/press-announcements/statement-acting-fda-commissioner-ned-sharpless-md-and-deputy-commissioner-frank-yiannas-steps-usher
4. https://cointelegraph.com/news/tracing-global-meat-related-risks-with-blockchain-amid-covid-19
5. https://thorax.bmj.com/content/75/8/693
6. https://www.foodandwine.com/news/new-york-seafood-labeling-attorney-general-report
7. https://cointelegraph.com/news/tracing-fishy-risks-with-blockchain-tech-amid-the-covid-19-pandemic
8. Ibid.

Chapter 20
Are NFTs Here to Stay?

Nonfungible tokens (NFTs) were the biggest disrupter in art in 2021, with artists minting, exhibiting, and auctioning, and investors buying, selling, and trading.

On November 14, 2021, Tezos-based NFT marketplace Hic Et Nunc—which in Latin means "here and now"—abruptly shut down. Artists became worried about their NFTs on exhibit at the Hermitage Museum's first-ever NFT exhibition, "Ethereal Aether" (November 10–December 10), as well as Art Basel Miami's first-ever NFT exhibition, "Humans + Machines: NFTs and the Ever-Evolving World of Art" (December 2–4).[1]

Diane Drubay, founder of We Are Museums and a minter of NFTs on Hic Et Nunc—who curated a panel discussion at Art Basel Miami—explained to me: "Of course, it was a shock to see Hic et Nunc shut down, but people took it right away as a new step over in their journey. Because when the website shut down, our NFTs were preserved on-chain, nothing was lost and artists were safe to keep making a living from their NFTs. We saw mirrors or new versions of HicEtNunc.art being opened only a few hours later, which provided the necessary backup for artists to keep selling and buying, exhibiting NFTs." She added: "The community is now organizing itself to create a decentralized autonomous organization [DAO] to keep experimenting with decentralization on Web 3.0."

This incident made me wonder: Will the "International Year of Creative Economy for Sustainable Development," as declared by the United Nations General Assembly, go down in history as the year NFTs entered the mainstream? Or will it go down as a passing global fad of invention lurking in the shadows of the COVID-19 pandemic? I conducted research and interviews to find the answer.

NFTs' Environmental Impact, Valuation, and Regulation

NFTs are digital assets that are built on a blockchain platform and are tradeable like digital trading cards in exchange for cryptocurrencies or even fiat currency. They generally act as evidence of ownership of digital assets, but the specific rights that attach to NFTs vary. Some NFTs incorporate "smart contracts" as part of the token that self-execute when defined events occur.

Computer scientist Antsstyle has critiqued NFTs: "In a nutshell, NFTs are bad for two reasons: 1. They are bad for the environment, as they rely on cryptocurrencies that cause huge amounts of carbon emissions. [. . .] 2. They are only valuable as tools for money laundering, tax evasion, and greater fool investment fraud."[2]

The long version of Antsstyle's analysis gives a comprehensive overview of proof-of-stake (energy-efficient) and proof-of-work (energy-intensive) NFT platforms.[3]

A. J. Woloszynski, manager at Eisner Advisory Group LLC of EisnerAmper, pointed out, furthermore, that NFTs have subjective valuations determined by however much somebody is willing to pay for them: "For example, take a look at the image below. You are not encountering an issue with the image loading on your computer; what you are seeing is a plain gray box. This is an NFT known as The Pixel, produced by an artist who goes by the name [Pak] and sold for roughly $1.3 million at a Sotheby's auction in April 2021." Other major art auction houses such as Christie's,[4] Phillips, and Portion also began auctioning NFTs minted on various NFT platforms this year.[5]

The Pixel, 2021, by Pak
SOURCE: Courtesy the artist and Sotheby's.

According to CryptoArt, Pak is the second-highest-selling crypto artist of all time, with around a $65 million market capitalization for his art pieces. NonFungible ranks Bored Ape Yacht Club at number one, with the "Bored Ape #9449" NFT last selling for more than $1 million.[6]

Bored Ape #9449
SOURCE: NonFungible.

While not ranked by NonFungible, the low-pixel 24×24 images of computer-generated CryptoPunks by Larva Labs were the first major NFTs. In March, CryptoPunk #3100 sold for 4,200 ether (ETH), or $7.6 million at the time. This sale was surpassed by the sale of "Everydays: The First 5000 Days," an NFT by graphic designer Mike Winkelmann, aka "Beeple," that raised $69.3 million that same day, amounting to $13,800 per each work of digital art included in the collage.[7] According to DappRadar, CryptoKitties by Dapper Labs—the first big Ethereum-based NFT project to use the ERC-721 standard—also registered a 22,106% day-over-day increase in trading volume amid the recent NFT market resurgence.[8]

Sustainable NFTs

NFTs were the biggest disruptors of the art world in 2021, with artists minting, exhibiting, and auctioning, and investors buying, selling, trading, and investing in them. Nash Islam, an early investor in NFTs, said: "For NFTs, the community action is primarily on Twitter and Discord." He added, "Investing in Pak across multiple projects has yielded massive multiples and also helped us understand and establish some principles for NFT investments."[9]

Even Damien Hirst, the United Kingdom's richest living artist, launched an NFT series titled "The Currency" in 2021, exploring the nature of value, art, and currency. It was minted on Palm, an NFT platform operating as an Ethereum sidechain, and pieces were offered for sale through Heni at $2,000 each.

Artist Ilya Shkipin told me he decided to mint his MonarxNFT series on the energy-efficient, open-source Tezos NFT platform: "Choosing Tezos wasn't a choice but an obvious decision once we spoke with our supporters. Both the Monarx team and the community valued low gas fees and a convenient minting experience. We ended up doing what our community told us to do because the art is for them, not us. My MonarxNFT series—merge of a neural network carefully guided by artistic vision—was inspired at a time of loss in my life."

Reid Yager, global director of communications and public relations for Tezos, explained that Tezos is presenting the first-ever NFT art exhibition occurring as an official partner of international art fair Art Basel, in collaboration with the host city's local institutions: "The Tezos Ecosystem Exhibition at Art Basel Miami Beach will feature more than 25 artists from 18 countries spanning 5 continents showcasing their work. Additionally, over 30 artists, gallerists, museum directors, celebrities, and thought leaders will participate in the Tezos Ecosystem Exhibition Speaker Series in the exhibit space." As part of the show, visitors will be able to create AI-generated portraits of themselves and mint them as NFTs on Tezos.

Yager added: "The leading Tezos NFT platform Hic Et Nunc, which recently completed the first-ever NFT marketplace Web3 transition from platform-owned to community-owned (DAO), has seen over half a million NFTs minted by users from every corner of the globe. The Tezos blockchain is booming with over 6 million contract calls in September, and November is on pace to top that. The Tezos blockchain is the choice for minting and collecting NFTs globally. In fact, one of the first ever NFTs from a Museum was minted on the Tezos blockchain by the Whitworth Museum—William Blake's 'The Ancient of Days.'"

According to DappRadar, Hic Et Nunc was the 14th-largest NFT marketplace in terms of all-time sales ($50.37 million) when it shut down, with the average sale at $25.19 per NFT. The leading marketplace for NFT trading is New York–based OpenSea, which operates on the proof-of-work Ethereum blockchain. Ethereum is in the process of transitioning to Ethereum 2.0, a proof-of-stake blockchain, which will be 99% less energy-intensive and more scalable, secure, and sustainable. But whether OpenSea or any of the other top-ranked marketplaces will be able to hold their place in this fast-changing market is yet to be seen, as some of the largest companies have been entering the NFT space to transform the Metaverse, including:

- Technology companies: TikTok, Twitter, Facebook, Alibaba, Tencent, Xiaohongshu, NetEase, Baidu, Microsoft, and eBay.
- Fintech companies: China's Blockchain-based Service Network, which will support future central bank digital currencies from various countries, launched infrastructure to support the deployment of NFTs in China and other countries.
- Cryptocurrency marketplaces: Coinbase and Binance NFT, which sold the Hermitage Museum's first nonfungible token.

NFTs and Museums

A study carried out by the International Council of Museums (ICOM) found that as a result of the COVID-19 pandemic, more than 30% of museums were forced to reduce their staff and nearly 6% may never be able to reopen to the public. But the digitization of museums is taking place at high speed, with some museums turning to NFTs for a variety of reasons.[10]

NFT Exhibitions

The Hermitage Museum's "Ethereal Aether" consisted of 36 NFTs from around the world, including Larva Labs' "Cryptopunk #5652," "Schrödinger's Cat" from Dapper Labs' CryptoKitties, and Mihai Grecu's "NeoPyongyang I," minted on Hic Et Nunc.

Hack of a Bear
Hackabao

Partial Equilibrium
Marco Brambilla

Organic Growth: Crystal Reef
Michael Joo and Danil Krivoruchko

Quantum
Kevin McCoy

Daily Truth
Siebren Versteeg

Cryptopunk #5652
Larva Labs

Celestial Hermitage's virtual exhibition
SOURCE: Celestial Hermitage.

The curators, Dimitri Ozerkov and Anastasia Garnova, explained: "Interest in digital art intensified during the COVID-19 pandemic, when millions of people sat at home for months on end with the museums closed. The first NFT exhibition will launch the creation of the 'Celestial Hermitage'—a new museum in the virtual noosphere, which in the future will be transformed into a digital branch of the actual museum." They added, "We are confident that the area of digital art, NFTs in particular, will develop in incredible ways, and that it can look forward to a great future—safe, smart and fascinating."

Guggenheim Partners cofounder Todd Morley announced plans to create the world's biggest museum dedicated to NFTs within a massive skyscraper located in New York City, just four blocks from the Museum of Modern Art.[11]

NFT Fundraising by Museums

Three out of the 20 largest museums in the world—the State Hermitage Museum in St. Petersburg (no. 2), the Metropolitan Museum of Art in New York City (no. 4), and the British Museum in London (no. 12)—turned to NFTs for fundraising during 2021. Other examples include the Uffizi in Florence, the Whitworth in Manchester, the Museum and Church of São Roque in Lisbon, the Kansong Art Museum in Seoul, the Museum of Broadcast Communications in Chicago, and the Academy Museum of Motion Pictures in Los Angeles. There's even an NFT of an entire museum based in the metaverse, called the Museum of Digital Life.

The Miami Institute of Contemporary Art accepted a donation of "CryptoPunk #5293" from one of its trustees.

CryptoPunk 5293
SOURCE: Larva Labs.

Jean-Sébastien Beaucamps, cofounder of French eco-friendly startup LaCollection—an Ethereum-based NFT platform—explained, "To coincide with its Hokusai: The Great Picture of Everything exhibition (September 30–January 30, 2022), the British Museum partnered with LaCollection.io to sell NFTs of 200 Hokusai works. For each NFT minted by our company, we will plant a tree to compensate for the wildfires of last summer and for our NFTs to be carbon neutral: we call it our NFTree program. The NFTs will consist of works in the exhibition, including the famed The Great Wave, while another 100 will be from the BM's own collection, including drawings from the recently re-discovered book which is the subject of the exhibition."[12]

NFTs and Environmental Education

The International Committee for Museums and Collections of Science and Technology (ICOM)'s 48th annual conference titled "Museums & Environmental Concerns, New Insights" (I held an art show there)[13]— addressed our planet's environmental concerns and the way science and technology museums can approach and present this important issue via education and exhibitions. Several museum directors told me about the role NFTs played in their museums:

- George Ma, head of the climate action section, social responsibility, and the sustainable development office at the Jockey Club Museum of Climate Change at The Chinese University of Hong Kong: "NFTs are currently not on our radar, but something we could keep an eye on. We digitized our exhibitions. We have a 360 Virtual Tour which is the digital version of our permanent exhibition. Since 2018, for every themed exhibition we developed, we also produced a digital version of it, either in a more website-like format or in 360 VR."
- Patrick Hamilton, director of climate change, energy, and the environment at the Science Museum of Minnesota: "The Science Museum of Minnesota is digitizing its collections but I'm not aware of any current plans to digitize its exhibits or sell NFTs."
- Julie Decker, director and CEO of the Anchorage Museum: "NFTs are a really interesting topic to think and read about. Currently, we do not have plans."
- Viviane Gosselin, director of collections and exhibitions and curator of contemporary culture at the Museum of Vancouver: "At the moment we are not selling NFTs for fundraising or collecting purposes—not yet. My understanding is that it is not by and large a 'green industry' so that is a bit of a red flag and turnoff for me!"
- Soren Brothers, Shiff curator of climate change at the Royal Ontario Museum: "ROM is digitizing its collections, which can be accessed here (https://collections.rom.on.ca/). I don't know anything about whether ROM has plans to sell NFTs."

It should be noted that the Los Angeles County Museum of Art has an Art + Technology Lab that runs a series to explore what NFTs mean for institutions collecting digital art.[14] It also examines the "artistic, curatorial, conservation, registration, and legal issues of this new digital format."[15]

COVID-19: Art Charity and Blockchain

The COVID-19 pandemic has created both a public health crisis and an economic crisis. The pandemic has disrupted lives, pushed the hospital system to its brink, and created a global economic slowdown resulting in losses totaling over $1.7 billion for the United States arts and cultural sector alone.[16]

According to X4Impact—a data insights, research, and consulting services company for social innovation in the United States—over 457,000 nonprofit organizations in the United States, which have a combined funding of around $2.9 trillion, continue to experience an increase in demand for their services against a significant decrease in income.[17] The extent to which the coronavirus has affected the US charitable sector remains unknown.[18]

Pinpointing the urgent need for funds for charities and artists as well as for COVID-19 victims (SDG 3), Bundeep Rangar—CEO of PremFina, the United Kingdom's first venture capital–backed alternative insurance premium finance company—explained to me, "Last June, Art & Co held a first of its kind blockchain technology-assisted charity art auction. The auction bidding sales process, tracking sale proceeds, and distribution of proceeds to charities was tracked by LuxTag Blockchain/NEM."

Since June 2020, when I held my first digital art show inspired by climate change and COVID-19 (SDGs 3 and 13),[19] NFTs and blockchain technology have steadily seeped into the art and charity world, enabling artists and museums to monetize their work and continue to receive payments for their work even after it is sold.

In August 2021, OpenSea—the largest nonfungible token marketplace—saw NFT sales volume balloon to $4 billion, followed by a bearish correction during September. But there is a race among artists, museums, and charities to tap into the NFT market to monetize their work.

Charitable, Sustainable NFTs for the UN's 17 SDGs

Twitter CEO Jack Dorsey sold his first-ever tweet as an NFT for $2.9 million and donated the proceeds in Bitcoin to GiveDirectly, a charitable organization that sends funds to families in Africa impacted by the COVID-19 pandemic (SDG 3).[20] Bids were handled on a sustainable platform called Valuables that lets people make offers on tweets that are "autographed by their original creators."

Other sustainable nonfungible token platforms where artists can mint NFTs and showcase and sell their creations to inspire greater awareness in the context of the UN's 17 SDG goals include DigitalArt4Climate, the Enjin NFT platform, and Doin-Gud, where I am launching my first NFT, "Recovery Roses," at the first-ever Origins Exhibition—with sale proceeds of my NFT to be donated to fund SDG-focused charitable organizations around the world.

Recovery Roses NFT by Selva Ozelli

DoinGud cofounder Manu Alzuru told me, "DoinGud's blockchain-based social media and marketplace is designed to facilitate charitable giving via NFT sales to vetted social impact organizations of the creator's choice. It will lead to ever-increasing opportunities to support worthy charitable causes that share the UN's 17 Sustainable Development Goals like ending world hunger, solving climate change and more."

William Quigley—a cryptocurrency investor, cofounder of NFT blockchain platform Worldwide asset eXchange (WAX), and cofounder of the first fiat-backed stablecoin Tether (USDT)—told me about WAX's new charitable initiative that addresses

SDGs 13 and 14. The company—which provides an eco-friendly blockchain for NFTs, video games, and collectibles—has released a new collection of "Carbon Offset vIRL" NFTs. As Quigley said, "For every $1 'composted' in WAX's sustainability-driven collection, the National Forest Foundation will plant one tree sapling, each of which offsets an average of one tonne of carbon dioxide over its lifetime. WAX is officially setting higher standards for responsibility across the blockchain. We've been working tirelessly to ensure our blockchain is both energy efficient and inspires our community to act with the environment in mind. With Carbon Offset vIRL® NFTs, we are confident we can all make a massive, positive difference together."

Cryptograph, on the other hand, is the first luxury and celebrity NFT auction platform to use blockchain technology to introduce a new way to do philanthropy in the digital age and make charitable fundraising easier, instantly global, and perpetual in nature. Tommy Alastra, a blockchain pioneer and Cryptograph's cofounder, explained, "Cryptograph is a major breakthrough for charitable organizations wanting to ride the wave to improved donations that are borderless and accessible from across the world. With the new post-COVID world and less in-person large-scale charity galas, Cryptograph will permit charitable foundations to continue to fundraise successfully and receive percentages of each NFT auction item even in the resale market on an ongoing basis."

Cryptograph sells NFTs made by Vitalik Buterin, Emin Gün Sirer, Erik Voorhees, Evan Van Ness—the writer of "Week In Ethereum News" and former director at ConsenSys—and others, with the proceeds funding organizations working toward SDGs 1, 2, 4, and 14. Creators can also choose their own SDG-focused charitable organization to fund. For example, the Autism Science Foundation, which is dedicated to supporting and funding innovative autism research (SDG 3), announced that it is accepting cryptocurrency and NFT donations via Every.org.[21]

Notes

1. https://cointelegraph.com/news/invisible-aether-world-s-largest-museum-launches-nft-art-exhibition
2. https://antsstyle.medium.com/why-nfts-are-bad-the-short-version-48acff22c54b
3. https://antsstyle.medium.com/why-nfts-are-bad-the-long-version-2c16dae145e2
4. https://cointelegraph.com/news/christie-s-auctions-its-first-purely-digital-artwork-in-form-of-blockchain-token
5. https://www.eisneramper.com/non-fungible-tokens-money-laundering-flvs-blog-0821/
6. https://nonfungible.com/project/boredapeclub/BAYC/9449
7. https://cointelegraph.com/news/beeple-nft-auction-closes-at-record-setting-69-3m
8. https://dappradar.com/blog/cryptokitties-suddenly-millions-of-dollars-in-trading
9. https://nashtyrhymes.substack.com/p/my-5-emerging-principles-for-investing?s=r
10. https://icom.museum/wp-content/uploads/2021/07/Museums-and-Covid-19_third-ICOM-report.pdf
11. https://news.artnet.com/art-world/nft-museum-111-west-57th-1973184
12. https://cointelegraph.com/news/2021-ends-with-a-question-are-nfts-here-to-stay
13. https://ubiverse.org/posts/cimuset-art-shows-by-selva-ozelli
14. https://www.lacma.org/lab/nfts-and-museum
15. https://cointelegraph.com/news/2021-ends-with-a-question-are-nfts-here-to-stay
16. https://www.americansforthearts.org/by-topic/disaster-preparedness/the-economic-impact-of-coronavirus-on-the-arts-and-culture-sector
17. https://x4i.org/all/money-flow
18. https://www.councilofnonprofits.org/nonprofits-and-coronavirus-covid-19
19. https://cointelegraph.com/news/review-cointelegraph-inspired-climate-change-art-exhibition
20. https://cointelegraph.com/news/nifty-news-jack-dorsey-sells-genesis-tweet-for-2-9m-nfts-save-wild-pandas-and-more
21. https://cointelegraph.com/news/charitable-sustainable-nfts-for-the-united-nations-17-sdgs

Chapter 21
Regulation of Digital Assets

In the United States, cryptocurrencies at a federal level are regulated by the Financial Crimes Enforcement Network (FinCen), the Office of Foreign Assets Control (OFAC), the Internal Revenue Service (IRS), the Commodity Futures Trading Commission (CFTC), and the Securities and Exchange Commission (SEC), which characterize cryptocurrencies as money, property, commodity, and a security, respectively.

The multi-classification of cryptocurrencies poses uncertainties about the regulation of cryptocurrency and blockchain technology transactions that industry participants are eagerly awaiting answers and clarification to.

In addition to federal laws, cryptocurrencies are also regulated at the state level in the United States.[1]

On March 11, 2022, the US Treasury Department issued new guidance clarifying that the Office of Foreign Assets Control's Russia-related sanctions extend to cryptocurrencies. It later followed up with its Russian Harmful Foreign Activities Sanctions program on March 24.

The Treasury Department's announcements came after it published new regulations on March 1 to address the Russian sanctions. The Department of Justice established Task Force KleptoCapture on March 2 to enforce the sweeping sanctions.

On March 9, US President Joe Biden signed his Executive Order on Ensuring Responsible Development of Digital Assets, with Russia's invasion of Ukraine having elevated crypto's national security significance. This executive order highlights the importance of digital assets in retaining the United States' technological leadership in a world of increasing competition and striking the right balance between sustainably fostering innovation, protecting investor rights, and mitigating the national security risks posed by the illicit use of digital assets. The executive order further requests a set of interagency reports from a wide range of executive branch stakeholders, including the Federal Reserve, which earlier released a report about CBDCs.[2]

Regulation	Regulator	Yes	No
ICO	SEC/CFTC	X	
AML/CFT	FinCen	X – proposed	
NFT	IRS		X
Sanctions	OFAC	X	
Whistleblowing law	SEC, CFTC, AML, Tax	X – awards	
Capital gains tax	IRS	X	

Notes

1. https://www.govtech.com/policy/states-are-split-on-how-to-regulate-cryptocurrency.html;https://www.ncsl.org/research/financial-services-and-commerce/cryptocurrency-2021-legislation.aspx
2. https://cointelegraph.com/news/the-world-has-synchronized-on-russian-crypto-sanctions

Part 2
Digital Asset Utilization and Regulation Around the World

Chapter 22
Portugal

Portuguese banking and finance regulators seek a coordinated regulatory solution for cryptocurrencies. The finance minister of Portugal, Mario Centano, who is also the president of the Eurogroup, said that he is looking to European regulatory guidance concerning cryptocurrencies since they are "overseeing the general picture." The Eurogroup is a group of 19 finance ministers of EU countries, who meet once a month to talk about major economic and monetary policies that are implemented across the EU.[1] Banks have been increasingly adopting blockchain technology after caving to customer pressure starting in the fourth quarter of 2017 to reduce costs and make cross-border payment transactions more efficient.

Blockchain Adoption: "We are committed to creating a leading international blockchain payment ecosystem that presents significant opportunity for cross-border payments globally," explained José Luis Calderón, the global head of Santander Global Transaction Banking. Banco Santander-UK began working with American Express and the Ripple network to allow American Express's US business customers to make instant, traceable, cross-border noncard payments using the blockchain network RippleNet to Banco Santander-UK.

"We're taking a huge step forward with American Express and Santander to solve the problems customers experience with slow cross-border global payments," Brad Garlinghouse, CEO of Ripple, revealed.[2]

Crypto Adoption: At the end of 2021, 2.37% of the population owned cryptocurrencies.[3] The Central Bank of Portugal is the financial services regulator responsible for the oversight and regulation of the banking and financial sector, notably banks, credit, and mortgage credit institutions, and payment, e-money institutions, and crypto exchanges. BOP issued licenses to Criptoloja and Mind The Coin as "virtual asset service providers."[4]

Crypto Mining: Crypto mining is not regulated; there are no restrictions.[5]

Startups: There are mostly blockchain-based fintech startups in Portugal such as Digital Legacy Vault, Cheapstaking, Cuffies, Velaspad, Revault, Token Bank, and Abypay [6]

Central Bank Issued Digital Currency (CBDC): Portugal, which is part of the EU's European Central Bank (ECB), is exploring creating a central bank digital currency (CBDC), the Digital Euro, according to the Atlantic Council.[7] Starting in May 2020, the Bank of France successfully experimented with using the Digital Euro in the sale of securities, digital bonds, and cross-border payment with the Monetary Authority of Singapore through blockchain technology.[8]

Nonfungible Tokens: Nonfungible tokens (NFTs) exploded during 2021, and Portugal followed the trend by hosting Europe's first crypto art festival, Rare Effect.[9] The country is quickly emerging as an attractive place for NFT startups because of its being free of regulation and taxes.[10] NFT artist Yard, who in a year went from being a window cleaner to an NFT millionaire artist, says that after her work was shown in Sotheby's Metaverse, and sold for $500,000, she was invited as a speaker to an Ethereum conference in Lisbon, Portugal.[11]

Illicit Use of Crypto:

	Yes	No
Known hacking groups	Lapsus$[12]	
Known crypto exchange hacks	Cryptojacking[13]	

Regulation of Digital Assets: Portugal's regulators have done a great deal to nurture the blockchain industry. In 2020, the Portuguese government instituted Resolution of the Council of Ministers No. 29/2020, which established general principles for a legislative framework that promotes and facilitates research, demonstration, and testing activities, in technology-free zones, of innovative technologies including blockchain and AI.[14] Coupled with no capital gains tax on crypto, Portugal hopes to promote the growth of the crypto industry within Portugal.

Regulation	Regulator	Yes	No
Markets in Crypto-Assets Regulation (MiCA)	European Securities Market Authority (ESMA), European Banking Authority (EBA)[15]	Proposed	
Sustainability	EU taxonomy	X	
Advertising			X
ICO	ESMA[16]	X	
AML/CFT		X	
NFT			X
Sanctions	EU restrictive measures	X	
Whistleblowing law	Directive (EU) 2019/1937	X – no awards	
Capital gains tax			X

Notes

1. https://www.emchat.net/emchat/2017/12/18/the-finance-minister-of-portugal-says-regulators-are-following-bitcoins-development
2. https://ripple.com/ripple_press/american-express-introduces-blockchain-enabled-cross-border-payments/
3. https://triple-a.io/crypto-ownership-portugal/
4. https://www.bportugal.pt/en/page/registration-virtual-assets-service-providers-0
5. https://www.globallegalinsights.com/practice-areas/blockchain-laws-and-regulations/portugal
6. https://tracxn.com/explore/Blockchain-in-Financial-Services-Startups-in-Portugal
7. https://www.atlanticcouncil.org/cbdctracker/
8. https://www.ecb.europa.eu/pub/pdf/other/Report_on_a_digital_euro~4d7268b458.en.pdf
9. https://arrozestudios.pt/events/rare-effect-vol2-nft-festival/
10. https://www.growinportugal.com/why-is-portugal-such-a-friendly-place-for-nft-companies/
11. https://www.the-sun.com/money/4494692/window-cleaner-depression-nft-artist/
12. https://www.wired.com/story/lapsus-hacking-group-extortion-nvidia-samsung/
13. https://seguranca-informatica.pt/hackers-are-attacking-portuguese-websites-with-crypto-jacking/#.YkM-5C0RqqA
14. https://www.europarl.europa.eu/RegData/etudes/STUD/2020/652752/IPOL_STU(2020)652752_EN.pdf
15. https://www.europarl.europa.eu/news/pt/press-room/20220309IPR25162/cryptocurrencies-in-the-eu-new-rules-to-boost-benefits-and-curb-threats
16. https://www.esma.europa.eu

Chapter 23
Netherlands

The Netherlands has an established tradition of being at the forefront of innovation. And it is following this same path when it comes to blockchain development. The Netherlands ranks in the top five countries when it comes to digital economies.

The Dutch Blockchain Action Agenda is the driving force for the innovative application of this technology in both products and services. Under the label "Dutch Digital Delta,"[1] government, industry, knowledge institutions, even the Royal family's Prince Constantijn, with over 20 organizations in the financial sector, energy, and logistics, are active in this initiative.[2]

Blockchain Adoption: The five Dutch banks, which control over 90% of the Netherlands' retail banking market, are exploring implementing blockchain technology in their operations. ABN AMRO and Rabobank joined the SWIFT global payments innovation project. ING has completed the testing of a blockchain-powered trade settlement platform in partnership with Calypso and the R3 consortium. And NIBC has set up an Innovation Lab to stimulate the adoption of technological advancements within the bank as well as to enter strategic partnerships with innovative blockchain companies.

Willem Vermeend, the first official "fintech ambassador" of the Netherlands, said, "Blockchain will become a critical part of the financial sector, but what's needed is collaboration. There is a lot of creativity in the Netherlands. The problem is that I have spoken to 20 parties who do not know what each other is doing."

The Dutch government is exploring how to use blockchain technology to improve service delivery to citizens as the catalyzer for democracy, transparency, and participation. So far, more than 30 pilots have been concluded utilizing blockchain technology in a variety of areas like income tax, identity, logistics, autonomous vehicles, debt counseling, and so forth.

During 2017, Prince Constantijn joined the high-level group of innovators that advises the European Commission (EC). On February 1, 2018, the EU Blockchain Observatory and Forum announced that "it is partnering with ConsenSys, an Ethereum powered global venture production studio, for the benefit of the single European Union (EU) market, ensuring they work collaboratively across borders to help integrate and consolidate views, analysis and visions coming from the Netherlands in a forum at EU level," explained EC spokesperson Nathalie Vandystadt.[3]

Crypto Adoption: At the end of 2021, 3.04% of the population owned cryptocurrencies,[4] which they traded on 20 registered cryptocurrency service providers with the Dutch central bank (DNB).[5]

Crypto Mining: Crypto mining is not regulated; there are no restrictions.[6]

Startups: With 3,200 startup tech companies hitting a scale-up phase in the Netherlands, initial coin offerings (ICOs) offer a new way of fundraising enabled by digital currencies and blockchain technology. Currently, the Dutch Authority for the Financial Markets (AFM) does not regulate ICOs.

"When it comes to innovation and developing markets, the Netherlands always held a forward-thinking stance. ICO initiatives are not an exception. The Dutch landscape comprises of bottom-up initiatives such as meet-ups and conferences, Ethereum DEV NL, Skycoin Netherlands, and Bitcoin Wednesday, a thriving startup ecosystem with (pre-) ICO fundraising entities. Not surprisingly, the advisors of some of the most successful ICOs of the caliber of Bancor, Kik, and Monetha live in the Netherlands," explained Emanuele Francioni, founder of Web3 Ventures.

Central Bank Issued Digital Currency (CBDC): A few years ago, the Central Bank of the Netherlands (DNB) created its own cryptocurrency called DNBcoin, for internal circulation only, to understand better how it works. After studying it, the DNB concluded that blockchain might be "naturally applicable in fintech" for the settlement of complex financial transactions, cross-border payments, securities transactions, and document and identity validation.[7]

The Netherlands, which is part of the EU's European Central Bank (ECB), is exploring creating a central bank digital currency (CBDC), the Digital Euro,[8] according to the Atlantic Council.[9] Starting in May 2020, the Bank of France successfully experimented with using the Digital Euro in the sale of securities, digital bonds, and cross-border payment with the Monetary Authority of Singapore through blockchain technology.[10]

Nonfungible Tokens: Dutch NFT Drops makes NFTs out of artists' work.[11] Dutch artist Dadara, in collaboration with RAIRTech, developed 7.9 billion Greyman characters for every person alive in the world, available on the Polygon Ethereum Scaling Network.[12]

Illicit Use of Crypto: Netherlands is a member of J5, FIU, and JCat to fight transnational tax, cyber, and sanctions crime. According to an annual survey by regulator DNB on information security, more than 15% of pension funds and insurance firms in the Netherlands have suffered significant damage from cyber-crime in 2021.[13]

	Yes	No
Known hacking groups	Ethical hackers[14]	
Known hacks	Global cyberattack[15]	
J5	X	
JCAT	X	
FIU	X	

Regulation of Digital Assets: The May 21, 2020, Dutch Implementation Act applied the fifth European Directive on anti-money laundering and counter-terrorist financing (AMLD V) to wallet providers and crypto exchanges.

Regulation	Regulator	Yes	No
MiCA	ESMA, EBA[16]	Proposed	
Sustainability	EU taxonomy	X	
Advertising			X
ICO	ESMA[17]	X	
AML/CFT		X	
NFT			X
Sanctions	EU restrictive measures	X[18]	
Whistleblowing law	Directive (EU) 2019/1937	X – no awards	
Capital gains tax		X	

Notes

1. https://dutchblockchaincoalition.org/en
2. https://cointelegraph.com/news/upbeat-dutch-blockchain-and-crypto-action-agenda
3. https://cointelegraph.com/news/upbeat-dutch-blockchain-and-crypto-action-agenda
4. https://triple-a.io/crypto-ownership-netherlands/
5. https://www.dutchnews.nl/news/2021/05/bitcoin-is-hype-in-the-netherlands-but-number-of-investors-is-unclear/
6. https://notabene.id/world/netherlands
7. https://cointelegraph.com/news/upbeat-dutch-blockchain-and-crypto-action-agenda
8. https://www.dnb.nl/en/innovations-in-payments-and-banking/digital-euro-what-why-and-how/
9. https://www.atlanticcouncil.org/cbdctracker/
10. https://www.ecb.europa.eu/pub/pdf/other/Report_on_a_digital_euro~4d7268b458.en.pdf
11. https://dutchnftdrops.com
12. https://economictimes.indiatimes.com/markets/cryptocurrency/dutch-artist-creates-nfts-for-every-person-in-the-world/articleshow/89896846.cms
13. https://www.ipe.com/news/15-of-dutch-pension-funds-fall-victim-to-cyber-crime/10057015.article
14. https://www.computerweekly.com/feature/How-Dutch-hackers-are-working-to-make-the-internet-safe
15. https://www.reuters.com/article/us-cybercrime-netherlands-university-idUSKBN1ZZ2HH; https://www.dutchnews.nl/news/2021/07/global-cyber-attack-affects-hundreds-of-dutch-companies-fd/
16. https://www.europarl.europa.eu/news/pt/press-room/20220309IPR25162/cryptocurrencies-in-the-eu-new-rules-to-boost-benefits-and-curb-threats
17. https://www.esma.europa.eu
18. https://www.government.nl/topics/international-peace-and-security/compliance-with-international-sanctions/implementation-of-sanctions-in-the-netherlands

Chapter 24
South Africa

South Africa has been relatively progressive on the subject of cryptocurrencies. The South African Reserve Bank (SARB) issued a 2014 position paper on cryptocurrencies and in July of 2017 began to work with Bankymoon, a blockchain-based solutions provider, on creating a "balanced" approach to cryptocurrency regulation.[1]

Blockchain Adoption: As a result of the Zupta scandal (the largest post-apartheid corruption scandal, resulting in the incarceration of South Africa's president, Jacob Zuma[2]), several South African financial institutions have embraced a blockchain technology called Springblock, which they hope to adopt for all financial transactions, explained Farzam Ehsani, chair of the South African Financial Blockchain Consortium. The SARB has established the Financial Technology Program, whose primary goals are to track and analyze developments and to assist policymakers in formulating frameworks in response to these emerging innovations. The program also intends to review the SARB's position on private cryptocurrencies to inform an appropriate policy framework and regulatory regime. Additionally, it will launch Project Khokha, which will experiment with Ethereum-based distributed ledger technologies in partnership with ConsenSys to replicate interbank transfers on Quorum, a platform built by JP Morgan.[3]

According to research by Finder.com, there is a strong correlation between cryptocurrency investment enthusiasm (56%) and government corruption (a Transparency International's Corruption Perceptions Index score of 44) in South Africa.[4]

Crypto Adoption: At the end of 2021, 7.1% of the population owned cryptocurrencies, which they traded on unregistered cryptocurrency service providers.[5] "There is no longer any room for doubt regarding the impact crypto assets are having on our global financial system," said Farzam Ehsani, CEO and cofounder of VARL, a South African crypto exchange that processed over $7.5 billion in trading volume since its 2019 launch.[6]

Crypto Mining: Crypto mining is not regulated; there are no restrictions. One of the world's most profitable cryptocurrency mines is located in Johannesburg, and it uses solar energy generation to power its operations.[7]

Startups: South Africa Crypto Valley Venture Capital initiated a public-private partnership with the Swiss State Secretariat for Economic Affairs (SECO) to build the first-ever, blockchain-focused Accelerator for Africa, focused on startups that work across supply chain, healthcare, fintech, and government sectors.[8]

Central Bank Issued Digital Currency (CDCB): South Africa is part of Russia's multinational stablecoin initiative with BRICS and EAEU countries. South Africa, like other BRICS countries, is also scheduled to issue CBDC this year that will be exchanged on smartphones, outside of the SWIFT and CHIPS systems. A new report on Project Dunbar from the central banks of Australia, Malaysia, Singapore, and South Africa confirms that cross-border CBDC payments are technologically possible.[9]

Nonfungible Tokens: Africa's largest NFT auction was hosted by Momint.[10]

Illicit Use of Crypto: Mirror Trading International perpetrated a crypto Ponzi scheme of 23,000 BTC worth $588 million in 2020, which the US Federal Bureau of Investigations is also investigating. In April 2021, two founders of Africrypt stole US $3.6 billion in crypto from investors.[11]

	Yes	No
Known hacking g	H.O.Z	
Known hacks	Africrypt	

Regulation of Digital Assets: Crypto-asset service providers will be regulated by the South African regulators when the proposed crypto laws, based on the Intergovernmental Fintech Working Group (IFWG) position paper,[12] are finalized in 2022.

Regulation	Regulator	Yes	No
Financial sector laws	FIC Act	Proposed	
Financial product laws	FAIS Act	Proposed	
AML/CFT	South African Treasury	Proposed	
NFT			X
Capital gains tax		X[13]	

Notes

1. https://cointelegraph.com/news/south-african-president-steps-down-as-banks-embrace-blockchain-technology
2. https://www.aljazeera.com/features/2018/3/27/investigating-south-africas-mire-of-gupta-linked-corruption
3. https://cointelegraph.com/news/south-african-president-steps-down-as-banks-embrace-blockchain-technology
4. https://www.finder.com/finder-cryptocurrency-adoption-index
5. https://triple-a.io/crypto-ownership-south-africa/
6. https://blockworks.co/in-one-of-africas-largest-crypto-raises-south-african-exchange-takes-in-50m/
7. https://mybroadband.co.za/news/cryptocurrency/425860-joburg-crypto-mine-among-the-most-profitable-in-the-world.html
8. https://africabusinesscommunities.com/tech/tech-news/south-africa-crypto-valley-venture-capital-initiates-an-investment-strategy-to-build-a-blockchain-accelerator-for-african-startups/
9. https://www.bis.org/press/p220322.htm
10. https://www.momint.so/events
11. https://issafrica.org/iss-today/africa-new-playground-for-crypto-scams-and-money-laundering
12. http://www.treasury.gov.za/comm_media/press/2021/IFWG_CAR%20WG_Position%20paper%20on%20crypto%20assets_Final.pdf
13. https://www.sars.gov.za/individuals/crypto-assets-tax/

Chapter 25
Switzerland

S witzerland has long been a global center for the wealth management industry, housing around $2 trillion, or 27%, of global offshore wealth. Since 1934, Swiss bankers and regulators have resisted the efforts of foreign tax regulators, including the Internal Revenue Service (IRS) in the United States, to obtain information about secret Swiss bank accounts. They claimed compliance with Swiss law and the need to protect the privacy of their customers, as Swiss private bankers smuggled US taxpayer wealth from the United States to Switzerland in all sorts of creative ways. From bundles of cash hidden inside rolls of newspaper, to setting up shell companies, to jamming diamonds into toothpaste tubes, Swiss bankers aided tens of thousands of wealthy American clients to evade US taxes by using secret offshore bank accounts.

After giving up on their famous banking secrecy laws with a little nudging from the US Department of Justice (DOJ) and the IRS Criminal Investigations Division (IRS-CI), which shut down the oldest private bank and slapped the largest and most prominent Swiss banks with billions of dollars in fines for aiding US tax evasion, Switzerland was on the verge of losing its competitive edge over rival financial markets.

But don't count Switzerland out just yet.[1]

Blockchain Adoption: By establishing a global hub for virtual currencies known as the "Crypto Valley" in Zug, and the implementation of forward-looking regulation by the Swiss Financial Market Supervisory Authority (FINMA),[2] Switzerland is emerging as one of "the world's leading ecosystems for crypto, blockchain, and distributed ledger technologies," according to Oliver Bussmann, the cofounder of the Crypto Valley Association. Johann Schneider-Ammann, the head of the Swiss Department of Economic Affairs, points out that the country is becoming a "crypto nation" for the digital revolution with a flourishing initial coin offering (ICO) market.[3] The number of companies in Crypto Valley grew to 1,128 at the end of December 2021, an 18% increase from the previous year.[4]

Similarly, Lugano is aspiring to become another hub for blockchain by adopting Bitcoin, Tether (USDT), stablecoin, and the city's own LVGA tokens as legal tender, as a means for payment of taxes, goods, and services.[5]

GlobalData estimates that the blockchain market will expand at a compound annual growth rate of 46% during 2020–2025,[6] and according to its Cryptocurrency Index ranks Switzerland as one of the top global markets in terms of blockchain and cryptocurrency development.[7]

Crypto Adoption: At the end of 2021, 1.82% of the population owned cryptocurrencies.[8] SEBA Bank launched the first regulated gold token to enable digital ownership of physical gold.

The token is designed to provide low-cost access to precious metals and set a new standard in the stablecoin sector.[9]

Crypto Mining: Crypto mining is not regulated; there are no restrictions.[10] Alpine Tech is the earliest and largest crypto mining company in Switzerland.[11]

Startups: Oliver Bussmann, a tech thought leader, is a member of the Global Token Awareness Initiative for startups and the founder and CEO of Bussmann Advisory, where he advises enterprises and startups around the world. In an interview, Bussman said, "One of the biggest drivers of financial institutions' interest in blockchain is the concept of smart contracts, which is probably the most discussed but least understood concept in blockchain. One of the leading smart contract platforms is Deon Digital based in Zurich."[12] Information about other Swiss startups can be found at Startup.ch and News Swiss Regtech.

Central Bank Issued Digital Currency (CDCB): In the first quarter of 2022, the Swiss National Bank undertook "Project Helvet" in cooperation with five established major banks that integrated a CBDC into their existing systems and processes.[13]

Nonfungible Tokens: In the third quarter of 2021, SIX Digital Exchange (SDX), the operator of the Swiss national stock exchange, obtained a license from FINMA to list NFTs and digital assets.[14] In 2020, SDX announced a partnership with Japan's banking and financial services giant SBI Group[15] to establish a Swiss-based crypto exchange and central securities depository (CSD) in Singapore. The SBI joint venture called "the Asia Digital Exchange or ADX" is designed to create a regulated, global liquidity pool between Asia and Europe for digital assets.

Illicit Use of Crypto:

	Yes	No
Known hacking groups	Tillie Kottmann[16]	
Known crypto exchange hacks	Carbanak cybergang[17]	
JCat	X	

Regulation of Digital Assets: For the first time, Switzerland imposed crypto sanctions, in response to the Russia-Ukraine war. "The provisions of the sanctions Ordinance of March 4th apply to crypto-assets in the same way as they do to other assets, including asset-freeze for listed persons and entities. Crypto companies/financial institutions must notify the authorities concerning crypto sanctions enforcement cases. Criminal charges apply for violation of prohibitions in accordance with the Embargo Act of 2002, to which the Ordinance refers in Article 32," explained Isabelle Rösch, press officer of Swiss Federal Department of Finance.[18]

Regulation	Regulator	Yes	No
Sustainability			X
Crypto trading	DLT Act	X	
ICO	FINMA	X	
AML/CFT	FINMA	X	
NFT			X
Sanctions	Embargo Act of 2002	X	
Capital gains tax		X – Businesses	X – Individuals

Notes

1. https://cointelegraph.com/news/why-switzerland-is-becoming-a-crypto-nation-with-a-flourishing-ico-market-expert-take
2. https://www.finma.ch/en/~/media/finma/dokumente/dokumentencenter/myfinma/faktenblaetter/faktenblatt-virtuelle-waehrungen.pdf

3. https://cointelegraph.com/news/why-switzerland-is-becoming-a-crypto-nation-with-a-flourishing-ico-market-expert-take
4. https://beincrypto.com/crypto-valley-roundup-early-2022/
5. https://www.ndtv.com/business/cryptocurrency-to-be-accepted-as-currency-in-swiss-city-of-lugano-2806382
6. https://www.globaldata.com/data-insights/macroeconomic/blockchain-habitat-for-cryptocurrencies-and-nfts/
7. https://www.electronicpaymentsinternational.com/comments/switzerland-is-a-global-leader-in-blockchain-adoption/
8. https://triple-a.io/crypto-ownership/
9. https://www.seba.swiss/media-and-investors/media-and-investors/seba-bank-launches-landmark-first-regulated-gold-token-to-enable-digital-ownership-of-physical-gold
10. https://www.globallegalinsights.com/practice-areas/blockchain-laws-and-regulations/switzerland
11. https://alpinetech.swiss
12. https://fintechnews.ch/fintech-influencer-switzerland/fintech-influencer-switzerland-interview-series-7-questions-to-oliver-bussmann/36269/
13. https://cvj.ch/en/focus/background/swiss-national-bank-continues-cbdc-experiments/
14. https://www.sdx.com
15. https://www.six-group.com/en/newsroom/media-releases/2020/20201208-six-sbi-jev.html
16. https://thehill.com/policy/cybersecurity/543255-swiss-authorities-raid-home-of-hacker-potentially-responsible-for/
17. https://www.entrepreneur.com/article/242964
18. Personal interview with author.

Chapter 26
Israel

Blockchain technology is being widely used by the Israeli government and businesses.

Blockchain Adoption: The government of Israel promotes the policy of open government, with the understanding that recent innovations in communication and information technologies could allow a significant improvement in parliamentary democracy. This approach fosters informed policy-making processes, improves governmental services, and has the potential to strengthen the trust between citizens and government.

The Israeli government funds, collaborates, and partners with businesses as well as educational institutions in fostering and continuously developing innovative technologies and science.

A startup blockchain technology company, CoaliChain, is designing an interactive political platform that promotes the policies of an open government and eliminates the communication gap between the elector and the elected. During interactive discourse between citizens and government, the platform produces heat maps and graphs conveying the citizen's interests, allowing politicians, in turn, to respond in real time to their constituent's queries. The data collected by the system traces the frequency of corporate influence and payments made to politicians. The system also utilizes smart contracts for enforcing campaign commitments made by politicians, such as budgets proposals and policies. The launch of a beta version was scheduled for release in Q1 2018, and the full version and blockchain-integrated app by the end of 2018, according to the company's website.

A tech rise fueled by the smartphone electronics industry has significantly accelerated the use of unmanned aerial vehicles (UAVs) in commercial applications. Drones initially came into existence for the sole purpose of reaching and traversing areas where it was arduous for man to maneuver. Over time, their use expanded to military applications, for example, to get a bird's-eye view of complex operational missions and perform intelligence, surveillance, and reconnaissance. With time, demand, and further progressions, drones began to be used for a variety of other purposes, including for inspections, surveys, surveillance, security, delivery, and wireless internet access. Israel is a leading drone exporter. Airobotics, a startup company based in Petah Tikva, Israel, is the world's first company to obtain authorization from the Civil Aviation Authority of Israel (CAAI) to fly commercial, fully unmanned drones in their nation's airspace.

To track and secure commercial drone flights and deliveries, another startup company, Applied Blockchain, founded by Adi Ben-Ari, developed the blockchain drone registry. "The blockchain platform brings together drone operators, drone manufacturers, and regulators together with a single source of truth. Flight path data captured by a drone during a flight can be uploaded onto the same shared ledger and represented visually on an interactive map. As this data is attached to a registered drone, aviation authorities can plot the flights of a specific drone, all drones of a given operator, or even all drones from a specific manufacturer, all on a single map and in real time to ensure the safe interoperation of UAVs within the airspace. This access to data is a paradigm shift from legacy-based systems, which inherently rely upon a single trusted party to maintain the data and provide the correct level of access to users" Ben-Ari explained.[1]

Crypto Adoption: At the end of 2021, 1.27% of the population owned cryptocurrencies.[2] Israeli bank Leumi was the first in the country to allow cryptocurrency trading.[3]

Crypto Mining: Crypto mining is treated as a business and is subject to income tax.[4]

Startups: According to Bloomberg, Israel ranks as the world's tenth most innovative country, ahead of the United States. This is because it has one of the highest percentages of engineers and scientists in the workforce, and the largest number of tech startups producing cutting-edge technologies such as Bancor, Zen, and DAGlabs, which is developing technology to improve crypto scaling issues.[5]

Central Bank Issued Digital Currency (CBDC): Israel has joined the growing list of countries planning to launch a state-backed cryptocurrency. The Israeli Finance Ministry and the Bank of Israel's interest in promoting a state-backed cryptocurrency is aimed at minimizing risks of corruption, money laundering, and tax evasion offenses.[6]

Nonfungible Tokens: An Israeli company, CryptoVerses, sold an NFT encrypted with a Bible verse for $8,400, representing the "technological development over thousands of years," from papyrus through parchment, paper, and now digital representations of the Bible.[7]

Illicit Use of Crypto:

	Yes	No
Known crypto fraudster	Moshe Hogeg[8]	
Known crypto terror financing	Hamas[9]	

Regulation of Digital Assets: The Israel Securities Authority (ISA) is the main cryptocurrency regulator. Recently, ISA partnered with the Ministry of Finance, Start-Up Nation Central, and tech providers like VMware, Digital Asset, and Algorand to host its first hackathon to attract blockchain-based solutions that can improve the infrastructure supporting the securities and sovereign debt markets in Israel as part of ISA's larger initiative to gather the expertise needed to regulate the fintech and the crypto sector.[10]

Regulation	Regulator	Yes	No
Sustainability			X
Crypto trading	Law 5776-2016	X	
ICO	ISA	X	
AML/CFT	BOA	X – Proposed	
NFT			X
Capital gains tax		X	

Notes

1. https://cointelegraph.com/news/blockchain-technology-takes-hold-in-israel-expert-take
2. https://triple-a.io/crypto-ownership/
3. https://www.al-monitor.com/originals/2022/03/israeli-bank-leumi-becomes-first-country-allow-cryptocurrency-trading
4. https://www.calcalistech.com/ctech/articles/0,7340,L-3732231,00.html
5. https://cointelegraph.com/news/blockchain-technology-takes-hold-in-israel-expert-take
6. https://cointelegraph.com/news/blockchain-technology-takes-hold-in-israel-expert-take

7. https://www.timesofisrael.com/israeli-company-cryptoverses-sells-nft-of-bible-verse-for-8400/
8. https://www.timesofisrael.com/alleged-dirty-dealings-and-sex-offenses-moshe-hogegs-long-history-of-deceit/
9. https://allarab.news/israel-seizes-cryptocurrency-accounts-liked-to-terror-group-hamas/
10. https://www.nasdaq.com/articles/israels-securities-regulatory-chief-lays-out-crypto-plans

Chapter 27
South Korea

Over the past five years, South Korea has come to be known as the world's global-innovation gold medalist. With a lightning-fast internet, the country is emerging as one of the world's biggest markets for trades in cryptocurrencies as well as its underlying blockchain technology. Behind South Korea's high-tech developments are 45 large chaebols, a term that combines the Korean words *chae* (wealth) and *bol* (clan)—family-run large industrial conglomerates that are incriminated in governance transgressions.[1]

Blockchain Adoption: Samsung Electronics Co. is the most valuable multinational tech company by market capitalization and is at the heart of blockchain innovation in South Korea. The Samsung Group is a member of the Enterprise Ethereum Alliance, as well as the Korean Blockchain Association (KBA), which was established in 2018 with 66 member companies to self-regulate the cryptocurrency market.

The Samsung Group has launched various integrated blockchain platforms that can be deployed across all industries, including fintech and govtech. Its permissioned blockchain system called NexLedger was jointly developed with Amazon Web Services and a Korean startup blockchain company, Blocko.[2] Similarly, LG Electronics recently revised its business development goals to include cryptocurrency and blockchain-based software.[3]

KT Corp, a major South Korean telecommunication company, announced that it will digitize its documents using blockchain technology to reduce carbon emissions.[4] And South Korea's Ministry of ICT, Science, and Future Planning pledged 223.7 billion Korean won ($186.7 million) to create a metaverse ecosystem to further support the growth of digitization.[5]

Crypto Adoption: At the end of 2021, 3.79% of the population owned cryptocurrencies, including memecoins.[6] Dogecoin (DOGE) is South Korea's fifth-most traded memecoin on the big four exchanges that operate legally in the country—Upbit, Bithumb, Coinone, and Korbit.[7]

South Korean pension funds are allowed to invest in Bitcoin ETFs.[8] KB Bank is the first to offer a crypto investment fund for individual investors, with several other financial institutions considering offering similar crypto-based products.[9]

Crypto Mining: Crypto mining is treated as a business and is subject to income tax.[10]

Startups: SK Square, the investment arm of South Korean conglomerate SK Group, is committed to spending 2 trillion won (US $1.6 billion) by 2022 on semiconductors and blockchain technology.[11]

Central Bank Issued Digital Currency (CBDC): The Bank of Korea completed the first phase of a CBCD pilot run on Kakao's Ground X, while the second phase is currently underway.[12]

Nonfungible Tokens: People are adopting NFT use at a high rate. Even President-Elect Yoon issued an NFT collection that followers can mint.[13] The South Korean NFT exchange of choice is Bithumb.[14]

Illicit Use of Crypto: South Korea was the first country to outlaw anonymity-enhanced currencies (AECs) in November 2020.[15]

	Yes	No
Known crypto hack groups	X[16]	
Known crypto fraud and money laundering	X[17]	

Regulation of Digital Assets: The Financial Services Commission (FSC) is the main crypto regulator that is working to introduce new NFT rules.[18]

Regulation	Regulator	Yes	No
Sustainability			X
Crypto trading	FSC	X	
ICO	FSC[19]	X	
AML/CFT	FSC	X	
NFT			X
Capital gains tax	NTS	X Corporations	X

Notes

1. https://cointelegraph.com/news/south-korea-wants-to-set-a-desirable-cryptocurrency-and-blockchain-policy-expert-take
2. Ibid.
3. https://cointelegraph.com/news/lg-electronics-adds-blockchain-and-crypto-as-new-areas-of-business

4. https://cointelegraph.com/news/leading-south-korean-telecom-firm-adopts-blockchain-for-carbon-ambitions

5. https://cointelegraph.com/news/south-korea-to-invest-187m-in-national-metaverse

6. https://triple-a.io/crypto-ownership/

7. https://cointelegraph.com/news/1-million-shiba-inu-users-can-t-be-wrong-can-they

8. https://cointelegraph.com/news/south-korean-pension-fund-to-invest-in-bitcoin-etf-report

9. https://cointelegraph.com/news/kb-bank-to-launch-south-korea-s-first-crypto-investment-fund

10. https://news.bitcoin.com/south-korea-to-impose-a-20-tax-on-crypto-mining-activities/

11. https://www.hankyung.com/finance/article/202203234757i

12. https://cointelegraph.com/news/bank-of-korea-completes-first-phase-of-digital-currency-pilot

13. https://finance.yahoo.com/news/korean-presidential-candidate-issues-over-052915843.html

14. https://cointelegraph.com/news/korean-bithumb-exchange-to-launch-nft-marketplace

15. https://cointelegraph.com/news/south-korean-financial-watchdog-to-ban-privacy-coins

16. https://www.wired.com/story/north-korea-hacking-zero-days-google/

17. https://cointelegraph.com/news/korean-investigation-finds-1-48b-in-illegal-overseas-crypto-transactions

18. https://cointelegraph.com/news/mixed-messages-on-crypto-tax-rules-create-confusion-in-south-korea

19. https://asia.nikkei.com/Spotlight/Cryptocurrencies/South-Korea-s-incoming-president-vows-big-cryptocurrency-push

Chapter 28
Brazil

On April 7, 2018, the 35th president of Brazil, Luiz Inácio Lula da Silva, was the nation's first former president ever to be jailed, for charges stemming from Brazil's Operação Lava Jato (Operation Car Wash) corruption investigation. Lula's incarceration followed after police in Rio de Janeiro uncovered a first-of-its kind Bitcoin-based money laundering scheme in which state officials misstated the budget spent on food for state-run prisons to the tune of $22.4 million. Luíz Henrique Casemiro, superintendent of the Internal Revenue Service (IRS) in Rio, said, "This was the first-time cryptocurrencies were used in such an operation to fly below the radar of the Central Bank and the IRS."

Operation Car Wash began as an investigation into money laundering in 2014, but quickly turned into something much greater, uncovering a vast intricate web of political and corporate racketeering involving the heads of states of Brazil, Peru, Guatemala, Ecuador, Mexico, Argentina, Venezuela, Colombia, and Panama. It is the biggest corruption scandal in global history that exposed a culture of systemic graft in Brazilian politics and provoked a backlash from the establishment fierce enough to bring down the government of the 36th president of Brazil,

Dilma Rousseff, and leave the administration of the 37th president, Michel Temer, on the brink of collapse.[1]

Blockchain Adoption: Blockchain adoption is widespread in govtech, fintech, and renewable energy applications.

To bring transparency to the popular petition process, the Brazilian government is supporting an innovative Ethereum blockchain solution with a mobile app that will allow people to register to the system online via their smartphones and submit a petition or place their signatures on petitions they support. The system would allow anyone to view the actual number of signatures for a certain petition, ensuring that no signature is lost or forged.

Another state-run blockchain initiative is a platform for property registration—for the world's fifth-largest country, occupying half of South America's land mass—to protect millions of trees in the Amazon rainforest. The aim of the initiative is to prevent illicit development of the biggest, most biodiverse nature reserve in the world. The southern city of Pelotas is among the first in Brazil to experiment with a fully computer-based blockchain-based land-titling system.

Several large Brazilian banks that have been caught in the crosshairs of the Operation Car Wash investigation for money laundering and tax evasion have begun exploring implementing blockchain technology in their banks. This includes Banco Santander, SA, which on the one hand, due to the lack of cryptocurrency regulation, has shut down or refused to open some cryptocurrency exchange brokers' accounts, while on the other hand recently has launched the first blockchain-based cross-border payment service for end consumers in Brazil.[2]

Mercado Bitcoin partnered with Comerc, one of the main retail energy providers in Brazil, to develop two types of renewable energy tokens. The first, set to launch in 2022, will be tied to a 15–20% cashback scheme for solar energy generation. The second token will be linked to certificates that document energy consumption from renewable sources.[3]

Crypto Adoption: High inflation and devaluation are generating a crypto boom in Brazil. According to a survey by Gemini, 51% of respondents in Brazil made their first purchase of a cryptocurrency in 2021.[4] At the end of 2021, 4.88% of the population owned cryptocurrencies.[5]

Brazil approved the first crypto ETF investment in 2021 with a fund that invests in carbon credits and green tech investments.[6] Visa aims to accept Bitcoin payments in Brazil,[7] and a Brazilian mayor will invest 1% of city reserves in Bitcoin.[8]

Crypto Mining: Crypto mining is treated as a business and is subject to income tax.[9]

Startups: Moss.Earth, a São Paulo-based startup founded by Luis Felipe Adaime, tokenizes carbon credits (MCO2 tokens) to offset carbon emissions, with the proceeds going toward "reputable environmental projects" working to save the Amazon rainforest.[10]

Central Bank Issued Digital Currency (CBDC): The Brazilian National Bank for Economic and Social Development (BNDES) wants to prove that documenting government funding through a visible public ledger based on Ethereum's blockchain will prove to be an efficient way to ensure transparency, as well as a deterrent to fraud and corruption. BNDES is tokenizing the Brazilian real for these purposes. Brazil is also involved in BRICS—Brazil, Russia, India, China and South Africa—a multinational cryptocurrency initiative led by the Central Bank of Russia that recently indicated that it could eventually be deployed atop an Ethereum-based platform as well.[11] Brazil is expected to pilot CBDC during 2022.[12]

Nonfungible Tokens: In Brazil, an eco-friendly, Tezos-based nonfungible token (NFT) marketplace offered creators a sustainable way to make a living at Hic et Nunc—which in Latin means "here and now." However, it abruptly shut down on November 14, 2021, when artists became worried about their

NFTs on exhibit at the Hermitage Museum's first-ever NFT exhibition, "Ethereal Aether" (November 10 to December 10, 2021), as well as Art Basel Miami's first-ever NFT exhibition, "Humans + Machines: NFTs and the Ever-Evolving World of Art" (December 2 to 4, 2021).

Illicit Use of Crypto:

	Yes	No
Known crypto hacking groups	Lapsus$[13]	
Known crypto fraud, money laundering, pyramid scheme	GAS Consultoria Bitcoin[14]	

Regulation of Digital Assets: Brazil's crypto bill was unanimously approved by the Senate's Economic Affairs Committee. Once passed by both the Senate and the lower house, it will be sent to President Jair Bolsonaro to be signed into law. The legislation states that it provides "guidelines for the provision of virtual asset services," defining what constitutes a virtual asset (VA), a broker, or exchange, and which arms of the federal government would have jurisdiction over the matter.[15]

Regulation	Regulator	Yes	No
Sustainability			X
Sandbox	CVM	X	
Crypto trading		X – Proposed	
ICO	CVM	X	
AML/CFT	COAF	X	
NFT			X
Capital gains tax	FRO	X	

Notes

1. https://cointelegraph.com/news/brazils-operacao-lava-jato-paves-the-way-to-blockchain-implementation-expert-take
2. Ibid.
3. https://cointelegraph.com/news/largest-cryptocurrency-exchange-in-latin-america-to-develop-renewable-energy-tokens
4. https://cointelegraph.com/news/new-crypto-owners-nearly-doubled-in-3-key-regions-in-2021-report
5. https://triple-a.io/crypto-ownership/
6. https://cointelegraph.com/news/new-brazilian-bitcoin-etf-pledges-carbon-neutrality
7. https://cointelegraph.com/news/visa-reportedly-aims-to-integrate-bitcoin-payments-in-brazil
8. https://cointelegraph.com/news/brazilian-mayor-to-reportedly-invest-1-of-city-reserves-in-bitcoin
9. https://www.globallegalinsights.com/practice-areas/blockchain-laws-and-regulations/brazil
10. https://agfundernews.com/nfts-crypto-carbon-credits-moss-earth-is-using-to-fight-climate-change and personal interview.
11. https://cointelegraph.com/news/brazils-operacao-lava-jato-paves-the-way-to-blockchain-implementation-expert-take
12. https://finance.yahoo.com/news/brazil-central-bank-plans-launch-225953568.html
13. https://www.theverge.com/22998479/lapsus-hacking-group-cyberattacks-news-updates
14. https://insightcrime.org/news/murder-drugs-god-and-crypto-downfall-brazil-pharaoh-bitcoins/
15. https://cointelegraph.com/news/bill-to-regulate-crypto-in-brazil-for-first-time-heads-to-senate-vote

Chapter 29
Canada

C anada has emerged as a leading crypto nation based on its innovation, low energy costs, high internet speed, and favorable regulatory regime.

Blockchain Adoption: While Canada ranks third in the world, behind the United States and the UK, when it comes to embracing blockchain technology, Ethereum blockchain technology adoption around the world, with a wide variety of applications in finance, government, legal, health, education, space, national and multinational cryptocurrencies, energy, initial coin offerings, and so forth is unparalleled.

A study conducted by Cornell University shows that "the Ethereum nodes are both in the latency space, and also geographically, more distributed around the world, as opposed to Bitcoin nodes, which tend to be located in data centers," explained Emin Gün Sirer, Cornell professor and computer scientist.[1]

Crypto Adoption: At the end of 2021, 3.20% of the population owned cryptocurrencies.[2] In 2018 the British Columbia Securities Commission approved Canada's first registered cryptocurrency investment fund, acknowledging that it views cryptocurrency investments as a new and novel way to invest. This ruling allowed pension, investment, and venture capital funds, including the Ontario Municipal Employees Retirement System's Ethereum Capital, to invest in cryptocurrencies and tokens. Amid extreme market volatility, Canada's first blockchain exchange-traded fund (ETF) began trading on the Toronto Stock Exchange in 2018.

In 2021, Canada's main securities regulator, the Investment Industry Regulatory Organization of Canada (IIROC), approved the world's first physically settled Bitcoin ETF that pays out a monthly yield.[3] Fidelity Canada launched its Fidelity Advantage Bitcoin ETF shortly thereafter.[4]

Crypto Mining: According to Hydro Quebec, the province has an energy surplus equivalent to 100 Terawatt hours over 10 years and offers some of the lowest electricity rates in North America. This has drawn cryptominers to the region, including from China, in droves. A cryptominer's easy, breezy lifestyle starkly contrasts that of a gold miner, who works 5,400 to 5,600 feet below the earth's surface, at suffocating temperatures, dripping with sweat, while punching holes into burning rock walls, in the dark, to find hidden gold.

Here is an example. China's Bitmain Technologies began mining in Canada in 2016, when ETH traded at $1. When ETH's price rose 63,600% to $636 with no implemented hard cap on the total ETH supply, Bitmain first announced a new specialized mining system for ETH, then set its eyes on cryptocurrency mining sites in Quebec, as it takes on average 29.05 TWh annually to operate a cryptocurrency mining operation. That's about 0.13% of total global electricity consumption.

While this may be potential bad news for smaller cryptominers in the region, a local ETH miner shrugged it off: "Quebec is one of the best places in the world for mining, thanks to low cost electricity, cool temperatures, and high-speed internet. There's a lot of data centers in Montreal and they'll rent you a space for your own server or ZTE smartphone—Sugar S11. Since you'd be paying about half to 1/3rd the electricity price of Ontario, then the added expense of rent is well worth it."

However, Quebec Premier Philippe Couillard warned that "Cryptominers planning to move to the region will not get cheap electricity from the government-owned utility Hydro-Quebec, as the utility may not have enough power to meet the demand."[5]

Crypto mining businesses are subject to income tax.[6]

Startups: Ron Resnick, executive director of the Enterprise Ethereum Alliance, which launched in 2017, explained: "EEA serves as the connective tissue between Ethereum blockchain and the evolving enterprise industry with over 450 members from all around the world—135 in the Banking Work Group—which are driving production deployments through a community of over 30,000 developers."

Take, for example, ConsenSys, an EEA member firm, with various Ethereum projects, including Quorum, and the EU Blockchain Observatory and Forum, which trains Ethereum developers at its Academy.

The EEA is also a member of Blockchain Research Institute (BRI), based in Toronto, which is dedicated to over 70 research projects that proposes ways in which blockchain technology can be utilized to impact various industries. BRI has partnered with the Information and Communications Technology Council (ICTC) of Canada to build a nationwide blockchain ecosystem alongside the Bank of Canada, which has explored and experimented with a national cryptocurrency.[7]

Central Bank Issued Digital Currency (CBDC): The Bank of Canada and the Massachusetts Institute of Technology (MIT) are collaborating on a 12-month research project on CBDC.[8]

Nonfungible Tokens: Canadian rapper Tory Lanez earned $1 million in a minute by selling his album "When It's Dark" as an NFT via platform Audius in August of 2021.[9] While this made waves in the Music NFT circles, the National Hockey League's

Montreal Canadiens joining the NFT league by launching their own series of collectibles was big news in the sports NFT area.[10]

Illicit Use of Crypto:

	Yes	No
Known crypto hacking groups	X[11]	
Known crypto fraud, money laundering, pyramid scheme		Vancouver Model[12]
JCAT	X	
FUI	X	
J5	X	

Regulation of Digital Assets: Excessive regulation could stifle innovation; accordingly, Canada lightly regulates cryptocurrency/ICO/tokens and offers a wide selection of government—federal and provincial—incentives and aid to startup tech companies.

As Danielle Prenevost of the Canadian Securities Administrators explained,

On March 14, 2022 the Canadian Securities Administrators (CSA) issued a statement imposing crypto sanctions by amending the Special Economic Measures (Russia) Regulations, which are applicable to all crypto market participants—including issuers, marketplaces, clearing agencies, custodians, all categories of registrants, including crypto-asset trading platforms, and pension, investment and mutual funds and their managers. The CSA took this step to encourage all market participants to do their due diligence and consider obtaining expert advice to understand, follow and continually monitor their obligations under the regulations."[13]

Regulation	Regulator	Yes	No
Sustainability			X
Sandbox	CVM	X	
Crypto trading	CSC	X	
ICO	CSA, OSC	X	
AML/CFT	FINTRAC	X	
NFT			X
Sanctions	FINTRAC	X	
Whistleblowing		X	
Capital gains tax	CRA	X	

Notes

1. https://cointelegraph.com/news/why-canada-has-emerged-as-a-leading-blockchain-and-crypto-nation-expert-take
2. https://triple-a.io/crypto-ownership/
3. https://cointelegraph.com/news/crypto-makes-history-in-2021-five-instances-of-governments-embracing-digital-assets
4. https://www.fidelity.ca/fidca/en/etfs/bitcoin-etf
5. https://cointelegraph.com/news/why-canada-has-emerged-as-a-leading-blockchain-and-crypto-nation-expert-take
6. https://www.canada.ca/en/revenue-agency/news/newsroom/tax-tips/tax-tips-2022/mining-cryptocurrency.html
7. https://cointelegraph.com/news/why-canada-has-emerged-as-a-leading-blockchain-and-crypto-nation-expert-take
8. https://www.bankofcanada.ca/2022/03/central-bank-digital-currency-collaboration/
9. https://www.rap-up.com/2021/08/10/tory-lanez-sells-1-million-nft-albums/
10. https://www.nhl.com/canadiens/news/canadiens-to-launch-line-of-nft-digital-collectibles/c-325897062
11. https://www.wired.com/story/teen-sim-swap-theft-fbi-email-hack-stripchat-leak-security-news/
12. https://fcpablog.com/2018/04/24/selva-ozelli-us-cracks-down-on-canadian-cross-border-cryptoc//
13. https://cointelegraph.com/news/the-world-has-synchronized-on-russian-crypto-sanctions

Chapter 30
Malta

Malta's Prime Minister Joseph Muscat has described his country as the global trailblazer in the regulation of blockchain-based businesses and the jurisdiction of quality and choice for world-class fintech companies. Muscat ties Malta's success to becoming a member of EU's Blockchain Partnership and to its cryptocurrency legal infrastructure, which he implemented in 2018, becoming the first country to regulate crypto.[1]

Blockchain Adoption: In unique govtech applications, the Family Ministry of Malta has used blockchain technology in child adoptions to speed up the adoption process,[2] and the Ministry of Transport has used NFTs to bundle together a digitized painting with the legal right to own a personalized numberplate depicted in an artwork.[3]

Crypto Adoption: At the end of 2021, 1.44% of Malta's population owned cryptocurrencies.[4] Malta's strategy to become a global center for digital assets was working up until 2021, as roughly $71 billion, or 60 billion euros, worth of cryptocurrencies passed through Malta since it first adopted its "blockchain island" strategy.[5] But more than 100 licensed firms and funds have surrendered their Malta license since June 23, 2021, when Malta was gray-listed by the Financial Action Task Force.[6]

Crypto Mining: Crypto mining is not regulated and businesses are subject to taxation.[7]

Startups: Malta has introduced various tax credits and loan assistance programs for blockchain startups and corporations looking to choose Malta as their operational ecosystem. Examples of such programs are businesses capital investment loan matches at a 1:1 ratio up to €200,000 and regressive tax credits for companies based on their Maltese employment numbers.[8]

Central Bank Issued Digital Currency (CBDC): Malta, which is part of the EU's European Central Bank (ECB), is exploring creating a central bank digital currency (CBDC), the digital euro, according to the Atlantic Council.[9] Starting in May 2020, the Bank of France successfully experimented with using the digital euro in the sale of securities, digital bonds, and cross-border payment with the Monetary Authority of Singapore through blockchain technology.[10]

Nonfungible Tokens: Soccer star Leo Messi joined forces with Maltese Fan Token creator Socios.com with the aim of empowering football fans with NFTs, allowing them to interact with the soccer club and weigh in on certain business decisions.[11]

Illicit Use of Crypto:

	Yes	No
Known hacking groups	X[12]	
Known illicit crypto use	X[13]	

Regulation of Digital Assets: Malta's crypto bills grant regulatory power to the Malta Financial Services Authority to publish and enforce specific rules regarding cryptocurrencies:

- *The Malta Digital Innovation Authority Bill:* Establishes the Malta Digital Innovation Authority, which, on a voluntary basis, will certify blockchain platforms to ensure credibility and provide legal assurances regarding cryptocurrencies.

- *The Innovative Technology Arrangements Bill:* Provides a framework for the registration of technology service providers and the certification of technology arrangements concerning system administrators and auditors.
- *The Services and Virtual Financial Asset Bill:* Provides the regulatory framework for cryptocurrencies and initial coin offerings (ICOs).[14]

Regulation	Regulator	Yes	No
MiCA	ESMA, EBA[15]	Proposed	
Sustainability	EU taxonomy	X	
ICO	FSA/ESMA[16]	X	
AML/CFT	FSA	X	
NFT			X
Sanctions	EU restrictive measures	X	
Whistleblowing law	Directive (EU) 2019/1937	X – No awards	
Capital gains tax		X – Business	X

Notes

1. https://cointelegraph.com/news/malta-emerges-as-world-s-cryptocurrency-hub-despite-eu-s-tax3-investigation-expert-take
2. https://timesofmalta.com/articles/view/blockchain-technology-introduced-to-speed-up-child-adoption.816174
3. https://decrypt.co/90549/how-one-nft-project-is-blurring-the-lines-between-artwork-and-assets
4. https://triple-a.io/crypto-ownership/

5. https://cointelegraph.com/news/71b-in-crypto-has-reportedly-passed-through-blockchain-island-malta-since-2017
6. https://cointelegraph.com/news/malta-emerges-as-world-s-cryptocurrency-hub-despite-eu-s-tax3-investigation-expert-take
7. https://www.globallegalinsights.com/practice-areas/blockchain-laws-and-regulations/portugal
8. https://www.trade.gov/country-commercial-guides/malta-blockchain-and-artificial-intelligence
9. https://www.atlanticcouncil.org/cbdctracker/
10. https://www.ecb.europa.eu/pub/pdf/other/Report_on_a_digital_euro~4d7268b458.en.pdf
11. https://lovinmalta.com/malta/messi-socios-com-football-fans-mark-favourite-teams/
12. https://newsbook.com.mt/en/hacker-arrested-in-malta-in-connection-with-us-100m-cryptocurrency-robbery/
13. https://cryptopotato.com/maltese-man-accused-of-stealing-700k-worth-of-crypto/
14. https://cointelegraph.com/news/malta-emerges-as-world-s-cryptocurrency-hub-despite-eu-s-tax3-investigation-expert-take
15. https://www.europarl.europa.eu/news/pt/press-room/20220309IPR25162/cryptocurrencies-in-the-eu-new-rules-to-boost-benefits-and-curb-threats
16. https://www.esma.europa.eu

Chapter 31
Germany

Move over, Singapore and the United States. Germany rises to the top spot in Coincub's crypto-friendly ranking guide for Q1 2022 for allowing crypto investments to form part of its long-term domestic savings industry, supported by its zero-crypto-tax policy on long-term capital gains, along with Germany's number of Bitcoin and Ethereum[1] nodes trailing those of the United States.[2]

Blockchain Adoption: In 2019 Germany became the first country to adopt a blockchain strategy to harness blockchain's potential for advancing digital transformation and to help make Germany an attractive hub for the development of blockchain, Web3, and metaverse applications in fintech, business, cleantech, and govtech, including its digital identities project.[3]

The German Savings Banks Association (known as Sparkasse, which is a network of 400 banks), Commerzbank, and Volks- und Raiffeisenbank started developing fintech blockchain applications to enable customers to buy and sell cryptocurrencies.[4] Sparkasse is also developing a cryptocurrency wallet.[5]

Various companies such as Volkswagen, About You,[6] SAP, BrainBot, and BigChainDB[7] have been developing NFTs, Metaverse,

Web3, govtech, and crypto payment applications that are widely used in e-commerce to purchase goods.[8]

Jacopo Visetti, an advisor to German-founded C-3, explained to me that "C-3 is a climate tech company developing advanced technological infrastructure by allowing carbon credits from international standards to be bridged to the blockchain by means of tokenization."[9]

To fund the development of these technologies, Roundhill Investments, an ETF sponsor focused on innovative thematic funds, launched the first Roundhill Ball Metaverse UCITS ETF (METV) on the Deutsche Börse Xetra.[10] Furthermore, Germany's "Fund Location Act" allows pension funds, insurance companies, family offices, and corporate investment funds to allocate up to 20% of their assets in digital assets.[11]

Crypto Adoption: At the end of 2021, approximately 2.6% of the population in the 18–34-year-old age group used cryptocurrency in Germany, with 44% of Germans being motivated to invest in crypto, according to a report released by Ku Coin.[12]

German investors can invest in crypto via German exchanges, such as 1inch Exchange, Bitwala, FinLab, Minespider, The NAGA Group, Tangany, Coindex, CryptoTax, Upvest, Fiona, Blocksize Capital, USDX Wallet, Bitbond, and IOTA Foundation, or shop at Sugartrends.com using Dash.[13]

"Dash is an alternative cryptocurrency that provides financial freedom without borders. It accelerates financial inclusion by allowing people to use their phones as bank accounts. It is decentralized, permissionless, and censorship-resistant," explained Mark Mason, Dash's communications and business relations manager.

Crypto Mining: Germany is within the top 10 countries for crypto mining and is home to the EU's largest mining company, Northern Data, which is powered almost entirely by renewable energy.[14] Crypto mining is taxable as a business.[15]

Startups: Numerous blockchain startups have settled in Germany's crypto capital, Berlin, with fintech angle investor Christian Angermayer's Apieron Investment Group backing Berlin's Denario, SME banking startup Penta, Nextmarket,[16] and crypto mining company Northern Data.[17]

Paycer, a Hamburg-based fintech startup company, specializes in cryptocurrencies and decentralized finance (DeFi) and is currently developing a bridge protocol that will aggregate DeFi and cross-chain crypto services and combine them with traditional banking services.[18]

Berlin-based fintech startup Forget Finance focuses on motivating young people to save and invest in crypto using an online coaching mix of AI bot and real financial experts.[19]

Central Bank Issued Digital Currency (CBDC): According to a Bundesbank survey, the share of cash payments in point-of-sale transactions made by German consumers dropped from 74% in 2017 to 60% in 2020.[20] Accordingly, Bundesbank has been working on distributed ledger technology asset settlements[21] and, as part of EU's European Central Bank (ECB), it is exploring creating a central bank digital currency (CBDC), the digital euro,[22] according to the Atlantic Council.[23] Recent ECB research, based on discussions with panels of EU citizens, emphasizes security and universal acceptance as main concerns.[24]

Nonfungible Tokens and the Metaverse: Ahead of the NFT craze in 2021, the ZKM Centre for Art and Media in Karlsruhe acquired a number of NFTs in 2017 and is exhibiting a selection of works from its own NFT collection as well as from private lenders on the cube screen.[25]

Following the NFT craze, German sportswear company adidas teamed up with the Bored Ape Yacht Club and Prada Re-Nylon adidas Forum for its charitable climate-focused NFT art project to raise climate awareness utilizing blockchain

Polygon Web3.[26] And the German auto company Volkswagen launched an interactive successful NFT ad campaign.[27]

The metaverse is the next wave of Web3, changing the way we interact, socialize, work, play video games, fund charities, purchase and sell NFTs, and attend concerts, sports events, and conferences.

Brian Shuster, founder and CEO of Utherverse.io, explained, "Utherverse has been building and operating an online virtual world community where one can socialize in real time, attend events, and start a business, since 2005. Utherverse has combined the best of the internet, gaming, and virtual reality for the ultimate metaverse experience. For example, Secret City is a game developed by Utherverse Digital Inc. with 81% of its users in Germany. Having developed more than 100 patents and pending patents to core internet technologies and the metaverse, we are the undisputed leaders of Metaverse Architecture and VR Economics. There's a ton of noise out there relating to the metaverse and frankly, most companies claiming to offer properties and token coins have dangerously underestimated the complexity of the task at hand. Almost every company that's tried to make a metaverse work has failed. The third generation of Utherverse and its utility token is expected to be unveiled in Q2 of 2022."

Illicit Use of Crypto: Germany is a member of the Joint Cybercrime Action Taskforce (J-CAT) to fight transnational cybercrime. According to a 2022 report by the Europol "The use of virtual currency for criminal activities and laundering of profits has grown over the past years in terms of volume and sophistication [. . .] the criminal use of cryptocurrency is no longer confined to cybercrime activities, but now relates to all types of crime that require the transmission of monetary value."[28]

After a tipoff, Germany's Federal Criminal Police Office, the Bundeskriminalamt (BKA), took down Hydra, the world's largest illegal dark web marketplace, which has cumulatively facilitated over $5 billion in Bitcoin transactions to date.[29] This was followed by the US Treasury issuing sanctions against Hydra "in a coordinated international effort to disrupt proliferation of malicious cybercrime services, dangerous drugs, and other illegal offerings" available through the Russia-based site.[30]

"The takedown of Hydra is notable not just because it was the largest darknet market in operation, but also because it offered money laundering services that enabled the conversion of cryptocurrency into Russian rubles. Taken together with the sanctions actions against Garantex as well as Suex and Chatex last year, government agencies are clearly targeting cashout points that cybercriminals use for ransomware, darknet market sales, scamming, and potentially sanctions evasion," explained Gurvais Grigg, CTO for Public Sector at Chainalysis.[31]

	Yes	No
Known hacking groups	Chaos Computer Club (CCC)[32]	
Known hacks	Hydra Dark Market[33]	
J-CAT	X	

Regulation of Digital Assets: Germany is one of the few states in Europe that started to regulate cryptocurrencies ahead of MiCA. According to Robin Matzke, a lawyer and blockchain expert who advised the German Bundestag, crypto custody regulation requires those addressing the German market and having control over private keys on behalf of others to get a license from BaFin, even if they hold other similar licenses within the EU.[34]

EU's new Transfer of Funds Regulation also provides disclosure rules for "unhosted" wallets—crypto accounts that are not managed by a custodian or centralized exchange. Lone Fønss Schrøder, CEO of the blockchain company Concordium, explained, "The new draft regulations require significant changes in the way current cryptocurrency transfers are made. It may be a huge challenge for the decentralized crypto solutions that hold anonymity as a core value and are committed to peer-to-peer (P2P) and self-custody. Moreover, many projects could be held back by their community from changing their solutions."[35]

Regulation	Regulator	Yes	No
MiCA	ESMA, EBA	Proposed	
Sustainability	EU taxonomy	X	
Advertising			X
ICO	ESMA	X	
AML/CFT	BaFin	X	
NFT			X
Sanctions	EU restrictive measures	X	
Whistleblow-ing law	Directive (EU) 2019/1937	X – No awards	
Capital gains tax			X – Long-term

Notes

1. https://cointelegraph.com/news/the-future-of-the-internet-inside-the-race-for-web3-s-infrastructure
2. https://www.prnewswire.com/news-releases/germany-takes-the-top-spot-in-the-latest-q1-international-crypto-ranking-guide-for-2022-says-coincubcom-301525845.html
3. https://www.bundesfinanzministerium.de/Content/EN/Standardartikel/Topics/Financial_markets/Articles/2019-09-18-Blockchain.html

4. https://cryptopotato.com/two-more-german-banks-planning-crypto-services-following-sparkasse/
5. Ibid.
6. https://www.fibre2fashion.com/news/fashion-news/germany-s-about-you-fashion-tech-firm-launches-hypewear-for-nfts-280125-newsdetails.htm
7. https://www.bloomingprairieonline.com/global-blockchain-in-government-market-to-witness-huge-gains-over-2022-2031/
8. https://triple-a.io/crypto-ownership-germany/
9. Jacopo Visetti, interview with author.
10. https://www.prnewswire.com/news-releases/roundhill-ball-meta verse-ucits-etf-metv-launches-in-germany-301507195.html
11. https://www.forbes.com/sites/philippsandner/2021/11/30/germanys-fund-location-act-allows-funds-to-allocate-up-to-20-of-their-assets-in-bitcoin-and-other-crypto-assets/?sh=67ba440a1569
12. https://cointelegraph.com/news/almost-half-of-germans-to-invest-in-crypto-report
13. Mark Mason of Dash, interview with author.
14. https://www.statista.com/statistics/1200477/bitcoin-mining-by-country/
15. https://www.primerus.com/international-business-articles/crypto currencies-how-will-mining-be-taxed-in-germany.htm
16. https://sifted.eu/articles/europes-top-fintech-angel-investors-2022/
17. https://sifted.eu/articles/largest-crypto-miner-europe/
18. https://finance.yahoo.com/news/german-fintech-startup-paycer-combine-155400031.html
19. https://www.eu-startups.com/2022/02/berlin-based-forget-finance-secures-e3-5-million-for-its-all-in-one-finance-platform-for-millennials/
20. https://www.bundesbank.de/en/press/speeches/exploring-a-digital-euro-875408
21. https://cointelegraph.com/news/eu-central-banks-work-on-dlt-based-asset-settlement
22. https://www.dnb.nl/en/innovations-in-payments-and-banking/digital-euro-what-why-and-how/
23. https://www.atlanticcouncil.org/cbdctracker
24. https://www.ecb.europa.eu/paym/digital_euro/investigation/pro fuse/shared/files/dedocs/ecb.dedocs220330_report.en.pdf

25. Margit Rosen, interview with author.
26. https://www.highsnobiety.com/p/adidas-prada-nft-collection-zach-lieberman/
27. https://www.ledgerinsights.com/volkswagen-sa-launches-interactive-nft-ad-campaign/
28. https://www.europol.europa.eu/cms/sites/default/files/documents/Europol%20Spotlight%20-%20Cryptocurrencies%20-%20Tracing%20the%20evolution%20of%20criminal%20finances.pdf
29. https://thehackernews.com/2022/04/germany-shuts-down-russian-hydra.html
30. https://cointelegraph.com/news/us-sanctions-russia-s-largest-darknet-market-and-crypto-exchange-garantex
31. Gurvais Grigg, interview with author.
32. https://www.ccc.de/en/
33. https://thehackernews.com/2022/04/germany-shuts-down-russian-hydra.html
34. https://fcpablog.com/2020/01/10/germany-imposes-licensing-requirements-on-banks-to-sell-and-store-cryptocurrencies/
35. https://cointelegraph.com/news/here-is-why-germany-is-ranked-the-most-crypto-friendly-country

Chapter 32
The United Arab Emirates

The United Arab Emirates (UAE) is the world's sixth-largest oil producer and one of the richest countries in the world, with a gross domestic product per capita of more than $43,000, as of 2019, according to the World Bank. As per its "Vision 2021," its petroleum- and natural-gas-reliant economy is committed to sustainable development in order to emerge as the Gulf Cooperation Council's, or GCC's, most diversified economy. This includes the digitization of the economy, which has become a priority during the COVID-19 pandemic.

At the first virtual Abu Dhabi Sustainability Week Summit 2021, in his opening address, Sultan Ahmed Al Jaber—the UAE's minister of industry and advanced technology, special envoy for climate change, and chairman of clean energy company Masdar—pointed out that with the COVID-19 pandemic, society is now witnessing the implementation of artificial intelligence, machine learning, and the digitization of different spheres of life all over the world. Accordingly, electrification, decarbonization, and digitization initiatives have become increasingly important across all industries.[1]

Blockchain Adoption: The UAE government has made the digitization of its economy a priority in order to bring efficiency to government and creativity to industry, and to build international leadership. To accomplish this goal, the UAE has established in Masdar City the world's first graduate-level, research-based artificial intelligence university, Mohamed bin Zayed University of Artificial Intelligence, which welcomed its first students in January 2021.

The UAE also adopted the Emirates Blockchain Strategy 2021 and the Dubai Blockchain Strategy, which have each undertaken several blockchain projects. SustVest is a crowd-investing blockchain-based platform that lets people invest in solar projects and earn returns from consumers who use their funding to install solar panels. The company is based in the Dubai Silicon Oasis Authority and has built its solution on the Nem blockchain. Its founder, Hardik Bhatia, explained:

> The global rooftop solar segment is booming with opportunities and is valued at over $66 billion. Emerging economies are looking to transition to solar as it offers a green and cheap alternative to conventional energy sources. SustVest enables this transition in emerging economies by crowdfunding rooftop solar projects in emerging economies on its platform. We tokenize solar projects granular to the level of individual solar cells, and investors purchasing these tokens can earn dividends generated by the sale of electricity from these individual solar cells. We are opening the gates for retail investment into solar space, and we do so by tokenizing the projects to reduce the barrier of entry and creating a secondary marketplace for providing liquidity to investors."[2]

Jeff Allison, president of Delta CleanTech Inc., a global technology leader in CO_2 capture, decarbonization of energy, solvent, and glycol reclamation, blue hydrogen production, and carbon credit tokenizing, explained that "to further educate and collaboratively work with global clean energy colleagues in the UAE, Delta will hold a series of CO_2 carbon capture and carbon credit workshops in Abu Dhabi during 2022."

Crypto Adoption: At the end of 2021, 1.54% of the UAE population owned cryptocurrencies.[3] According to a survey conducted by Gemini, the number of cryptocurrency owners massively increased in 2021, with nearly 35% of owners in the UAE buying crypto for the first time.[4] The world's largest crypto exchange, Binance, received approval from Dubai[5] as well as the Abu Dhabi Global Market to operate as a broker-dealer in digital assets.[6]

Crypto Mining: Crypto mining is not regulated in the UAE. Epazz Inc., a provider of blockchain cryptocurrency mobile apps, will use solar power technology to convert sunlight into Bitcoin via its CryObo Project in the UAE.[7]

Startups: Developed by Masdar, Abu Dhabi's Masdar City is one of the world's most sustainable urban communities, offering a strategic base through which companies can build their networks locally and globally and can explore multiple investment opportunities and test innovative new technologies from inception through to implementation to help the UAE diversify its economy.

Housing a free zone area, the city has more than 900 organizations, from international conglomerates to startups, developing innovative technologies in the areas of energy, water efficiency, mobility, space, blockchain technology, and artificial intelligence to address the world's most critical sustainability challenges in more than 30 countries.[8]

Central Bank Issued Digital Currency (CBDC): The Central Bank of the United Arab Emirates, along with the Saudi Central Bank, is developing a state-backed bilateral central bank digital currency, Aber. Aber is initially set to help the UAE and Saudi Arabia make more cost-effective bank-to-bank, cross-border payments and financial settlements using blockchain technology on a probationary basis; according to official statements, it will be exclusively available to a limited number of banks. Eventually, Aber will be used globally on China's blockchain-based service network BSN, which will support future CBDCs from various countries such as the UAE.[9]

Nonfungible Tokens: In a first-of-its-kind application, a rug given as a gift to Pope Francis by Sheikh Mohamed bin Zayed Al-Nahyan, crown prince of Abu Dhabi, was minted as an NFT,[10] and the Middle East's first NFT stamps were issued by UAE.[11]

Illicit Use of Crypto:

	Yes	No
Known hacking groups	Al Qaeda[12]	
Known crypto exchange hacks	Russian sanction avoidance[13]	

Regulation of Digital Assets: Law No. 4 of 2022 regulates digital assets and apply throughout Dubai (including free zones and special development zones but excluding the Dubai International Financial Centre). It is the first such law in Dubai, coming into effect on March 11, 2022.[14]

On March 21, 2022, the Abu Dhabi Global Market published a consultation paper entitled "Proposals for Enhancements to Capital Markets and Virtual Assets," which contains draft guidelines that cover, among other asset classes, nonfungible token (NFT) trading. The paper proposes that companies with a license from the free zone's financial regulator be allowed to facilitate NFT trading.[15]

Regulation	Regulator	Yes	No
Advertising			X
ICO	VARA	X	
AML/CFT	SCA	X	
NFT		X – Proposed	
Capital gains tax		X	

Notes

1. https://cointelegraph.com/news/the-united-arab-emirates-green-digitization-vision
2. Ibid.
3. https://triple-a.io/crypto-ownership/
4. https://cointelegraph.com/news/new-crypto-owners-nearly-doubled-in-3-key-regions-in-2021-report
5. https://cointelegraph.com/news/it-s-official-binance-secures-a-license-to-operate-in-dubai
6. https://cointelegraph.com/news/binance-receives-in-principle-approval-to-operate-in-abu-dhabi
7. https://finance.yahoo.com/news/epazzs-cryobo-nft-project-uae-125100861.html
8. https://cointelegraph.com/news/the-united-arab-emirates-green-digitization-vision
9. Ibid.
10. https://cointelegraph.com/news/2021-ends-with-a-question-are-nfts-here-to-stay
11. https://cointelegraph.com/news/uae-issues-first-nft-stamps-in-the-middle-east
12. https://journals.sagepub.com/doi/abs/10.1177/10439862211001606
13. https://cointelegraph.com/news/the-world-has-synchronized-on-russian-crypto-sanctions
14. https://cointelegraph.com/news/dubai-establishes-virtual-asset-regulator-and-announces-new-crypto-law
15. https://www.adgm.com/documents/legal-framework/public-consultations/2022/consultation-paper-no-1/consultation-paper-no-1-of-2022-proposals-for-enhancements-to-capital-markets-and-virtual-assets.pdf

Chapter 33
Turkey

Turkey—the cradle of civilization—is quietly digitizing despite its high-inflation economy, and the lira's volatility might be correlated with the prices of Bitcoin (BTC) and Ether (ETH). During the fourth quarter of 2021, the TRY/USD exchange rate crashed from 9 to 18.5 liras per dollar in the six weeks leading up to mid-December before strengthening to as high as 10 liras and then falling back to 13.87 liras at the time of this writing, rendering the currency a highly volatile asset.

The lira's volatility stemmed from a contrarian interest rate cut made by Turkish President Recep Tayyip Erdoğan amid high inflation and against the advice of central bankers. High inflation tends to devalue cash and drive investors—including major professional and institutional investors as well as top hedge fund managers like George Soros—to invest their money in cryptocurrencies.[1]

Blockchain Adoption: While Satoshi Nakamoto is credited with designing the first cryptocurrency, it was actually Turkish-American Emin Gün Sirer—CEO of Ava Labs, professor at Cornell University, and codirector of the Initiative for Cryptocurrencies and Smart Contracts—who designed the first in 2003, six years before the launch of Bitcoin. Named Karma, it was based on a proof-of-work protocol.

Since 2019, Sirer has been focused on building Avalanche, an eco-friendly blockchain that uses a novel consensus mechanism for high-transaction throughput. As Sirer explained: "Avalanche is a high-performance, eco-friendly blockchain that scales hard math and science, rather than expensive, energy-intensive hardware. At its core, the innovation of the Avalanche consensus reduces the amount of communication required between validating nodes, which also decreases the hardware and power required to secure the many billions of dollars in value on the network. Taken a step further, Avalanche is a 'quiescent' protocol, meaning that if network activity slows, nodes will not perpetually expend energy as we see on almost every other platform. Nodes will simply wait until they hear another transaction to broadcast and move swiftly toward the next decision." He added: "Sustainability is critical to the blockchain industry's ability to overtake traditional infrastructures, as well as a core ethic of this entire ecosystem of using innovation to better the lives of people." Sirer continued: "Much of the inertia that climate activists have faced is from incumbents who wield far too much power. Decentralizing their power and putting more economic control in the hands of individuals, rather than institutions, is an incredible step forward. Momentum toward mass adoption of decentralized services continues to accelerate, and users are also witnessing that high performance and eco-friendliness of a blockchain platform are not enemies. In fact, they are necessary companions to achieve mass adoption, doing right by both people and the planet."[2]

Sierra Nevada Corporation (SNC), a cybersecurity and aerospace company cofounded by Turkish-American couple Eren and Fatih Ozmen, partnered with Ultra to modernize the cryptographic infrastructure of SNC's legacy AN/PYQ-10 Simple Key Loader devices to protect against mounting cyber and electronic warfare threats and to protect, store, and distribute sensitive information. SNC has joint ventures with Aselsan and Havelsan, which are state-owned defense, software, and electronics companies that are part of the Digital Turkish Lira Collaboration Platform.

President Erdoğan has said that Turkey's main objective is to produce all its equipment used in high-tech and aerospace systems, including cyberdefense systems.[3]

Crypto Adoption: At the end of 2021, 2.94% of the population owned cryptocurrencies.[4] With inflation soaring above 20%, Erhan Kahraman, news editor at Cointelegraph, told me that during 2021, "Bitcoin and other cryptocurrency usage in Turkey increased elevenfold."

Unexpectedly, the cryptocurrency market crashed during the first trading week of 2022, and, as a result, Bitcoin and Ether—which rose 100 and 300%, respectively, in 2021—entered bear market territory. The crash was blamed on a combination of three events.

The first event was the release of the minutes from the US Federal Reserve's December meeting. They hinted that the US central bank would reduce its pandemic-era stimulus and begin raising interest rates sooner than expected. This news triggered a selloff in the global stock markets that spilled over into the cryptocurrency markets, with Bitcoin's price ultimately crashing over 40% from its all-time high set in November 2021. Similarly, Ether dropped over 13% after the news to as low as $3,300.

The second event was the anti-government riots in Kazakhstan, the world's second-largest Bitcoin mining hub, which led to the country's government being sacked and internet services shut down, leaving an estimated 13% of the world's Bitcoin mining operations offline.

The third event was the rapid worldwide spread of the Omicron variant of COVID-19, which wreaked havoc on long-term social and economic development by leaving millions sick and inundating healthcare systems that were already buckling under the cumulative toll of every previous surge. Reinforcing the idea that people shouldn't live in constant fear of the virus, Ugur Sahin, the German-Turkish cofounder of COVID-19 vaccine maker BioNTech, highlighted that despite the virus being here to stay for a couple more years, the COVID-19 variants are becoming controllable and that BioNTech is keeping its eye on new variants and new strains.

Nevertheless, the unexpected market crash was not enough to shake Turkish investors' faith in cryptocurrencies being a hedge against a weakening lira and double-digit inflation.[5]

Crypto Mining: Crypto mining is not regulated in Turkey. According to a study, cryptominers in Turkey profitably exploit the speculative arbitrage opportunities in crypto markets.[6]

Startups: Cointelegraph Turkey's Kahraman explained to me that "Turkey's digital banking, or 'fintech,' industry is already miles ahead of many regions across the world in terms of adoption and technologies used. Local banks are offering a myriad of digital services to their customers. Cashless payments are already above 50% of all transactions, per PwC's 2020 payments research." DigiliraPay is a blockchain payment company based out of Eskisehir, Turkey.[7]

Central Bank Issued Digital Currency (CBDC): According to the Atlantic Council, there are 87 countries—including Turkey—that are exploring a central bank digital currency (CBDC). As part of the Central Bank Digital Turkish Lira Research and Development Project, the Central Bank of the Republic of Turkey established the Digital Turkish Lira Collaboration Platform in close collaboration with Aselsan, Havelsan, and Tübitak Bilgem. The project is researching the potential benefits of introducing a digital lira to complement the nation's existing payments infrastructure. The results of the first phase of this research are expected to be announced in 2022 after the tests are completed.

"So, while there are clear benefits for the Turkish government and financial institutions in issuing a central bank digital currency, I don't see a significant advantage for the citizens," explained Cointelegraph Turkey's Kahraman.[8]

Nonfungible Tokens: "Machine Hallucinations: Coral Dreams," a work by Refik Anadol—an award-winning Turkish-American new media artist—was the talk around town during 2021 Art Basel Miami Beach.

Anadol is the first artist to use artificial intelligence in a public immersive artwork, partnering with teams at Microsoft, Google, Nvidia, Intel, IBM, Panasonic, the US National Aeronautics and Space Administration's Jet Propulsion Laboratory, Siemens, Epson, Massachusetts Institute of Technology, Harvard University, the University of California–Los Angeles, Stanford University, and the University of California–San Francisco. He applies the latest, cutting-edge science, research, and technologies to his work, which consists of data-driven machine learning algorithms that create abstract, dreamlike environments.

Kahraman explained to me that "There are several platforms that Turkish artists are actively using to create and sell their NFTs. The first one is OpenSea—it's probably the most popular NFT marketplace globally. Turkish artists like Refik Anadol, Cem Yılmaz, and others have already created and sold their NFTs on the Ethereum-based platform. However, the Ethereum network's high gas fees (multiplied by the exchange rates in Turkey) place a barrier for many lesser-known artists and their communities. Coupled with the popularity of Avalanche in Turkey, I am seeing several artists publish their NFTs on eco-friendly Avalanche-based platforms, then sell their collections on Kalao. But to be honest, the majority of Turkish users are also using global apps like Binance, Huobi, etc. BtcTurk and Paribu are the top two heavyweights of the local NFT ecosystem. Icrypex and Bitci are also rising in popularity with new partnerships and global projects."

Avenue 10 Gallery, founded by Luc Navarro and with branches in Paris and Bangkok, digitizes physical artworks to offer high-end NFTs sold on Ethereum-based OpenSea. Navarro invited me, a Turkish-American artist, to make NFTs out of my "Art in the Time of Corona" series of oil paintings, which includes, among others, a portrait of Erdal Arikan—the inventor of the world's first channel coding scheme (polar codes) for 5G technology.[9]

Illicit Use of Crypto:

	Yes	No
Known hacking groups	Mezopotamia Hackers[10]	
Known crypto exchange hacks	Thodex, Vebitcoin[11]	

Regulation of Digital Assets: As Kahraman explained to me, "There is currently no clear regulator governing all the crypto-related developments in Turkey. President Erdoğan said the legislation regarding crypto assets is ready for the parliament (TBMM), but there's no definitive date yet." He added:

Cryptocurrencies are referred to as "crypto assets" in published government documents. Different bodies working on different aspects of crypto assets are: The Financial Crimes Investigation Board (MASAK) is actively overseeing crypto service providers (crypto exchanges) on AML and compliance issues. The central bank is regulating the payment aspect of crypto assets. In April 2021, it banned the use of crypto assets from being used as a payment method. The Capital Markets Board (SPK) governs the crypto market, including ICOs and token offerings in a case-by-case manner.[12]

Regulation	Regulator	Yes	No
Advertising			X
ICO	SPK	X	
AML/CFT	MASAK	X	
NFT			X
Capital gains tax		X	

Notes

1. https://cointelegraph.com/news/crypto-and-nfts-meet-regulation-as-turkey-takes-on-the-digital-future
2. https://cointelegraph.com/news/crypto-and-nfts-meet-regulation-as-turkey-takes-on-the-digital-future
3. Ibid.
4. https://triple-a.io/crypto-ownership/
5. https://cointelegraph.com/news/crypto-and-nfts-meet-regulation-as-turkey-takes-on-the-digital-future
6. https://www.researchgate.net/publication/359392940_Bitcoin_Mining_in_Turkey_as_an_Example_of_Speculative_Entrepreneurship
7. https://www.fintech.coffee/research/61-turkey
8. https://cointelegraph.com/news/crypto-and-nfts-meet-regulation-as-turkey-takes-on-the-digital-future
9. Ibid.
10. https://www.aa.com.tr/en/turkey/pkks-hacker-group-admits-to-cybercrimes-against-turkey/2451366
11. https://cointelegraph.com/news/crypto-and-nfts-meet-regulation-as-turkey-takes-on-the-digital-future
12. Ibid.

Chapter 34
Singapore

Singapore is a major financial center and shipping hub and has the tenth-highest GDP per capita. It has emerged in a short period as a global cryptocurrency hub amid its favorable regulatory and tax infrastructure and by utilizing blockchain technology in many areas of its economy.

Blockchain Adoption: In a statement, the Monetary Authority of Singapore (MAS) said that while it "strongly encourages" blockchain technology development and innovative crypto use cases, cryptocurrency trading is "highly risky and not suitable for the general public." As such, cryptocurrencies should not be portrayed "in a manner that trivializes the high risks of trading" them. Singapore utilizes blockchain technology in the finance, energy, and shipping sectors.[1]

Crypto Adoption: At the end of 2021, 43% of the population owned cryptocurrencies. MAS has been selective in issuing licenses to cryptocurrency businesses, with a large number of applicants failing to receive licenses to operate in the country. Retail investors can trade cryptocurrencies on a multitude of crypto exchanges, including Coinbase, Kraken, FTX, Bybit, KuCoin, Vauld, Independent Reserve, Gemini, Coinhako, Tiger Brokers, Futu's Moomoo, and Syfe.

The SIX Digital Exchange—a sister company of SIX Swiss Exchange, which operates Switzerland's national stock exchange—announced a partnership with SBI Digital Asset Holdings, a division of Japanese banking and financial services giant SBI Group, to establish a crypto exchange and central securities depository in Singapore. The joint venture, called the Asia Digital Exchange, is designed to create a regulated, global liquidity pool for digital assets between Asia and Europe.[2]

Crypto Mining: Bitdeer, Saitech, Sharemine AI, and BitFuFu are all Singapore-based cryptocurrency mining companies with mining operations outside the country. Bitdeer and Saitech are seeking to be publicly listed on Nasdaq. Saitech recycles the waste energy from mining for use in residential, agricultural, and industrial applications. Bitdeer and Sharemine AI mine with clean energy generated from hydroelectric and solar power.[3]

Persistence, the multi-asset protocol focused on liquid staking, NFTs, and commodities, partnered with global private equity firm BridgeTower Capital to focus on blockchain infrastructure to bridge digital assets to traditional institutional investors.[4]

Startups: Tribe Accelerator is a blockchain accelerator launched by Trive Ventures, a Singaporean venture capital firm, with the core goal of increasing and streamlining blockchain adoption in Asia, beyond financial services applications. It is the first blockchain accelerator supported by the Singaporean government (it is backed by Enterprise Singapore). It is also supported by ecosystem partners including Temasek, MAS, Citibank, IBM, Intel, and BMW.

Tribe has accelerated more than 50 startups with a combined value of more than $1 billion. In November 2021, Microsoft launched its Singapore GreenTech Challenge to accelerate progress in startups in an effort to implement Singapore's Green Plan.[5]

Central Bank Issued Digital Currency (CBDC): Singapore, through its Project Ubin, is one of 87 countries exploring a central bank digital currency (CBDC), according to the Atlantic Council. MAS has been testing CBDCs and discussing the creation of multiple CBDC arrangements to improve the speed, cost, and transparency of cross-border payments. It has developed a prototype multicurrency wholesale settlement network to enable the issuance and distribution of various CBDCs on a common network in partnership with China.[6]

Nonfungible Tokens: Singapore Art Week 2022, which ran from January 14 through January 23, hosted TZ APAC, which celebrated Asian digital artists in an industry-first nonfungible token (NFT) showcase at the S.E.A. Focus showcase.

ArtScience Museum in Singapore—the first museum in Asia with major exhibitions to integrate art, science, culture, and technology—opened its newest exhibition, "Radical Curiosity: In the Orbit of Buckminster Fuller," in conjunction with the final weekend of Singapore Art Week, according to Adrian George, director of programs, exhibitions, and museum services at ArtScience Museum.

Known as the "grandfather of the future" by his admirers, Richard Buckminster Fuller was an American architect, systems theorist, inventor, and author, who predicted a technology similar to blockchain, on which cryptocurrency is based. In a video interview from 1967, Fuller states: "I'll have to talk about something which will be one of the very big, new realizations by 2000 AD, which will be a realistic scientific accounting system of what is wealth. [. . .] Wealth is energy."[7]

Illicit Use of Crypto:

	Yes	No
Known hacking groups		X
Known crypto exchange hacks	Crypto.com[8]	

Regulation of Digital Assets: Singapore's regulators have done a great deal to nurture the blockchain industry.

The Monetary Authority of Singapore (MAS), the country's main financial regulatory body, promptly implemented regulatory measures, when the cryptocurrency market began crashing in January 2022 and entered bear market territory,[9] and quickly implemented crypto sanctions in March 2002 when the Ukraine war broke out.

Jacqueline Ong, deputy director of communications at MAS, said to me in an interview: "The sanctions apply equally to all financial institutions (FIs) in Singapore, including digital payment token service providers. This is to ensure that Singapore's financial system is impervious to attempts to circumvent the sanctions, given the extensive interlinkages among different players in the financial system. FIs dealing in cryptocurrencies are required to comply with the sanctions. All FIs must have robust controls such as procedures to know their customers and the beneficial owners of customers. They are required to screen their customers and their transacting counterparties to avoid dealing with prohibited entities or activities. If FIs have any information on prohibited entities or activities, they are required to inform MAS immediately. They are also required to demonstrate their compliance to MAS and are subject to scrutiny and inspection by MAS."

She added: "MAS will take appropriate regulatory action against FIs, including imposing financial penalties, if they are found to have breached the sanctions."[10]

Regulation	Regulator	Yes	No
Advertising	MAS	X	
ICO	MAS	X	
AML/CFT	MAS	X	
NFT			X
Sanctions		X	
Whistleblowing		X	
Capital gains tax			X

Notes

1. https://cointelegraph.com/news/why-singapore-is-one-of-the-most-crypto-friendly-countries
2. Ibid.
3. https://cointelegraph.com/news/why-singapore-is-one-of-the-most-crypto-friendly-countries
4. Interview with author, April 2022.
5. https://cointelegraph.com/news/why-singapore-is-one-of-the-most-crypto-friendly-countries
6. Ibid.
7. Ibid.
8. https://www.cbsnews.com/news/wormhole-ether-cryptocurrency-320-million-hack/
9. https://cointelegraph.com/news/why-singapore-is-one-of-the-most-crypto-friendly-countries
10. https://cointelegraph.com/news/the-world-has-synchronized-on-russian-crypto-sanctions

Chapter 35
Puerto Rico

Without electricity, life came to a standstill in Puerto Rico, in the aftermath of hurricanes Irma followed by Maria, which ripped out the island's fossil-fuel-powered electric grid in 2017. Puerto Rico's blackout lasted for 11 months—the longest blackout in US history—leaving 3.4 million citizens without power. Schools shuttered and hospitals struggled to serve patients as the island's electrical grid failed; thousands lost their lives as a result of government ineptitude following Hurricane Maria.

About 60 private utilities across the United States arrived in Puerto Rico to rebuild the power grid. This included solar energy company Tesla, which arrived on the island a week after Hurricane Maria made landfall on September 20, 2017. Previously, with funding from the US Department of the Interior and the American Samoa Power Authority, Tesla had successfully transformed the whole island of Ta'u in American Samoa with Tesla's microgrid and photovoltaic solar panels.

The almost-year-long green energy restoration of Puerto Rico's micro electrical grid faced several infrastructural, financial, and regulatory/tax hurdles until the island of Vieques was able to install a solar microgrid without ever connecting to the mainland. Virtual power plants that took advantage of the home microgrids were established with the help of private companies like Sunnova and Sunrun, which provided solar power to the grid.[1] On the mainland, rooftop solar systems are expected to generate 18% of the energy—a ninefold increase in renewable energy use since Hurricane Maria.[2]

Blockchain Adoption: After so many back-to-back corruption scandals, the government of Puerto Rico is taking steps to improve its anticorruption efforts by adopting blockchain technology. Puerto Rican House Speaker Rafael "Tatito" Hernández, at the Puerto Rico Blockchain Trade Association (PRBTA) meeting at the end of 2021, announced that lawmakers will hold meetings with blockchain organizations such as Blockchain Puerto Rico to discuss the potential adoption of blockchain technology to bring more transparency and accountability to the public sector, Bloomberg reported on December 6, 2021.[3]

After all, 2021 was a bull market year for cryptocurrencies and NFTs with a market cap of $3 trillion. Venture capital investment in 15,829 cryptocurrencies traded on 446 cryptocurrency exchanges, reaching $30 billion over the year.

Bitcoin's price witnessed an all-time high at $70,00 in 2021, with the number of Bitcoin addresses reaching 917 million. Similarly, there was a 256% increase in DeFi addresses on ETH.

More companies moved toward the metaverse, with countries embracing cryptocurrencies and developing Central Bank Digital Currencies (CBDC). El Salvador declared Bitcoin legal tender, the first country in the world to do so.[4]

The trend of adopting blockchain technology as part of the recovery efforts from hurricanes Irma and Maria is regionwide via the CoinAgenda Caribbean project. Eastern Caribbean

Islands St. Lucia, Grenada, Antigua and Barbuda, and St. Kitts and Nevis created their own form of digital currency, DCash,[5] meant to help speed transactions and serve people without bank accounts, according to Eastern Caribbean Central Bank.

Crypto Adoption: At the end of 2021, 1.25% of the population owned cryptocurrencies.[6] Puerto Rico is already home to cryptocurrency funds Pantera Capital and Redwood City Ventures. FV Bank, a digital bank, offers accounts[7] that can hold digital assets alongside fiat currencies and convert cryptocurrencies to US dollars or other traditional currencies.[8]

Crypto Mining: Puerto Rico is headquarters to Bitcoin miner Coinmint, which utilizes green energy.[9]

Startups: Puerto Rico's government created an advisory council aimed at spurring the development of blockchain businesses and offering tax breaks to people who spend at least 183 days there every year. According to Act 60, bona fide residents do not have to pay taxes on US-source capital gains if they bought digital assets after establishing residency. Puerto Rico-based blockchain startup Tea raised $8 million in a seed round led by crypto exchange Binance.[10]

Nonfungible Tokens: NFT investor gmoney—which is included in Fortune's NFTy 50 and is a general partner of Delphi INFINFT, a fund dedicated to investing in the NFT ecosystem—hosted Metaverso, Puerto Rico's first-ever NFT summit, which that took place on December 7, 2021, in San Juan, Puerto Rico. Metaverso served as an inaugural event to kick off Puerto Rico Blockchain Week (December 6–12, 2021) by gathering NFT creators, collectors, and leading global players. During the week Puerto Rico's first NFT gallery, Lighthouse Gallery, opened in San Juan, where NFTs by established and emerging digital artists from Puerto Rico and the world were on exhibition.[11]

Illicit Use of Crypto:

	Yes	No
Known hacker	X[12]	
Known crypto fraud	X[13]	

Regulation of Digital Assets: As a semi-autonomous territory that belongs to, but is not part of the United States, Puerto Rico is regarded as a foreign jurisdiction by the IRS for tax purposes, even though the Foreign Account Tax Compliance Act (FACTA) does not apply.

Prior to hurricanes Irma and Maria, the Puerto Rican government created tax breaks in 2012 to infuse the island's struggling economy that exempted new residents from paying taxes on capital gains and dividends, according to the island's Department of Economic Development and Commerce. In 2019, Puerto Rico enacted Act 60 to attract investment from cryptocurrency, fintech, and other industries to be used to rebuild the economy from the impact of the hurricanes, offering residents full tax exemptions on Puerto Rican–sourced dividends and capital gains earned from the appreciation of securities—like cryptocurrencies.

In March of 2019—a year and a half after hurricanes Irma and Maria—the Puerto Rican legislature approved a bill mandating that 100% of the island's electricity be generated from renewable sources by 2050.[14]

Notes

1. https://microgridknowledge.com/prepa-storage-and-microgrids-puerto-rico/
2. https://www.tiredearth.com/interviews/mutual-connection-between-taxes-and-environmental-problems-part-3

3. https://linktr.ee/blockchainpuertorico?fbclid=IwAR3pZ6HhAOjS0O PhlHUuY-AVzdJ82ozKOFv8xEFmGsbDNez0xdLZexSgvfQ

4. https://blog.bitgo.com/2021-year-in-review-2e077548afba

5. https://www.dcashec.com

6. https://triple-a.io/crypto-ownership/

7. https://www.eccb-centralbank.org/p/what-you-should-know-1

8. https://apnews.com/article/technology-antigua-and-barbuda-st-kitts-and-nevis-blockchain-caribbean-5e06534b1d67c5039667ebc5ac 518c89

9. https://www.smart-energy.com/industry-sectors/energy-grid-management/data-centres-and-cryptomining-demonstrate-support-for-the-grid/

10. https://yourstory.com/the-decrypting-story/tea-blockchain-funding-binance-labs-max-howell/amp

11. https://roundtablecrypto.io/news/crystal-rose-gallery

12. https://cointelegraph.com/magazine/2022/04/12/bizarre-the-fbis-takedown-of-an-eth-dev-who-went-to-north-korea

13. https://www.bnnbloomberg.ca/crypto-mystery-where-s-the-us-69b-backing-the-stablecoin-tether-1.1663664

14. https://www.tiredearth.com/interviews/mutual-connection-between-taxes-and-environmental-problems-part-3

Part 3
Solarized Around the World

Chapter 36

Is US Environmental Tax Policy Hindering Solar Power to Fuel Digital Technologies?

The United States—both the government and private industry—is at the forefront of blockchain and artificial intelligence (AI) technology adoption. And Bitcoin's volatility recovery is fueling this process.

According to reports, US government spending on blockchain is expected to increase by 1,000% between 2017 and 2022, while US investors are expected to increasingly invest in digital assets to add diversity to their investment portfolios and resume cryptocurrency mining as it once again becomes profitable.[1]

Blockchain Transformation

The announcement by Facebook (Meta)—with 2.7 billion users—that it will be issuing cryptocurrency monetizing tools[2] to compete with China's blockchain-based mobile payment system—with 1.5 billion users—has put pressure on the largest US financial institutions for a quick blockchain transformation. Already, JPMorgan Chase has announced that it will be issuing a utility settlement cryptocurrency (USC) coin called JPM Coin. BNY Mellon, Nasdaq, and State Street Bank, on the other hand, are backing the development of USCs denominated in five major fiat currencies: the US dollar, the Canadian dollar, the British pound, the Japanese yen, and the euro.

Blockchain applications are not limited to fintech and are being adopted across various industries in the United States. For example, the shipping-focused blockchain TradeLens, developed by IBM and Maersk, recruited two major marine cargo carriers to help usher in the digital transformation of the global supply chain. Separately, IBM piloted a blockchain and Internet of Things (IoT) sensor solution to track sustainable groundwater usage. Pfizer Inc. and other leading American pharmaceutical companies joined a project to build a blockchain network for the health and pharmaceutical industries.

In the aerospace industry, blockchain technology is being implemented in myriad ways, including flight recorders, airspace management, cybersecurity, tracking parts during the manufacturing process, and in establishing secure, efficient and prioritized data, as well as command communication pathways among ground- and space-based sources. In addition, US energy companies Brooklyn Microgrid, Clearway Energy Group, and Grid are developing applications for trading renewable energy credits on a blockchain.

These new digital technologies will replace many jobs and necessitate a very large consumption of electric energy that is currently produced with coal and fossil fuels—which has adverse environmental effects, according to the United Nations World Meteorological Organization. Cryptocurrency mining alone generates about 22 megatons of carbon dioxide emissions each year, based on a study by the Technical University of Munich and the Massachusetts Institute of Technology (MIT).[3]

A report issued by LUT University in Finland and the Energy Watch Group in Germany states that transitioning to green energy—69% solar—can be accomplished globally in an economically competitive way in order to reduce greenhouse gas emissions in the energy system to zero by 2050.[4] Among other important options, solar power satellite (SPS) systems remain one of the most promising, but is currently a largely undeveloped option to accomplish this goal.

Solar Power Satellites

Paul Jaffe, an electronics engineer who has investigated SPS systems for the US Naval Research Laboratory (NRL), explained that "anything we can do to wean away from coal and fossil fuels is a step in the right direction. Implementing SPS might result in a clean, constant, and globally distributable energy supply—unmatched by any earth-bound source."[5]

The SPS transmission idea—in which energy captured from the sun is transmitted via microwave beams to nearby planets from a space station—was first mentioned in a short story in 1941 titled "Reason" by Russian-born US science fiction writer Isaac Asimov.

In 1968, the concept for SPS technology emerged when aerospace engineer Peter Glaser published the first technical article,

"Power from the Sun: Its Future," in the journal *Science*, in which he described collecting solar power in outer space via solar cells on a satellite system at geosynchronous orbit, where sunlight is available almost continuously (more than 99.8% of the time each year), that would be capable of converting sunlight directly into electricity and distributing it to Earth via a wireless transmission system to a receiver.

There are two potentially viable options: laser and microwave beams. According to an NRL research report from 2009, SPS systems offer one of several possible solutions to the energy independence and dominance of the United States and its military, but there remain significant system risks in many areas. For example, safe power densities for wireless energy transmission generally restrict applications to large, relatively immobile receiver sites. Jaffe explained, "While safety is a concern, wireless power transfer can be implemented to stay below existing safety limits. In general, microwave transmission requires larger diameter transmitters and receivers than laser."

Unlike land-based solar power, which has been inefficient due to the atmospheric, day/night light interference, an SPS system could continuously harness the sun's energy, working not only when there is daylight but also at night, during rain or snow, and even on cloudy days—24 hours a day, 365 days a year. For these reasons, the concept of SPS initially attracted a lot of attention during the 1970s, when NASA technical reports indicated that SPS was technically feasible but economically unrealistic—and thus, the US government and its agencies cut funding for solar cell research during the 1980s. According to Jaffe, "For space solar to work, it will almost certainly need to offer some compelling advantage in a given application before it can compete on cost. There are several segments involved: launch, manufacture of the space and ground portions, and the industries associated with each. The logistics will be challenging."

The International Academy of Astronautics completed the first international assessment of SPS during 2008–2011, with diverse subject matter experts from some 10 countries concluding that it is technically feasible and that it might be realized in as little as 10–15 years. "Space solar is an enabling technology that could leapfrog the electric-power transmission grid on Earth, and have a similar effect that previous satellites have had on communications," Jaffe said, but it has yet to electrify US terrestrial grids. Instead, ground-based solar energy has been making an important contribution of one-sixth of the US energy mix.

The world's largest renewable energy company, Nextera, forecasts solar energy costs at $30–40 per watt, post-2023, while utility-scale solar farms in India already generate solar energy for $0.03–0.04 a watt, according to Greg Nemet, a professor at the University of Wisconsin–Madison's La Follette School of Public Affairs, who has written a new book on global policy and market forces that combined to make solar electricity one of the cheapest forms of energy.[6] He said, "It's possible solar prices could have bottomed out a decade or two sooner had the U.S. not slashed funding in the 1980s"—or had the US environmental tax policy been more favorable toward solar energy and SPS by including it in government incentive programs as opposed to heavily subsidizing fossil fuels since the enactment of the US tax code in 1873.

US Environmental Tax Policy

Environmental taxes are used as an economic instrument to address environmental problems by taxing activities that burden the environment (e.g., a direct carbon tax) or by providing incentives to reduce the environmental burden and preserve environmentally friendly activities (e.g., tax credits and subsidies). It is used as part of a market-based climate policy that was pioneered in the United States, which also includes cap-and-trade energy emission allowance trading programs that attempt to limit emissions by putting a cap and price on them.

Environmental taxes are designed to internalize environmental costs and provide economic incentives for people and businesses to promote ecologically sustainable activities, to reduce carbon dioxide emissions, to promote green growth, and to fight climate change via innovation. Some governments use them to integrate climate and environmental costs into prices to reduce excessive emissions while raising revenue to fund vital government services.

Carbon Tax

Under a carbon tax regime, the government sets a price that emitters must pay for each ton of greenhouse gas emissions they emit so that businesses and consumers will take necessary steps—such as switching fuels or adopting new technologies—to reduce their emissions in order to avoid paying the tax, as taxes have distortionary effects that influence free-market decisions. Carbon taxes are favored because administratively assigning a fee to CO_2 pollution is relatively simple compared to addressing climate change by setting, monitoring, and enforcing caps on greenhouse gas emissions as well as regulating emissions of the energy-generation sector. There are four subsets of environmental taxes: energy taxes, transport taxes, pollution taxes, and resource taxes.

The United States is the world's number-two producer of CO_2 emissions,[7] owing 84% of its greenhouse gas emissions to fossil fuels. Currently, it does not impose a federal carbon tax. However, the Congress, in a bipartisan effort, is aiming to introduce a carbon tax in the United States because, according to the Organisation for Economic Co-operation and Development (OECD), greater reliance on environmental taxation is needed to strengthen global efforts to tackle the principal source of both greenhouse gas emissions and air pollution.

A carbon price/tax of between $50 and $100 per ton will be needed to be implemented by signatories to deliver on Paris Agreement commitments by 2030, according to a report titled "High-Level Commission on Carbon Prices," written by Nobel Laureate Economist Joseph Stiglitz and Nicholas Stern (2017).

Tax Credits

Through tax credits, subsidies, and other business incentives, governments can encourage companies to engage in behaviors and develop technologies that can reduce CO_2 emissions. Just as tax credits for fossil fuel energy sources have enabled growth and development, renewable energy tax credits are incentives for the development and deployment of renewable energy technologies.

According to an International Monetary Fund (IMF) report, subsidies to the hydrocarbon industry accounted for 85% of global subsidies of $4.7 trillion (6.3% of global GDP) in 2015, which were projected at $5.2 trillion (6.5% of GDP) in 2017, with the United States ranking number two in subsidies to the hydrocarbon industry at $649 billion. In stark contrast, during 2016, subsidies for renewable energy totaled $6.7 billion—dropping 56% from 2013 levels, according to a report prepared by the US Energy Information Administration. About 80% (or $5.6 billion) of the 2016 renewables subsidies came in the form of tax breaks, half of which went to biofuels like ethanol and biodiesel; the other half benefited wind and solar in the form of tax credits, which are set to expire at the end of 2024, although a permanent 10% investment tax credit (ITC) for solar and geothermal installations will remain. In December 2020, Congress passed an extension of the ITC, which provides a 26% tax credit for systems installed in 2020–2022, and 22% for systems installed in 2023. (Systems installed before December 31, 2019, were eligible for a 30% tax credit.) The tax credit expires starting in 2024 unless Congress renews it.

According to the IMF as well as the International Energy Agency, the elimination of fossil fuel subsidies worldwide would be one of the most effective ways of reducing greenhouse gases and battling global warming.[8]

Increased digital technology adoption in the United States and around the world will continue to push CO_2 emission to its highest levels in history if the electricity used to fuel it is largely produced with hydrocarbon energy. To cut down on CO_2 emission during the height of the cryptocurrency bull market in 2017, the use of an SPS system was proposed to electrify cryptocurrency mining.

Transitioning to clean energy has become inevitable—a survival concern—so much so that investment advisors who manage nearly half the world's invested capital, more than $34 trillion in assets, are urging the G20 for compliance with the Paris Agreement to save the global economy $160 trillion. The alternative will result in damages of $54 trillion.

Nevertheless, switching to solar energy will likely necessitate—among other actions—adjustments to the US environmental tax policy, which currently heavily favors fossil fuels.

Notes

1. https://cointelegraph.com/news/us-govt-blockchain-spending-expected-to-increase-1-000-between-2017-2022-study
2. https://cryptopotato.com/meta-unveils-metaverse-monetizing-tools-for-facebook-and-instagram-creators/
3. https://www.sciencedaily.com/releases/2019/06/190613104533.htm
4. http://energywatchgroup.org/wp-content/uploads/EWG_LUT_100RE_All_Sectors_Global_Report_2019.pdf
5. Interview with Paul Jaffe
6. https://www.howsolargotcheap.com/
7. https://www.wri.org/insights/interactive-chart-shows-changes-worlds-top-10-emitters
8. https://www.imf.org/en/Publications/WP/Issues/2019/05/02/Global-Fossil-Fuel-Subsidies-Remain-Large-An-Update-Based-on-Country-Level-Estimates-46509

Chapter 37
Japan to Solarize Its Burgeoning Digital Economy

The global financial crisis of 2007–2008 wreaked havoc in the world economy and resulted in a decline in consumer wealth, widespread real estate foreclosures, evictions, business bankruptcies, prolonged unemployment, and a worldwide downturn in economic activity. But not everything related to the crisis was negative. Poor banking decisions and practices faced a rude awakening by coming to a crashing halt, allowing for new ideas to emerge, garner attention, and be put into use, especially in Japan, the Land of the Rising Sun.

As the credit crisis was in full force, Japan passed its Basic Space Law, which established Space Solar Power—the concept of collecting solar power in outer space and distributing it to Earth via satellites—as a national goal with the Japanese Space Exploration Agency. On January 9, 2009, a new triple-entry accounting ledger system and the first cryptocurrency, Bitcoin, made its world debut by the programmer using the pseudonym Satoshi Nakamoto.

SoftBank Group CEO Masayoshi Son, Japan's wealthiest citizen—who is changing startup technology investing with his large checkbook, upending Silicon Valley finance—refers to these technological developments as the "disruptive, foundational technologies that are building the infrastructure for tomorrow." In 2017 Masayoshi Son, backed by investors who gave him on average $1 billion per minute, launched the $100 billion technology-focused SoftBank Vision Fund in partnership with tech companies Apple, Qualcomm, Foxconn, and Sharp. And because investing in BTC is considered to adhere to Islamic law, investors in the fund include Saudi Arabia's Public Investment Fund and Abu Dhabi's Mubadala Investment Company. More foreign country wealth funds are eager to gain access to shares and initial coin offerings (ICOs) in tech companies, and are pushing for a second SoftBank Vision Fund, which plans to raise about $880 billion.

Masayoshi Son believes that with improvements in both internet connectedness and solar power utilization, there will continue to be more global demand for digital assets. As a result, he has made investments in low Earth orbit satellite company OneWeb and in solar power businesses all around the world.[1]

Solarized Blockchain Technology Adoption

The Ministry of Economy, Trade and Industry (METI) of Japan sets the strategic energy plan for the world's fourth-largest energy consumer and the sixth-largest emitter of CO_2, 90% of which is tied to hydrocarbon energy. METI believes that the impact of blockchain—which consumes large amounts of electricity—is huge and that its importance is similar to the emergence of the internet.

According to a World Economic Forum survey, global GDP stored on blockchain technology is expected to reach 10% by 2027. Therefore, in June 2018, Japan introduced a sandbox regime to accelerate the introduction of new business models and innovative technologies such as blockchain, AI, and the Internet of Things.

The world's largest technology investment fund—the $100 billion SoftBank Vision Fund, which announced the launch of a second fund—and Japanese megabanks have been investing in and funding blockchain startups concerning applications in telecommunications, SWIFT-payment systems, solar energy, identity, healthcare, messaging, transportation, data security, and fintech industries, both in Japan and globally.

Japan's Ministry of Technology and Industry (MITI) views solar photovoltaic power as an essential part of its digital economic transformation. Japanese fiction author Haruki Murakami concurs: "Japan, as an economic power, should find another source of power besides atomic energy. It may cause a temporary economic dip, but we will be respected as a country that does not use nuclear power."[2]

Solar photovoltaic (PV) technology—which converts light into electrical current—was born in the United States at Bell Labs when engineer Daryl Chapin, chemist Calvin Fuller, and physicist Gerald Pearson worked together to develop the first silicon solar PV cell in 1954. An article in the New York Times suggested that the silicon solar cell "may mark the beginning of a new era, leading eventually to the realization of one of mankind's most cherished dreams—the harnessing of the almost limitless energy of the sun for the uses of civilization."[3]

First launched in 1974 by MITI, with METI joining in 2001, the Sunshine Project was a long-term comprehensive plan for the research and development of new solar energy technologies to resolve Japan's energy and climate change problems.

The program was heavily funded by the government because PV technology emits no CO_2 while also being highly reliable and modular, with lower construction and operational costs.

Starting in the 1980s, Japanese manufacturers began incorporating solar PV cells into electronic applications in various areas. In the late 1990s, Japanese government programs began promoting solar houses. In 2009, Tsutomu Miyasaka and his colleagues in Japan reported on perovskite compounds being light absorbers for solar energy applications, which outperform the efficiency of more established PV technologies and can be printed or woven into fabric. As a result, Japan emerged as the world's third-largest solar energy power producer, with 45% of PV cells in the world being manufactured in Japan.

With the rise of Bitcoin and in the aftermath of the Fukushima nuclear plant disaster in 2011, the government boosted the proliferation of decentralized solar energy by encouraging the production of more energy-efficient buildings, cars that combine solar panels with some form of energy storage, as well as other devices. This compelled the solar energy sector to begin using blockchain technology. Professor Umit Cali of the University of North Carolina provided an exclusive comment, saying: "In the solar energy sector, decentralized blockchain technology is used in person-to-person (P2P) energy trading, labeling, energy provenance and certification, smart metering and billing, electric vehicle charging and payments, and wholesale power trading and settlements."

Reports published by Fitch Solutions Macro Research and Globadata conclude that over the next decade, decentralized solar technology may replace PV solar farms as the main growth driver in Japan. Already, a blockchain-enabled solar energy-trading pilot project is set to link 100 solar rooftops of smart, zero-energy homes in the country, while another pilot project will administer an energy-trading marketplace using blockchain to connect a number of Japanese power production facilities with homes, offices, factories, batteries, and electric vehicles.

Toyota Motor Corp., which began testing high-efficiency solar cells for electric cars, has joined forces with the University of Tokyo and online renewable energy retailer Trende to test peer-to-peer vehicle-to-grid electricity trading using blockchain technology, which allows for electric vehicles to communicate with the power grid to buy and sell electricity to smooth out peak and low demand times.

Japan's Marubeni Corp. has recently backed a blockchain-based power-purchasing platform called WePower that makes it easy for small and medium-sized businesses to buy power from solar project developers, offering standardized, digital power purchase agreements to help underwrite new projects.

Japan is a predominantly mountainous land with varied weather conditions, and the area that a PV solar farm occupies is an important consideration, as it determines the yield. Accordingly, Japan has been creative in developing new PV solar energy generation stations at home and abroad—in seas, lakes, deserts, and space.

Japan built the world's first and largest floating solar plants. Its lakes and reservoirs are now home to 73 of the world's 100 largest floating solar plants, which are up to 16% more efficient than land-based solar systems.

In cooperation with the National University of Mongolia, Japan is also participating in the project "Energy from the Desert," with the Japan International Cooperation Agency (JICA) providing financial support covering up to half of the initial investment costs. Marubeni Corp. built the world's largest PV farm, the Noor Abu Dhabi photovoltaic power project, in the Sweihan Desert of the United Arab Emirates, which recently began producing solar energy at $0.024 per kilowatt hour.

On August 12, 2019, Australian energy technology company Power Ledger and Japanese Kansai Electric Power Co. (KEPCO) announced that they had completed a joint trial of a blockchain-based peer-to-peer trading system for post-feed-in tariff (FIT) surplus solar power in Osaka. Their announcement came on the heels of a report that highlighted multiple ways blockchain technology could disrupt the peer-to-peer solar energy trading sector. According to the report:

> Blockchain technology could alter the manner in which electricity customers and producers interact. Traditionally electric utilities are vertically integrated. Blockchain could disrupt this convention by unbundling energy services along a distributed energy system. For instance, a customer could directly purchase excess electricity produced from their neighbor's solar panels instead of purchasing electricity from the utility.[4]

Japan intends to replace the FIT's fixed price system with a competitive bidding/blockchain-based peer-to-peer trading system for a post-FIT surplus solar power system. This would thereby reduce inequality and provide cheaper, cleaner energy that reduces CO_2 emissions and would help promote digital development in Japan as well as across the world.

The Japanese Space Agency (JAXA) began its SPS program in 2009, with the goal to set up a one gigawatt solar farm in space that can transmit energy back to Earth by 2030. In 2015, Japan came closer to harvesting solar energy from space when it transmitted condensed solar power converted to microwaves to a receiving antenna, which converted only 5–10% of the power required to power three PCs.

For space solar power generation to become commercially viable, 50% of the solar power generated in space needs to be transmitted to Earth. JAXA is also designing kite-like orbiters that will travel in low-earth orbit above the equator, with a transmitting antenna on the Earthward face and solar collectors on the spaceward face in order to transmit solar energy to Earth. In 2010, JAXA had already successfully launched Ikaros, a solar space kite, that sailed through deep space and was propelled by solar energy. Small satellites are ideal candidates for this type of solar propulsion.[5]

Crypto Adoption

Japan has a ravenous appetite for cryptocurrencies, with 1.64% of its population using it.[6] The first Bitcoin exchange—Bitcoin Market—was established there on February 6, 2010, when BTC traded for $0.30. However, the exchange was shut down six months later after being scammed. In the aftermath, Japanese Mt. Gox quickly rose to prominence during the same year but met its end four years later after being hacked. This was the largest heist of a BTC exchange at the time, which has been recently superseded by the $530 million hack of an unregistered exchange, Coincheck (Japan). Coincheck is not alone, as crypto-related cybercrime is on the rise, with users and exchanges struggling to keep up with hackers and the constantly evolving methods they employ to steal money and information.

So Saito, partner at Japanese law firm So-Law, explains that "the first BTC regulations in Japan were proposed after the Mt. Gox hack, when the Banking Act and the Act on the Prevention of Transfer of Criminal Proceeds were amended, to prohibit banks and securities companies from dealing in BTC for customer accounts without registration, but allowing for proprietary trading in Bitcoin. These laws came into effect on April 1, 2017, along with the Payment Services Act recognizing cryptocurrencies as a means of payment, granting them the same legal status as any other currency. So far the Financial Services Agency (FSA) of Japan has granted licenses to 16 cryptocurrency exchanges."[7]

After history's biggest Coincheck hack, the FSA stepped up its efforts to investigate Bitcoin exchanges, as well as Bitcoin's illicit use in money laundering transactions. The FSA is also pushing for the merger of two business groups—the Japan Blockchain Association and the Japan Cryptocurrency Business Association—to establish a general incorporated association under the revised Payment Services Act in order to create a regulatory framework applicable to the crypto industry.

This is important, as regulations have allowed SoftBank Investment, the Sumitomo Mitsui Banking Corporation, the Mizuho Financial Group Inc., and the Dai-ichi Life Insurance Company to continue to invest in Bitcoin exchanges to the point of making Japan the top Bitcoin exchange market in the world, beating out both China and the United States.[8]

Central Bank Issued Digital Currency (CBDC)

The Bank of Japan (BoJ) is working on a CBDC, which it will roll out after a three-phase trial. The first two phases of the trial, with the first ending on March 22, 2022, and the second beginning on March 24, 2022, of the trial focused on testing the proofs-of-concept, while the third phase would see a pilot currency be launched. The governor of the BoJ, Haruhiko Kuroda, indicated at Japan's FIN/SUM fintech summit during April of 2022 that it has no plans to introduce a CBDC anytime soon.[9]

Nonfungible Tokens

Since 2001, TeamLab, an art collective, interdisciplinary group of ultratechnologists whose collaborative practice seeks to navigate the confluence of art, science, technology, design, and the natural world, has been exhibiting their digital art around the world. The team consists of artists, computer programmers, engineers, computer graphics animators, mathematicians, and architects.

Their digital artworks are in the permanent collection of the Art Gallery of New South Wales, Sydney; the Art Gallery of South Australia, Adelaide; the Asian Art Museum, San Francisco[10]; the Asia Society Museum, New York; the Borusan Contemporary Art Collection, Istanbul; the National Gallery of Victoria, Melbourne; and Amos Rex, Helsinki.[11]

Nonfungible tokens (NFTs) in the visual arts, videos, music, collectibles, brand awareness raising, gaming, publishing, carbon trading, and fundraising sectors are also rapidly gaining popularity worldwide, and consequently are receiving significant attention in Japan as well. Since 2018, there has been an NFTokyo conference to cultivate and discuss the future of NFTs beyond the border.[12]

Tokyo launched its first crypto art exhibition, not with world-renowned Japanese pop artist Takashi Murakami's Avatars[13] on RTFKT or Teamlabs' digital artwork, but with tattoo NFTs over the summer of 2021.[14] The first NFT auction, "NFT in the history of Contemporary Art," was launched by the SBI Art Auction House on October 29–30, 2021, since NFTs changed the structure of the art world and are shifting the types of ideas artists will be addressing moving forward.[15] PolkaFantasy, the world's first NFT marketplace dedicated to Japanese animation, comics, and games culture, launched at the end of 2021,[16] although manga artist Hiro Ando, the creator of Samurai Cats, listed his NFTs at Studio Crazy NOOdles instead.[17]

Other Japanese NFT platforms include Japan: .mural,[18] Nanakusa, NFT Studio, Token Link, Miime, Coincheck, Doki Finance, Rakuten, and Genies.

Environmental, Regulatory, and Tax Policy

Japan has inadequate energy resources and imports 87.4% of its hydrocarbon energy. It is the world's largest importer of liquefied natural gas and third-largest importer of oil and coal.

Japan has lower levels of subsidies for fossil fuel consumption when compared to other G7 countries, but higher subsidies for oil and gas exploration and coal production. Because efforts to compensate for the drop in nuclear power generation after the Fukushima nuclear crisis—which was triggered by the magnitude 9.1 Tōhoku earthquake that generated a tsunami in Japan and which forced the shutdown of Japan's entire fleet of nuclear 48 reactors, effectively terminating the plan to supply half the country's electricity with nuclear power—resulted in far more support for fossil fuels and increased CO_2 emissions compared to renewable energy.

Japan provides billions in taxpayer dollars for building highly polluting coal plants in Japan as well as overseas. Japan's largest banks—MUFG and SMBC Group—along with other banks, have reportedly continued to finance fossil fuels with $1.9 trillion since the adoption of the Paris Climate Agreement. Therefore, Japan is the second-worst performer when it comes to reforming fossil fuel subsidies, according to a report by the Natural Resources Defense Council.[19]

In October 2012, Japan implemented a carbon tax of 289 Japanese yen (about $3) per ton of CO_2 equivalent. The government plans to use the revenues of $2 billion generated from this carbon tax to finance clean energy and energy-saving projects. Hydrocarbon air pollution is a drag for renewable energy. Dust and other sky-darkening air pollutants slash solar energy production by an estimated 11.5–13%. The haze blocks sunlight from reaching the solar panels, and if the particles land on a panel's flat surface, they cut down on the area exposed to the sun.

Japan also introduced a FIT system in 2012 to lower solar power generation costs, which are double those of Europe, thereby shifting the price of solar energy on the public to the tune of 2.4 trillion yen (roughly $22 billion) in the 2019 fiscal year alone, with a cumulative total of about 10 trillion yen (nearly $100 billion) since its introduction in July 2012. The government's steady lowering of the FIT purchase price, which stands at 14 yen ($0.13) per kilowatt hour in 2019, has brought a drastic drop in profits for solar energy companies, triggering a wave of bankruptcies, which reportedly rose year-on-year for five consecutive years beginning in 2013.

Globally, subsidies and financing for fossil fuels continue to remain stubbornly high. According to reports, 2018 actually saw an increase in money going into new upstream oil and gas projects, while investment in renewable power of all kinds dipped 2%. The World Bank still funds the fossil fuel industry at an amount that is at least three times greater than that of renewable energy.

This is despite G20 finance ministers' commitment to working together in redirecting public investments to renewable energies through fiscal policy and the use of public finance. Despite the International Renewable Energy Agency reporting that the cost of solar electricity has tumbled 80% in recent years and with three-quarters of coal production now more expensive than solar energy, the fossil fuel industry still receives benefits from governments.[20]

In the 2019 G20 meeting in Osaka, Japan reiterated its dedication to the Paris Agreement and to phasing out fossil fuel financing and subsidies in order to tackle climate change. Enhancing zero-carbon energy is an urgent task for the Japanese government, which is aiming to derive 44% of Japan's power from renewable (7% from solar energy) and nuclear power by 2030 to fuel its burgeoning digital economy. Fossil fuel subsidies significantly reduce the use of renewables, according to an OECD report.[21]

According to scientific reports, earthquakes, volcanic eruptions, giant landslides, and tsunamis become more frequent as global warming changes the Earth's crust, swells sea levels, and triggers a repetitive cycle of severe natural disasters that cause extensive environmental and economic damage (e.g., it cost $315 billion to $728 billion to clean up the Fukushima nuclear reactor site alone).[22]

Regulation	Regulator	Yes	No
Crypto asset	Payment Services Act	X	
Security token	Financial Instruments Exchange Act (FIEA)	X	
ICO	Financial Services Agency (FAS)	X	
AML/CFT	Act on Prevention of Transfer of Criminal Proceeds (CAESP)	X	
NFT			X
Sanctions[23]		X	
Whistleblowing[24]		X	
Capital gains tax[25]	National Tax Agency (Kokuzeichou)	X	
FIU[26]		X	

Notes

1. https://cointelegraph.com/news/bitcoin-and-solar-energy-fuel-investment-in-japan-expert-take
2. https://soranews24.com/2015/04/09/haruki-murakamis-solution-to-the-nuclear-power-debate-in-japan-actually-call-it-nuclear-power/
3. https://www.nytimes.com/packages/pdf/science/TOPICS_SOLAR_TIMELINE/solar1954.pdf
4. https://www.powerledger.io/media/power-ledger-and-kepco-bring-p2p-energy-trading-to-osaka-japan
5. https://cointelegraph.com/news/japan-to-solarize-its-burgeoning-digital-economy-expert-take
6. https://triple-a.io/crypto-ownership/
7. Interview

8. https://cointelegraph.com/news/bitcoin-and-solar-energy-fuel-investment-in-japan-expert-take
9. https://cointelegraph.com/news/boj-official-says-digital-yen-won-t-be-used-to-achieve-negative-interest-rate
10. https://exhibitions.asianart.org/exhibitions/teamlab-continuity/
11. https://futurepark.teamlab.art/en/about/#about
12. https://nonfungible.tokyo/about/
13. https://www.instagram.com/takashipom/
14. https://www.dailysabah.com/arts/events/tokyo-launches-1st-crypto-art-exhibition-with-tattoos-nfts
15. https://news.artnet.com/buyers-guide/japan-first-ever-nft-auction-sbi-2024199
16. https://polkafantasy.medium.com/worlds-first-ever-japanese-acg-themed-nft-marketplace-going-live-6d81c37c01c9
17. https://augustafreepress.com/how-did-hiro-ando-introduce-his-iconic-samurai-cats-in-the-nft-space/
18. https://www.billboard.com/business/tech/japan-mura-nft-ecosystem-musicians-1235010378/
19. https://www.nrdc.org/experts/han-chen/japan-second-worst-g7-reforming-fossil-fuel-subsidies
20. https://www.irena.org/costs
21. http://www.oecd.org/environment/oecd-companion-to-the-inventory-of-support-measures-for-fossil-fuels-2018-9789264286061-en.htm
22. https://cointelegraph.com/news/japan-to-solarize-its-burgeoning-digital-economy-expert-take
23. https://cointelegraph.com/news/the-world-has-synchronized-on-russian-crypto-sanctions
24. Ibid.
25. https://cointelegraph.com/news/bitcoin-and-solar-energy-fuel-investment-in-japan-expert-take
26. https://cointelegraph.com/news/the-world-has-synchronized-on-russian-crypto-sanctions

Chapter 38

Green Policy and Crypto Energy Consumption in the EU

Proving the heliocentric model of our solar system put forward by European scientists Aristarchus of Samos (310–230 BC, Greece), Nicolaus Copernicus (1473–1543, Poland), Galileo Galilei (1564–1642, Italy) and Johannes Kepler (1571–1630, Germany) took 2,200 years, when the German-American spaceflight, the *Helios 2* solar probe, cruised within 26.55 million miles (42.73 million kilometers) of the sun in April of 1976. Now, the European Union is solarizing its digital economy at a much faster pace.

With renewable energy projected to comprise 90% of the electricity mix in Europe by 2040, the following three major factors are contributing to this paradigm shift in energy.

1. **Technological:** Blockchain-based digital technologies are decentralizing and democratizing the electricity supply by enabling the interoperability of solar cell photovoltaic (PV)

energy produced from diversified PV assets with micro- and macro-utility electric grids. This is keeping EU-based companies that perform efficiently, even in cloudy conditions, at the forefront of space-grade and liquid PV innovation.

2. **Economic:** Solar energy is an increasingly attractive alternative from an economic standpoint due to its declining cost, the demand for solar PV panel installations in the EU's smart cities, an increase in CO_2 costs attributable to carbon taxes and environmental lawsuit fines, net metering subsidies, as well as funding—including from the European Investment Bank—in the renewable energy sector, as reported by the United Nations Environment Program.

3. **Environmental:** Solar energy does not produce CO_2 emissions, thereby improving air pollution and pollinator habitats to avoid a climate change apocalypse. A potential meltdown is relevant to the EU, as it ranks third in the world for CO_2 emissions.

Space Power Satellites

The EU's commitment to solarizing its digital economy in order to lower its CO_2 levels in accordance with the United Nations Framework Convention on Climate Change's (UNFCCC's) 2015 Paris Agreement is backed by various initiatives undertaken both in space and on Earth.

The European Space Agency (ESA) is a space, weather, and CO_2-emission watchdog. With the Copernicus Climate Change Service satellite, it keeps tabs on the CO_2 levels of all countries around the world. But since satellites are expensive to build and launch, and are difficult to update once in orbit, the ESA also utilizes a fleet of PV-energized, high-altitude pseudo-satellites (HAPSs). A zeppelin-like HAPS called the Stratobus is currently being manufactured by Thales Alenia Space in Cannes to track CO_2 emissions.

The ESA has also been actively evaluating the possibilities of utilizing solar-powered satellites by formulating a European strategy to solarize earthbound electric grids based on a study from Frazer-Nash Consultancy, which found that space-based solar power is both technically feasible and affordable with a competitive levelized cost of electricity and that its development could bring substantial economic benefits.[1]

France's Airbus Defense and Space is building an SPS that intends to beam earthbound solar energy via high-powered infrared lasers by 2030. Airbus is also making a HAPS called Zephyr, as well as a larger version of it that can be used for communications, reconnaissance, deliveries, and even laser solar energy transmission. The world's first HAPS base is already in operation at Wyndham Airfield in Australia.

The ESA also continues to develop the different areas of solar electric propulsion required for deep-space exploration missions. With the first picture of a black hole published in the spring of 2019, the future may involve "using solar electric propulsion to explore black holes for alternate energy sources," according to Andrew Lauren, producer of the French science fiction film *Highlife*, which centers on the same topic.[2]

Smart Cities

As part of the EU Green deal, the EU Commission announced that 100 EU cities will participate in the EU Mission for 100 climate-neutral and smart cities by 2030.[3]

Over half of the world's population live in cities that contribute 70% of global energy-related greenhouse gas emissions. "Cities around the world are the main cause of climate change

but can also offer a part of the solution to reducing the harmful greenhouse gases that are causing global temperatures to
rise," explained U.N.-Habitat Executive Director Maimunah
Mohd Sharif.

Germany became the EU's climate change pioneer with its
Energiewende (energy transition) policy when it began installing
PV rooftop solar panel systems in 1999 that now represent about
23% of all solar power generation capacity installed worldwide.
More than a million German buildings now have solar panels on
their roofs, with one out of every two new orders accompanied
with a battery storage system.

A decade later, the Danish island of Samsø emerged as the
poster child of action against climate change, as it has been
carbon neutral for over 10 years. This inspired Spain's Balearic
Islands, followed by another 26 European islands—including the
world's cryptocurrency hub, Malta—to commit earlier in 2019
to transition to 100% renewable energy and ditch coal power.

So far, most EU countries have committed to phasing out
coal plants by 2038, since they are the most significant source
of air pollution, indifferent to political agendas, and not con-
tained by the national or city borders of the 28 EU member
states. Austria—which finished phasing out coal in 2020, ahead
of other EU countries—is home to solar company Smartflower,
which manufactures intelligent solar panels shaped like flow-
ers that move along with the position of the sun. Coal-fired
power generation can be replaced by installing solar PV panels everywhere—on coal mining sites, building rooftops, and
agricultural land—to reduce CO_2 pollution. Already, a former
coal plant in Germany—where solar energy tops the list of
sources for public electricity supply—is reinventing itself as a
cultural center for experimental/electrical art that is fueled by
green energy.

Under the Horizon 2020 project, 70 EU cities are switching to clean energy sources that are digitally distributed using artificial intelligence, the Internet of Things, and blockchain-enabled networks. Germany leads the way in the EU's digitalization of the energy sector, as outlined in its blockchain strategy. "Generating cheap green energy is no longer a challenge. The price of PV installations has tumbled over the last 10–20 years, so we're now seeing huge investments in this particular energy source. The challenge is to link energy production from myriads of small installations across the landscape with a country's total energy demand and energy production from other sources, some of which is also linked across national borders," explained Marta Victoria, a professor who investigated and mapped the capacities of solar PV generation in the European countries that vary considerably from one state to another.

Providing the solar digital link by creating smart-city energy districts are: Hivepower, ABB, Space10, Sonnen-TenneT, EDF Energy and the UK Power Reserve, Insolar, SMA Solar Technology and Iota. On the latter, "The IOTA Tangle brings the promise of Distributed Ledger Technologies (DLT) to the Internet of Things. A growing energy community of private and public enterprises and academia are now coming together to explore its potential in real world testbed environment, paving the way for a more open, transparent, and decentralized energy system," Wilfried Pimenta de Miranda—the business development director at the Iota Foundation, which is part of the CityxChange H2020 consortium—said in an email.[4]

Solarized Electric Transportation

"Pollution often is a silent killer and is one of the greatest health hazards in Amsterdam," explained the city's traffic

councilor, Sharon Dijksma, about Amsterdam's ban on gas-
oline and diesel-fueled cars and motorcycles by 2030. Similarly, other zero-carbon smart cities of the EU will need to
address the role of solarized electric transportation and the
blockchain-based energy network that will enable the interoperability between PV-energized transportation—such as
cars, bikes, flying water taxis, and roads—and the electric grid,
particularly in light of Volkswagen's "dieselgate" emissions-
cheating scandal.[5]

The German Fraunhofer Institute for Solar Energy Systems
has developed a solar car roof with highly efficient solar cells
to extend the driving range of electric cars as well as a new
solar cell textile that is woven into truck tarps to power onboard
equipment. Audi's A8 already features a solar sunroof, and
another two PV electric car companies—German Sono Motors
and Dutch Lightyear—are working toward putting their cars
on the road by 2021. US electric car manufacturer Tesla plans to
invest $4.4 billion in a Berlin factory to manufacture the com-
pany's SUV Model Y, which was produced by March 2022.[6] The
Mobility Open Blockchain Initiative is developing a blockchain-
based Electric Vehicle Grid Integrator that will connect electric
cars to the grid, while other solar energy blockchain projects
include an electric car charger and a car wallet with a wide
variety of use cases, including ride-sharing technology that
allows the deployment of underutilized personal vehicles to
provide rides.

The world's first dockless ride-sharing program was designed
by Luud Schimmelpennink in Amsterdam in 1965 to counter
the rise of pollution from cars. Called the "white bike" program,
bicycles could be borrowed and left anywhere in the city to be
borrowed again by the next individual. However, the dockless
bike-sharing system was unsuccessful due to vandalism and theft.

Ever since, there have been at least five generations of bike-sharing programs put forward, driven mostly by advances in digital and PV technology. The second-generation bike-sharing program was born in Denmark in 1991, which allowed bikes to be picked up and returned to several central locations with a coin deposit. Theft was also a problem in this case, largely due to user anonymity. The third generation of bike-sharing systems was born in Portsmouth University in England and involved several technological improvements, such as bike docks that locked electronically, onboard electronics tracking user identity, swipe cards, and telecommunication capabilities. The French cities of Lyon and Paris launched highly successful third-generation bike-sharing programs during the early 2000s and were followed by many cities around the world. The fourth-generation bike-sharing program, BikeBlockchain, which won the Genomineerd voor de Computable Award in 2017, utilizing blockchain technology to track the identities of electric bike users and accepting payment in cryptocurrencies, was jointly developed by the Netherland Vehicle Licensing Agency and IBM. Today, UK electric bike company 50 Cycles manufactures cryptocurrency-mining e-bikes, enabling electric bike-share riders to mine cryptocurrency while pedaling to earn their crypto fees, with German company Mobility House producing the chargers for these electric bikes. The Swiss city of Zug—or "Crypto Valley"—was the first city to implement this fourth-generation bike-sharing program, which utilizes uPort's eID program to track user identity and AirBie for payments in Ether (ETH).

The fifth-generation, solarized, docked electric bike-sharing program was designed by Christopher Cherry, Stacy Worley, and David Jordan of the University of Tennessee, Knoxville in 2010. US bike company Electric Bike Company began manufacturing solarized electric bikes. However, Cherry said in an email, "I haven't seen anything more than a pilot test like ours," regarding the implementation of the fifth-generation bike-sharing program so far. Nevertheless, PV panels are already energizing bike paths and roads of European cities.

The world's first solar bike path, SolaRoad—a 70-meter stretch of bike path between two suburbs of Amsterdam that generates solar power from rugged, textured, glass-covered photovoltaic cells—has been in operation since 2014. The world's first solar PV road—a patented French innovation that combines road construction and photovoltaic techniques—was installed in 2016 in France by Wattway. Similarly, the world's first electrified road that recharges the batteries of electric cars and trucks from two rails opened in Stockholm in 2018.[7]

EU Regulatory and Tax Policies

The EU has the authority to develop a unified energy policy under the 2009 Lisbon Treaty. The European Commission's Directorate-General for Energy is responsible for implementing the EU's Renewable Energy Directive to transition to a low-carbon economy with the aim of becoming the global leader in renewable energy. The Renewable Energy Directive foresees EU member states reaching 27% of renewable energy by 2030.[8] However, member states are free regarding the choice of support instruments for reaching these targets. The EU launched the Blockchain Observatory and has developed various blockchain-related legislative and policy under the European Data Protection Supervisor.

High-level industry standards for data protection, interoperability, and sharing of key blockchain technologies used in peer-to-peer energy trading, smart grids, metering, and aggregators was established by the Digitalization & Solar Task Force of Solar Power Europe. Danish blockchain company DataHub is developing a system to ensure meeting these standards in the electricity market.

Environmental Tax Policy

The power to levy taxes is central to the sovereignty of EU member states, which have assigned only limited competences to the EU in this area. Therefore, the EU lacks a coherent renewable energy or digital tax policy.

Carbon taxes provided the 28 EU nations and Norway more than 400 billion euros ($450 billion) in gas and oil taxation revenues in 2015.

The EU ranks number four in subsidies to the hydrocarbon industry, at $289 billion, which is failing to decrease despite the bloc's commitment to the Paris Agreement on climate change targeting net-zero emission levels.

State Aid Issues

Since the EU lacks a uniform tax regulator, energy tax and renewable energy subsidies are monitored by the EU Anti-Trust Commission, which is in charge of policing state aid that skews competition within the EU.

The guidelines on state aid for 2014 through 2020 allow aid to renewable electricity generation granted as a premium in addition to the market price (feed-in premium) in an open, competitive bidding process on a nondiscriminatory basis.

For example, EU state aid law does not allow Germany's tax rebates on solar power modules and other renewable energy installations of up to 2 megawatts, while Germany's parliamentary finance committee (Finanzausschuss) has voted to align national taxation with EU laws.

The collective commitment to renewable energy made by the International Renewable Energy Agency and the United Nations Framework Convention on Climate Change did not stop the record-hitting heat waves that extended across Europe and shut down power plants in the summer of 2019. "Time is running out—we are already seeing worsening climate change impacts around the world—including unprecedented heatwaves—and we need to grasp all opportunities to rapidly deploy clean, renewable energy at scale to prevent the worst climate scenarios from becoming a reality," Patricia Espinosa, executive secretary of the UNFCCC pointed out. The World Meteorological Organization published new data showing 2021 one of the seven warmest years on record.[9]

Further digitization in the EU is inevitable, with the financial sector set on establishing a blockchain payment system to compete with blockchain-based payment systems developed by China and the United States, a cryptocurrency-based trade finance mechanism called Instrument in Support of Trade Exchanges and the digital currency Eurocoin.[10]

Blockchain in the energy market is set to grow fivefold from its current market value to over $25 billion by 2024, as reported in a study by Global Market Insights, Inc.[11] But on the bright side, the EU's digitization will be solarized, with PV installations doubling in the next three years, according to a Wood Mackenzie report, and self-consumption accounting for almost 40% of all new capacity installed, according to the Europe Solar PV Market Outlook 2019. France has opened Europe's largest floating solar farm. "The EU and China are the parties that can take this forward," said Frank Rijsberman, director general of the Global Green Growth Institute.[12]

Regulation	Regulator	Yes	No
MiCA	ESMA, EBA	Proposed	
Sustainability	EU taxonomy	X	
AML/CFT		X	
NFT			X
Sanctions	EU restrictive measures	X	
Whistleblowing law	Directive (EU) 2019/1937	X – No awards	

Notes

1. https://www.powerengineeringint.com/solar/space-based-solar-power-gains-growing-interest/
2. https://cointelegraph.com/news/green-policy-and-crypto-energy-consumption-in-the-eu
3. https://ec.europa.eu/commission/presscorner/detail/en/IP_22_2591
4. https://cointelegraph.com/news/green-policy-and-crypto-energy-consumption-in-the-eu
5. https://fortune.com/longform/inside-volkswagen-emissions-scandal/
6. https://www.teslaoracle.com/2022/03/29/tesla-has-started-delivering-giga-berlin-made-model-y-suvs-outside-of-germany/
7. https://cointelegraph.com/news/green-policy-and-crypto-energy-consumption-in-the-eu
8. https://theicct.org/sites/default/files/publications/RED%20II_ICCT_Policy-Update_vF_jan2017.pdf
9. https://public.wmo.int/en/media/press-release/2021-one-of-seven-warmest-years-record-wmo-consolidated-data-shows
10. https://ec.europa.eu/digital-building-blocks/wikis/display/ebsi
11. https://www.gminsights.com/industry-analysis/blockchain-in-energy-market
12. https://cointelegraph.com/news/green-policy-and-crypto-energy-consumption-in-the-eu

Chapter 39

Chinese Blockchain-Based Mobile Payment Revolution

C hina leads the blockchain-based mobile digital payment revolution.

For the past three decades, China has been on an economic and technological growth path unequaled in size and duration in human history. Its government is playing an active role in shaping the global digital economy, serving as one of its biggest backers and building a world-class infrastructure to support digitization by acting as an investor, green developer, and consumer.[1]

China's leadership role in the digital payment area comes as no surprise and includes establishing the world's first blockchain-based central bank issued digital currency—stablecoin and mobile payment system DCEP.[2] After all, China pioneered the issuance of paper money during the Tang Dynasty (AD 618–907), which finally caught on in Europe and the United States during the seventeenth century, and still remains at the foundation of the modern economy.

The World's First Central Bank Issued Digital Currency

The chairman of the China International Economic Exchange Center, Huang Qifan, explained that the organization has been working on DCEP for seven to eight years now, and it was introduced by the People's Bank of China (PBoC) to seven institutions:

1. The Industrial and Commercial Bank of China
2. The China Construction Bank
3. The Bank of China
4. The Agricultural Bank of China
5. Alibaba
6. Tencent
7. Union Pay

DCEP will eventually be available to the general public. Pilot programs are continuously being rolled out.[3]

The DCEP's partial blockchain-based design will provide the PBoC with unprecedented oversight over money flows, giving them a degree of control over the Chinese economy that most central banks do not have. DCEP will be pegged 1:1 to the Chinese yuan, with the overall objective that it will eventually become a dominant global currency like the US dollar.

It will not be possible to mine or stake on the DCEP network.[4]

Stablecoins

Despite concerns from G7 and G20 regulators, Tether launched an offshore yuan-pegged stablecoin dubbed CNHT after launching a stablecoin pegged to the US dollar, which was blamed for causing the world's largest cryptocurrency bubble in 2017 by several class action attorneys in the United States who sued the company for trillions of dollars in damages. Steven Mnuchin, former secretary of the US Treasury, supported the launch of stablecoins, as long as US financial regulations are followed.[5] EU finance ministers, on the other hand, banned the launch of stablecoins in the region until the bloc has a common approach to regulation, since the EU parliament acknowledged in its latest report on financial crimes, tax evasion, and tax avoidance[6] that cross-border cryptocurrency transactions remained a very high risk in terms of money laundering, financing of terrorism, and tax evasion in the EU.[7]

Users all over the world are able to earn stablecoins by mining.

Blockchain-Based Mobile Payment System

Chinese President Xi Jinping passed a cryptography law and called on his country's tech community to accelerate efforts in blockchain adoption.[8] So far, China dominates in global blockchain patents,[9] and, according to a study conducted by the Central Committee of the Political Bureau of the Communist Party of China, there are over 700 blockchain companies in China.[10] But according to the PBoC, the number of Chinese black market blockchain companies is about 40 times higher—at 28,000—with 25,000 of these companies issuing their own crypto assets valued at over 110 billion yuan ($15 billion).[11]

In a report, Cipher Trace estimated cryptocrime activity at $4.4 billion for the first nine months of the year, noting that it had risen 150% compared to a year earlier. According to global monetary watchdog the Financial Action Task Force,[12] this sharp increase is due to criminals constantly developing new and more sophisticated methods to obfuscate the flow of illicit funds via blockchain-based mobile devices.[13]

Crypto Assets Can Be Earned by Mining, Even on Cell Phones

For better or worse, mobile blockchain payment technology adoption seems unstoppable. Huawei—a leader in the fifth generation of cellular network technology, or 5G—boldly implemented the world's first channel coding scheme (polar codes), pioneered by professor Dr. Erdal Arikan, and is collaborating with the PBoC on mobile blockchain payment projects.[14]

China Telecom is actively developing blockchain-enabled 5G SIM cards to become one of the world's leading platforms for mobile-based crypto asset transactions.[15] At the end of October 2019, 5G services were launched in more than 50 Chinese cities, creating one of the world's largest 5G networks, with as many as 110 million 5G users.[16]

China's Belt and Road Initiative (BRI), a massive free-trade plan involving over 130 other countries across Asia, Europe, Africa, and South America, is creating the Digital Silk Road of the twenty-first century and transforming China into a cyber superpower. Chinese tech behemoths Alibaba and Tencent have already led the way in cross-border mobile digital payments by driving the shift away from cash, and now collectively control 90% of the $17 trillion mobile payments market, sharing a combined 1.5 billion users between them. Traders of the Digital Silk Road are sending cross-border payments from Hong Kong to the Philippines in mere seconds using blockchain-based, mobile digital wallets from Alipay and WeChat Pay.

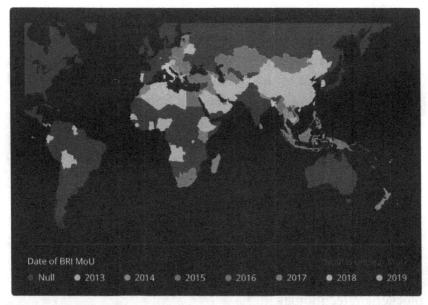

Date of BRI MoU

Null   ● 2013   ● 2014   ● 2015   ● 2016   ● 2017   ● 2018   ● 2019

cointelegraph.com

Countries of the Belt and Road Initiative Memorandum of Understanding
SOURCE: HKTDC Research, *Cointelegraph*.

Hong Kong Becomes a Fintech Hub

Before the Chinese crypto ban—which, notably, the government put in place only three months before the crypto market crash—the Chinese crypto market accounted for 90% of all global trades, according to a report in the *Asia Times*. Enacted on September 11, 2017, the crypto ban shut down all domestic cryptocurrency exchanges, and it was the main factor in a massive exodus of crypto exchanges and other related businesses, along with investors, out of China and to Hong Kong. Already known as Asia's financial center, Hong Kong emerged as a financial technology hub.

Officially known as the Hong Kong Special Administrative Region of the People's Republic of China, Hong Kong enjoys constitutionally mandated autonomy. Serving as a conduit between China and the rest of the world, numerous factors have helped support Hong Kong's emergence as a fintech hub: the presence of the rule of law; a free trade policy, including the absence of restrictions on inbound and outbound investment; the lack of capital or cryptocurrency controls; transparency; low headline tax rates; a technologically advanced ecosystem; and the Hong Kong Securities and Futures Commission's recent proposals for favorable legislation in the crypto space. As of 2019, Hong Kong hosted 48 of the world's leading fintech companies, which were reaping the rewards of useful regulatory initiatives. Conferences also helped to attract blockchain talent to the city and test new blockchain technology ideas.

The Hong Kong government's 2018 budget allocated HKD 500 million (about $64 million) to fintech development, illustrating the government's support for the city's forward momentum in the blockchain technology scene. In September 2017 the chief executive for the Hong Kong Monetary Authority delivered a speech entitled "A New Era of Smart Banking," introducing seven measures that it hoped would further bolster fintech development in the city, including a cross-border e-trade finance platform and a global trade connectivity network with the Monetary Authority of Singapore. Also, the Hong Kong Federation of Insurers created an e-platform to record and track motor insurance data.

Hong Kong's blockchain revolution has also affected the globalization of Chinese cross-border mobile payment systems. Tencent, which operates Hong Kong's version of WeChat Pay, has partnered with China UnionPay and its subsidiary UnionPay International Co. Ltd. to allow users in Hong Kong to pay for their purchases in mainland China using Hong Kong dollars.

Ant and WeChat Pay have launched blockchain-based cross-border mobile digital wallet remittance services in Hong Kong that, *inter alia*, allow Filipinos working in the city to safely and securely send funds to family members at home in seconds. Alibaba intends to expand its global cross-border blockchain mobile digital wallet remittance services via nine partnerships.

In the education arena, the Chinese government pledged an HKD 20 million research grant to the Hong Kong University of Science and Technology to explore ways that blockchain technology can enhance the security and efficiency of existing electronic and mobile payment systems. On the private side, Alibaba's cofounder Jack Ma stepped down from his role as the company's executive chairman to focus on philanthropy, including a not-for-profit foundation that he created to fund fintech entrepreneurship among Hong Kong's younger population.[17]

Nonfungible Tokens and the Metaverse

Web3 will be key to the future of China's internet, with Web3 reorganizing the organizational form and business model of the internet economy by offering a level playing field for all.[18]

Yifan He, CEO of Red Date (Hong Kong) Technology Ltd., told me, "the Blockchain-based Service Network (BSN) will launch the national NFT infrastructure in China."

The nonfungible token (NFT) is a digital certificate or a unit of data being stored on the blockchain. Owing to its uniqueness and indivisibility, NFTs are widely used in digital art and copyrighted content. However, their potential use cases go well beyond what we see today in the art world. Technically, NFT technology can be applied to any scenario where proof of interest is required, from collectible ownership and IP of creative works to documentation such as ID cards, academic certificates, real estate licenses, and so on. The technology can be used to verify the authenticity of documents while also preventing them from being tampered with or stolen, as well as facilitating verification, confirmation, and tracking.

However, most NFTs today are minted on public chain technologies that are not allowed in the Chinese market. To support NFT technology development in China, the BSN has modified the public chain technologies to "open permissioned blockchains" (OPBs) to overcome the regulatory hurdles in China by replacing cryptocurrency with fiat currency to pay gas fees and requiring permission for node deployment. To decouple the natural association with public chains and cryptocurrency, NFT is renamed Decentralized Digital Certificate (DDC).

BSN-DDC is a digital certificate infrastructure network on BSN China that includes 10 OPBs. BSN-DDC offers network access, core APIs, and SDKs—a one-stop shop for businesses to develop user portals or apps for all types of NFT applications. All payments and transaction fees are paid in fiat currency via BSN-DDC portals. BSN-DDC encourages digital certificate usage beyond the field of art and entertainment collectibles with support for all types of digital certifications, documents, tickets, identification, intellectual property, and more.

The BSN-DDC network currently is the most diverse, transparent, affordable, and user-friendly blockchain infrastructure that supports the legal deployment of NFTs within China.

It officially launched in January 2022 to support the mass adoption of NFTs in China.[19]

Crypto Asset Mining

Inspired by its new focus on blockchain, China up until May 2021 was committed to maintaining its world-leading position in cryptocurrency mining and keeping its massive mining farms in business.[20] The specialized processors used for mining proof-of-work cryptocurrencies (the world's supply of which is largely provided by China) consume large amounts of electricity, mostly fueled by coal—a resource that has been fundamental to China's unparalleled economic growth. China burns about half of the coal used globally each year. Between 2000 and 2018, its annual carbon emissions nearly tripled, now accounting for about 30% of the world's total. China emerged as the world's top CO_2 polluter starting in 2017, when cryptocurrencies experienced an unprecedented global bubble, and continues to maintain this ranking to date.[21]

During 2018 China accounted for roughly 60% of the global Bitcoin hashrate, down from a previously estimated high of 90% in 2017.[22] In a private email, Tsou Yung Chen, global CEO of RRMine—a cloud mining company—explained, "Our platform doesn't own data centers, we are a Hashrate service provider. We cooperate with global data centers, convert Hashrate into liquid asset and provide it to investors. Most of our cooperative data centers are in Southwest China, which has abundant hydropower for cryptocurrency mining."

Inner Mongolia is home to the world's largest solar power plant, Ordos, and, is one of the big three Bitcoin mining bases in China, together with Xinjiang and Sichuan. All three provinces also have the worst air quality.[23] Susanne Köhler and Massimo Pizzol at Aalborg University in Denmark found that coal-heavy Inner Mongolia accounted for 12.3% of Bitcoin mining but resulted in more than a quarter of the total country's CO_2 emissions,[24] which has only increased since countries signed on to the Paris Agreement.[25]

Liu Cixin, the celebrated Chinese science fiction writer, has advocated for abolishing crude technologies such as fossil fuels and nuclear energy and keeping gentler technologies such as solar power and small-scale hydroelectric power. During the past 25 years, China went from having virtually no solar panels to leading the world by a margin of more than 100%. The country surpassed Germany to become the world's largest producer of photovoltaic power based on its 2011 five-year plan for energy production in 2015, and became the first country to surpass the 100 GW of installed capacity in 2017. Estimates see China's photovoltaic panel installations hitting a cumulative total of 370 GWdc by 2024—more than double the projected capacity for the United States.

During the past 10 years, China has also ranked number one in terms of the sums invested in renewable energy capacity by committing $758 billion between 2010 and the first half of 2019, with Chinese companies emerging as technology leaders in green transport and energy as well as digital infrastructure. Currently, China accounts for around 24% of global investment in renewables, with solar and wind capacity in BRI countries surging from 0.45 GW to 12.6 GW between 2014 and 2019 as a result.

According to an Energy Transitions Commission report, it is technically and economically feasible for China to become a fully decarbonized and green-developed economy by reaching net-zero carbon emissions by mid-century, with solar energy comprising 44% of all renewable capacity additions until 2040, according to the International Energy Agency's World Energy Outlook report. Subsidy-free solar projects can be built not only in most Chinese cities—and at a significantly cheaper price than coal, hydropower, nuclear, and other grid-fed generation sources—but also in the nations covered by the BRI.

The reality is, wind and solar only accounted for 5.2 and 2.5%, respectively, of China's national power generation in 2018, and in May of that year, the Chinese National Energy Administration announced that it would stop providing subsidies for onshore renewable energy projects, which must now compete directly at auction with other forms of power generation. Solar energy also competes with the thick, gray air pollution that dims Chinese sunlight by about 13%. Renewable energy investment in China already dropped by 39% in the first half of 2019 compared to a year earlier, and starting January 1, 2020, the pricing of electricity underwent a seismic change that may impact the competitiveness of renewable energy pricing in favor of coal.

China's Space Power Satellites

China is very serious about the idea of building renewable-energy projects in space to beam the sun's energy back to Earth, fundamentally reshaping the way grids receive electricity. If scientists can overcome the formidable technical and economic challenges involved, space power satellite (SPS) projects could represent a monumental leap in combating China's addiction to coal power sources, which worsen air pollution and global warming. Pang Zhihao, a researcher from the China Academy of Space Technology Corporation, described SPS as an "inexhaustible source of clean energy for humans."

China's solar power station plans under contemplation include the launch of small solar power stations into the stratosphere between 2021 and 2025 to generate electricity, followed by a space-based solar power station that can generate at least a megawatt of electricity in 2030, as well as a commercial-scale solar power plant in space by 2050. A receiving station will be built in Xi'an—the region's space hub—to develop the world's first SPS power farm.

The China National Space Agency has been collaborating with India Space Research Organization in fields such as lunar and deep space exploration. On January 2, 2019, China made a historic first landing on the far side of the moon. The milestone marked a turning point for China's space exploration and may factor into China's SPS ambitions.

China's Energy Tax Policies

China is the world's most populous country and number one in CO_2 emissions as well as coal consumption. It is number two in the consumption of oil products, and number three in natural gas consumption. The country taxes 8% of CO_2 emissions from energy use.

According to an IMF report, China ranks number one in subsidies to the hydrocarbon industry, at $1.4 trillion, and is third in the world in terms of total coal reserves, behind the United States and Russia. Fossil subsidies are used as a tool to influence the energy mix and energy prices in both China and at coal-fueled electricity plants across the BRI countries it heavily lends to and invests in.

It is undeniable that China is once again taking the lead, this time by providing the world with a new blockchain-based mobile payment system, with the steep energy requirements that come with this new payment system being electrified by coal. Taking a proactive stance on the matter, Ziheng Zhou, partner and chief scientist at blockchain company VeChain, explained: We recognize that traditional carbon reduction is mainly driven by administrative orders. To counter this, we rolled out a market oriented Digital Carbon Ecosystem (DCE), the world's first blockchain-based program that incentivizes people for protecting the environment.

Only time will tell whether VeChain's blockchain-based, market-oriented approach will end up contributing to environmental protection and reversing the effects of climate change.

The failure of free markets to consider environmental costs and damages is being addressed by climate-change-based class-action lawsuits against governments and corporations—originally a uniquely American undertaking and historically prohibited in most other countries. These lawsuits have ramped up and spread across 28 countries, including China, where public interest claims for such damages have seen some success.[26]

Crypto Regulation in China

The guidance issued by the Central Bank of China during 2021 to prohibit domestic financial services institutions from providing crypto asset-related services was bolstered when foreign companies were likewise prohibited in the fourth quarter from offering crypto asset products to Chinese persons.[27]

Both Binance and Huobi, two of the largest crypto asset exchanges by daily volume, have begun to unwind their relationships with Chinese citizens. Also, major e-commerce platforms have begun prohibiting the sale of equipment that might be used to facilitate either the exchange or mining of crytpo assets as well.[28]

It should be noted that the metaverse and NFTs are in the crosshairs of the People's Bank of China, which wants to track them with anti-money-laundering tools.[29] And in the fourth quarter of 2021, China's tax official newspaper called for a tax on crypto and said that the exchange's taxation scale was very large. But since the PBoC defines all crypto activities as illegal activities, taxation seems to indirectly recognize their legalization.[30]

Notes

1. https://www.cgap.org/research/publication/china-digital-payments-revolution
2. https://beincrypto.com/chinas-dcep-to-be-worlds-first-national-digital-currency-says-ccie-vice-chairman/
3. https://english.news.cn/20220514/18c29e06fb264f00a6d85672104d2c31/c.html
4. https://boxmining.com/dcep/#Deployment_and_Distribution
5. https://www.bloomberg.com/news/articles/2019-12-05/mnuchin-powell-see-no-need-for-fed-to-issue-digital-currency
6. https://www.europarl.europa.eu/cmsdata/161562/TAX3%20Final%20Report_A8-0170_2019_EN.pdf
7. https://fcpablog.com/2020/01/10/germany-imposes-licensing-requirements-on-banks-to-sell-and-store-cryptocurrencies/
8. https://cointelegraph.com/news/breaking-chinas-xi-jinping-urges-accelerated-blockchain-technology-adoption
9. https://cointelegraph.com/news/us-and-china-battle-for-blockchain-dominance
10. https://cointelegraph.com/news/china-has-700-blockchain-companies-according-to-industry-study
11. http://www.nbd.com.cn/articles/2019-11-21/1387869.html
12. https://www.rand.org/content/dam/rand/pubs/research_reports/RR3100/RR3117/RAND_RR3117.pdf
13. https://www.fatf-gafi.org/publications/fatfgeneral/documents/statement-virtual-assets-global-stablecoins.html
14. https://cointelegraph.com/news/huawei-signs-deal-with-digital-currency-research-unit-of-chinas-central-bank
15. https://forkast.news/video-audio/watch-china-telecom-introduces-its-blockchain-sim-card-project/
16. https://www.bbc.com/news/business-50515426
17. Selva Ozelli, "How China's Cryptocurrency Ban Led to Hong Kong's Leadership In the Blockchain Arena," Tax Notes International, January 14, 2019.
18. https://cointelegraph.com/news/web3-will-be-key-to-the-future-of-china-s-internet-says-security-regulator

19. Interview with Yifan He, CEO of Red Date (Hong Kong) Technology Ltd.
20. https://cointelegraph.com/news/how-will-china-pursue-xi-jinpings-blockchain-adoption-plan
21. https://www.thestandard.com.hk/breaking-news/section/4/137976/China,-US-biggest-carbon-polluters,-study-finds
22. https://coinshares.com/assets/resources/Research/bitcoin-mining-network-june-2019-fidelity-foreword.pdf#page=9
23. https://www.sciencedirect.com/science/article/abs/pii/S0959652619344166
24. https://www.newscientist.com/article/2224037-bitcoins-climate-change-impact-may-be-much-smaller-than-we-thought/
25. https://wedocs.unep.org/bitstream/handle/20.500.11822/30797/EGR2019.pdf?sequence=1&isAllowed=y
26. https://cointelegraph.com/news/chinese-blockchain-based-mobile-payment-revolution-how-is-the-biggest-co2-polluter-becoming-leading-world-solar-panels-producer
27. https://www.china-briefing.com/news/china-makes-cryptocurrency-transactions-illegal-an-explainer/
28. https://www.elliptic.co/blog/china-continues-crackdown-on-the-crypto-industry
29. https://cointelegraph.com/news/china-s-central-bank-proposes-to-monitor-metaverse-and-nfts
30. https://twitter.com/WuBlockchain/status/1450647410011619330?ref_src=twsrc%5Etfw%7Ctwcamp%5Etweetembed%7Ctwterm%5E1450647410011619330%7Ctwgr%5E%7Ctwcon%5Es1_&ref_url=https%3A%2F%2Fu.today%2Fchina-seeks-to-tax-bitcoin-exchanges-despite-recent-crypto-ban

Chapter 40
India Is Fostering
a Solarized Digital Future

How can emerging technologies help one of the world's most populous countries and one of the largest energy consumers toward sustainable and renewable energy development?

India is fostering a digital future via Prime Minister Narendra Modi's "Digital India" initiative: a national blockchain strategy that includes quantum computing, machine learning, and artificial intelligence as digital technologies become the primary platform for economic activity and growth.

The IMF and the World Bank have forecasted that India's GDP will grow at the rate of 7–8% for the next few years, driving a rapid rise in its hydrocarbon-fueled energy demand tied to growing urbanization, rising incomes, and a steadily increasing population. Studies suggest that India's share of total global primary energy demand is set to roughly double to around 11% by 2040. This has become among India's most formidable challenges to sustained GDP growth.

India is the world's second-most populous country, the third-largest energy consumer and CO_2 emitter, and has the highest death rates among G20 countries attributable to air pollution and related calamities. While the country contributes 7% of the world's CO_2—half that of the United States—India's CO_2 emissions are increasing faster than they are in China and the United States, seeing a 4.8% rise in 2018. It is the fourth-largest consumer and importer of oil and natural gas while housing the fifth-largest coal reserves (after the United States, Russia, Australia, and China), which fuels three-quarters of India's power.

India intends to solarize its digital future. It became a world leader in the fight against climate change when Prime Minister Modi launched the International Solar Alliance with 121 member countries ahead of the Paris Agreement in 2015, with the primary objective of working for the efficient exploitation of solar energy to reduce dependence on fossil fuels.

With support from the government, foreign investors, technological breakthroughs, and falling solar power prices, India has seen an exponential growth in its renewable energy sector in the past five years, fueling 10% of its electrical power with renewable energy. The country's target for 2030 well exceeds the G20 average of 25%, at an impressive 40% of power fueled by renewables.

India's Blockchain-Based Mobile Payment Systems

Similarly to China, India put the brakes on the promotion of fintech services tied to cryptocurrencies in April of 2018 by imposing ring-fencing on banks and cryptocurrency exchanges, announcing that financial firms could not provide cryptocurrency services. The Supreme Court is currently listening to further hearings on this. However, on March 4, 2020, the Supreme

Court of India struck down the Reserve Bank of India's controversial ban on banks dealing with crypto-related firms.

The Reserve Bank of India confirmed that cryptocurrency is not banned in India in response to concerns raised by the country's Internet and Mobile Association, as the country is the second-largest telecommunications market, with 1.2 billion mobile phone customers and just 582 million bank accounts, a void often filled by cryptocurrencies. Accordingly, the Digital India initiative includes plans for a:

- Central bank-issued digital Rupee run on a permissioned blockchain.
- Multijurisdictional digital stablecoin backed by commodities and a cloud platform that will bypass SWIFT to connect BRICS national payment systems through a mobile payment app.
- Permissioned blockchain payments solution called Vajra.[1]

India has yet to finalize a crypto regulatory framework but has imposed a 30% crypto tax effective April 1, 2022.[2]

Smart, Solar Cities

The Ministry of New Renewable Energy has various programs focused on harnessing, democratizing, and decentralizing solar energy, as India is endowed with vast solar energy potential, allowing the country to shift away from new coal-fired power faster than anticipated.

Grid-Connected

This program aims to generate competitively priced solar thermal and photovoltaic power. Currently, India houses two of the largest solar plants in the world, which produce the world's cheapest solar power at $0.03 – 0.04 per watt, according to the International Renewable Energy Agency. At the end of 2019, India topped the Asia Pacific region for solar photovoltaic tenders. At the beginning of 2020, the Solar Energy Corporation of India concluded the world's largest renewables-plus-energy-storage capacity tender at a prespecified tariff of $0.04/KWh. According to a 2021 report, India is among the top 10 countries in terms of energy transition investment levels.[3]

Solar Cities

This program aims to support and encourage Urban Local Bodies to prepare a road map to guide their cities in becoming "renewable energy cities" or "solar cities" by promoting solar water heating systems in homes, hotels, hostels, hospitals, and industry; deploying solar panel systems and devices; and designing solar buildings. A total of 60 cities and towns are proposed to be supported for development into solar cities during the country's 11th Plan period.

Grid-Connected Rooftop

This program aims to install 40 gigawatts of electricity capacity from rooftop solar plants by 2022 in states, cities, railways, airports, and manufacturing facilities.

A key component to the adoption of solar energy to meet the Paris Climate Agreement is enabling consumers to store and trade excess solar energy that can be produced even at night with University of California Davis Professor Jeremy Munday's reverse solar panels. Accordingly, India's Energy and Resources Institute developed a mobile blockchain prototype for solar power trading that allows consumers to sell excess power generated from homes or electric vehicles peer-to-peer to their neighbors or power distribution companies. So far, electricity distributor BSES Rajdhani Power Limited has partnered up with Power Ledger, an Australian blockchain company, to test a blockchain peer-to-peer solar power trading solution in a New Delhi suburb.

Electric Vehicles

Under its National Electric Mobility Mission Plan, the Transport Ministry of India is aiming for 30% of vehicles in India to be all-electric vehicles by 2030, complete with a charging infrastructure as well as a developed solution for domestic battery raw materials and processing facilities.

India's electric vehicle revolution is aided by advances in qualified lithium-ion (Li-ion) cell technology—one of the most promising electrochemical energy storage technologies. Today, Li-ion has wide applications in electronic gadgets, telecommunications, industrial applications, aerospace, and electric and hybrid electric vehicles across India's innovation scene, including a bus from Ashok Leyland, a truck from Rhino, a car from Tata, a rickshaw from Mahindra, a bicycle from Yulu, drones from Skylark, and ridesharing by Uber, Ola, SmartE, and Yulu.

Drones, Solar Power Satellite Systems, and Solar Missions

The MARAAL is a series of multipurpose solar-powered unmanned aerial vehicles (UAVs), which are developed in India by the aerospace department of IIT Kanpur. Such solar-powered UAVs could be re-energized by laser-power beams, according to Paul Jaffe, who has been conducting space-based solar energy research at the US Naval Research Laboratory and focusing in part on transmitting solar energy from space to Earth for more than a decade.[4]

Jaffe recently conducted a "historic" laser power-beaming demonstration—the first of its kind—that could be used to send power to locations that are remote, hard to reach, or lack infrastructure, or to power electric UAVs whose flight time is currently severely limited by onboard battery life.

"If you have an electric drone that can fly more than an hour, you're doing pretty well," Jaffe said. He added: "If we had a way to keep those drones and UAVs flying indefinitely, that would have really far-reaching implications. With power beaming, we have a path toward being able to do that."

The Indian Space Research Organization has partnered with both the United States' National Space Society and China to harness solar energy via solar-powered satellites. Later in 2022, they will launch the satellite Aditya L-1 (Sanskrit for "sun") to study the solar corona after shooting down a satellite with a missile from Earth for the mission Shakti ("power").[5]

Environmental Tax Policy in India

The government is moving India away from a reliance on imported coal through targeted measures to encourage industry investment in now-least-cost renewable energy while progressively taxing the externalities of coal use. On July 1, 2010, India introduced a nationwide carbon tax of 50 rupees per ton ($1.07 per ton) of coal both produced and imported into India. Currently, the carbon tax stands at 400 rupees per ton ($5.73 per ton).

In India, hydrocarbon subsidies have been cut by around 75% since 2014, freeing up funds to support the development of world-leading wind and solar industries. Nevertheless, according to an IMF report, India ranks number five in subsidies to the hydrocarbon industry, at $209 billion, and has an expanding energy deficit.

According to a report by the International Institute of Sustainable Development (IISD), India's subsidies for renewable energy totaled $2.2 billion for 2017. The new government, in its 2020 budget, announced tax breaks for setting up mega-manufacturing plants for solar cells, lithium storage batteries, EV, and charging infrastructure.

Switching just 10 to 30% of subsidies supporting fossil fuels to renewables would unleash a runaway clean energy revolution, significantly cutting the carbon emissions that are driving the climate crisis. Due to rigorous lobbying efforts, subsidies and finance to the coal and fossil fuel industries are at least three times greater than they are for renewable energy, putting climate goals at risk.[6]

Nonfungible Tokens

During 2021 many Bollywood stars launched NFTs at Fantico.[7]

Notes

1. https://cointelegraph.com/news/india-is-fostering-a-solarized-digital-future
2. https://cointelegraph.com/news/30-crypto-tax-becomes-law-in-india-following-finance-bill-approval
3. https://mercomindia.com/global-investment-energy-transition-report/
4. Interview
5. https://www.indiatoday.in/science/story/chandrayaan-3-aditya-l-1-to-lunch-this-year-europe-readies-deep-space-network-to-track-two-big-indian-missions-1931587-2022-03-30
6. https://cointelegraph.com/news/india-is-fostering-a-solarized-digital-future
7. https://www.news18.com/news/business/cryptocurrency/nft-craze-in-india-2021-was-a-year-of-nfts-for-indian-celebrities-experts-decode-why-4600931.html

Chapter 41
Russia Leads Multinational Stablecoin Initiative

Russia is taking the lead in issuing a multinational stablecoin backed by commodities with the Eurasian Economic Union (EAEU) and BRICS countries (Brazil, Russia, India, China, and South Africa).

Russian President Vladimir Putin is the most influential person in the blockchain industry, according to Changpeng Zhao, the CEO of major cryptocurrency exchange Binance, which added five trading cryptocurrencies: Binance Coin (BNB), Bitcoin (BTC), Ether (ETH), and XRP at the beginning of December 2020, as well as adding Tether (USDT) later the same month against the Russian ruble.

Putin was the first to propose a multinational cryptocurrency along with the EAEU and BRICS countries after being advised by Vitalik Buterin in the wake of the 2017 cryptocurrency bubble.

With the EAEU's Agreement on Trade and Economic Cooperation with China coming into effect during 2020, Russia, with full support of the EAEU countries and BRICS Business Council, sought to establish a multinational stablecoin backed by commodities, along with BRICS pay, a cloud platform that will connect the countries' national payment systems through a mobile payment app. Russia, India, and China are planning to link national payment messaging systems, China's CIPS and Russia's FMSB, to accomplish this. This will be a major step on the path to dedollarization and a decoupling from the current United States–controlled global banking system and could lay the foundation for BRICS member state integration. The Bank of Russia, the country's central bank, has already begun testing stablecoins pegged to commodities in a regulatory sandbox.

Digitalization Is a Priority

Russia is the world's largest country. It is a leader in technology and a primary energy producer and exporter, with 80% of its economy dependent on exporting natural gas, oil—including high-sulfur fuel oil—metals, and timber.

In Soviet times, Russia's centralized electricity plants powered many Iron Curtain countries from Romania to Ukraine, and still remains an important player in the global energy system, providing 10% of global primary energy production and 16% of international energy trade. Russia ranks fourth in the world in primary electricity production, energy consumption, and carbon dioxide emissions, as the country is 70% electrified by hydrocarbon energy. Russia's CO_2 emissions are almost double the G20 average.

Recently, Russian scientists discovered a massive fountain of methane gas—emitting up to nine times the global average—bubbling from the seafloor in the East Siberian Sea and further polluting the air. Oceans act as the largest carbon sink of our planet and host 80% of all life while providing half of the planet's oxygen. According to the US National Oceanic and Atmospheric Administration, more than 90% of the warming that has happened on Earth over the past 50 years has occurred in the ocean.

Oceans are warming at the same rate as if five Hiroshima bombs were being dropped into them every second. The Russian Natural Resources and Environment Ministry acknowledged that Russia is heating faster than the rest of the world—warming 2.5 times quicker than the planet's average—as wildfires raged across country-size tracts of Siberian forest, followed by extreme flooding. This has contributed to the rise of sea levels from the melting of ice sheets in the Arctic, which is also warming faster than the rest of the world.

To diversify Russia's hydrocarbon energy–intensive economy, President Putin signed a decree in 2018 establishing a special "Digital Economy" state program, with digital energy infrastructure mentioned as a key component. It also includes the goal to increase the share of renewable energy sources in its Energy Strategy, so that 4.5% of the total energy consumption by 2030 comes from renewable energy sources to boost science and technology development, environmental improvement, and energy supply for isolated power systems, which in turn will strengthen the economy and create new jobs. The Digital Development and Energy Ministries have also developed projects focused primarily on digitalization, regulation, and coordination of the energy sector.

The expansion of the global digital economy created many new economic opportunities, with Russians behind some of the most successful digital platforms in the world. For example, Sergey Brin cofounded Google, which now claims some 90% of the market for internet searches, and Vitalik Buterin cofounded Ethereum, which allows programmers to develop decentralized blockchain applications—so much so that it's losing its scalability, resulting in very high gas fees, as slow transaction times require a substantial electricity supply for processing. In December 2019, the Russian government said it had completed a multi-day test of a national intranet known as RuNet.[1]

The Russian Association of Cryptocurrency and Blockchain counts over 2,000 members. Companies involved in cryptocurrency payments include Yandex, WebMoney, Mail.ru, Vkontakte, Odnoklassniki, QIWI/QBT, MirPay, and Wex. Companies involved in cryptocurrency mining include BitRiver, Minery, and the Russian Mining Company, which utilize Siberian hydropower plants to metabolize electricity into money very cheaply at $0.04 per Kw/h, comparable to the solar energy prices in India, at $0.03 to $0.04 per Kw/h.

Digitalization of the energy sector as a whole, and of the power sector in particular, is part of a global trend that both the EAEU and BRICS countries are involved in. According to the International Energy Agency (IEA), investments in digital technologies globally are higher than in gas-fired power generation. So far, Rosseti—Russia's national energy grid operator—has developed a blockchain solution for payments for the retail electricity sector with tech startup Waves, commencing pilot testing in the regions of Kaliningrad and Sverdlovsk in 2020.[2]

Solar Digital Initiatives for Power Plants and Waterways

Currently, solar energy utilization in Russia stands at just around 0.3%, but plummeting solar energy costs and breakthroughs in high-efficiency solar cells could aid the transition to renewable energy use.

In 2019, the Moscow-based Skolkovo Institute of Science and Technology demonstrated an organic solar cell able to withstand 6,000 gray units of gamma radiation—an achievement the institute says is a record high. Solar company Hevel is producing solar modules with an energy conversion efficiency of 22% and is behind building solar and storage into diesel power plants, hydro plants, oil and gas refineries, and solar plants in EAEU countries, with green-finance funding from both the European Bank for Reconstruction and Development and the Green Climate Fund. Hevel will audit the emissions in these solar-energized facilities with the world's first blockchain-issued green certificates.

Water pollution—which includes CO_2 pollution—is also a major issue in Russia, which houses 25% of the world's freshwater. Approximately 70% of Russia's drinking water comes from surface water, and the remaining volume from groundwater. More than 10 million Russians currently lack access to quality drinking water, with around 35–60% of total reserves of drinking water not meeting sanitary standards, according to Russian regulatory bodies. This exacerbates health issues in many cities and villages across the country, with only 8% of wastewater correctly treated before being returned to the waterways.

Worsening this situation is Russia's plans to delay complying with the International Maritime Organization's mandate to lower marine sector emissions by over 80% by switching to lower-sulfur fuels starting on January 1, 2020. This lack of compliance implies that Russia will not be auditing its huge inland waterway and deep-sea fleets in Russian-controlled waters, which account for 53% of the Arctic Ocean coastline, as it unveils major plans for Arctic oil and gas drilling and shipping. "Permafrost is undergoing rapid change," cautioned the Ocean and Cryosphere in a Changing Climate report by the Intergovernmental Panel on Climate Change. The changes threaten the "structural stability and functional capacities" of oil industry infrastructure, the authors warned.

To monitor and measure water pollution in the Kuybyshev Reservoir, the largest water reservoir in Eurasia, robotics research center Airalab Rus and Tolyatti State University have developed a solar-and-battery energized drone boat, *Drone on the Volga*, that monitors water pollution and distributes its readings through the Ethereum blockchain, including data such as the drone boat's exact location at the time the readings were taken. Nevertheless, satellites remain a crucial and efficient instrument in providing valuable environmental data.[3]

Solar Power Satellite (SPS) Systems

Space-based science fiction has been part of mainstream Russian literature since 1784, with Vasily Alekseyevich Lyovshin's novel *The Newest Voyage*. The book describes the first Russian flight to the Moon. Centuries later, on October 4, 1957, Soviets ushered in the space age when the Soviet Space Agency launched the first battery-operated satellite, *Sputnik 1*, into an elliptical low Earth orbit from the *Baikonur* spaceport in Kazakhstan. From then on, the country served as the locomotive of space-age technological advancements with innovations such as the first probe to impact the Moon (1959), the first man in space (1961), and a number of other space-related "firsts."

Russia's Znamya SPS project began in the late 1980s and consisted of a series of orbital mirror experiments that were intended to beam solar power to Earth by reflecting sunlight to increase the length of a day, with the goal of boosting productivity in farms and cities. In 2011, Russia and India launched a scientific-educational satellite called *YouthSat* to study solar–terrestrial relationships. On July 14, 2017, the Russian Space Agency, Roscosmos, successfully launched *Mayak* satellites that focused the sun's solar rays onto Earth. *Mayak*—complete with an Android tracking app—circled the planet at a height of about 600 kilometers (372 miles) in a pole-to-pole, low Earth orbit.

During the Eleventh BRICS Summit in November 2019, the BRICS space agencies that are leaders in world space initiatives agreed to build a "virtual constellation of remote sensing satellites" for various applications, including environmental monitoring and natural resource management.[4]

Nonfungible Tokens

Russia's Hermitage Museum took the world lead in holding the Hermitage Museum's first-ever NFT exhibition, "Ethereal Aether" (November 10–December 10, 2021). The curators, Dimitri Ozerkov and Anastasia Garnova, explained: "Interest in digital art intensified during the COVID-19 pandemic, when millions of people sat at home for months on end with the museums closed. The first NFT exhibition launched the creation of the 'Celestial Hermitage'—a new museum in the virtual noosphere, which in the future will be transformed into a digital branch of the actual museum." They added: "We are confident that the area of digital art, NFTs in particular, will develop in incredible ways, and that it can look forward to a great future—safe, smart and fascinating." During 2021 the museum also raised funds using NFTs.[5]

Undoubtedly, Russians fully embraced NFTs. Rarible is one of the most active NFT marketplaces for arts, according to DappRadar. The multi-purpose digital asset exchange is host to NFT Russia, which is an art platform for Russian artists who exhibit their NFTs. Other popular Russian NFT platforms include SketchAR , Foil Network, and Disartive.[6]

Tax Policy in Russia and Member States

Russia taxes 13% of CO_2 emissions from energy use. According to an IMF report, Russia ranks number three in subsidies to the hydrocarbon industry, at $551 billion, and holds the world's largest natural gas reserves (27% of the total). It has the second-largest volume of coal reserves and the eighth-largest volume of oil reserves. Approximately 60% of the subsidies go to natural gas, with the remainder spent on oil extraction and electricity, including renewable power generators.

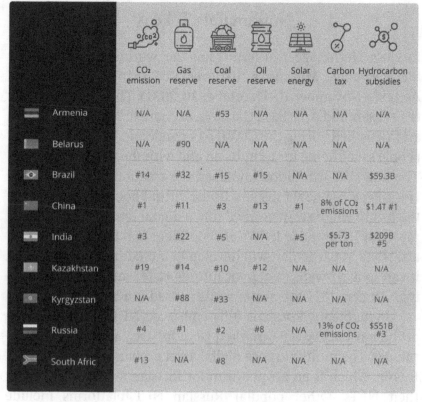

	CO_2 emission	Gas reserve	Coal reserve	Oil reserve	Solar energy	Carbon tax	Hydrocarbon subsidies
Armenia	N/A	N/A	#53	N/A	N/A	N/A	N/A
Belarus	N/A	#90	N/A	N/A	N/A	N/A	N/A
Brazil	#14	#32	#15	#15	N/A	N/A	$59.3B
China	#1	#11	#3	#13	#1	8% of CO_2 emissions	$1.4T #1
India	#3	#22	#5	N/A	#5	$5.73 per ton	$209B #5
Kazakhstan	#19	#14	#10	#12	N/A	N/A	N/A
Kyrgyzstan	N/A	#88	#33	N/A	N/A	N/A	N/A
Russia	#4	#1	#2	#8	N/A	13% of CO_2 emissions	$551B #3
South Afric	#13	N/A	#8	N/A	N/A	N/A	N/A

cointelegraph.com

Tax policy of member states
SOURCE: Selva Ozelli, "Russia Leads Multinational Stablecoin Initiative," *Cointelegraph*, February 14, 2020.

As the warmest decade on record—marked by extreme storms, deadly wildfires from Siberia to Brazil's Amazons to Australia, and heavy flooding—came to a closure, a study found that decarbonization of the energy sector is not yet on the horizon for Russia, which retains a skeptical attitude toward the problem of global climate change. The share of solar in the world's energy balance is insignificant and not expected to exceed 1% by 2040, driving hydrocarbon CO_2 emissions higher and higher.[7]

Russia ratified the Paris Agreement during the longest-ever United Nations climate summit, which ended without a deal to regulate carbon markets. The major powers, responsible for over 75% of global emissions, are set to miss emissions reduction goals, undermining the climate pact despite developing a revolutionary solar cell technology with an efficiency of 27.3–32% that could trounce the energy market.

Amid European Central Bank officials urging European banks to develop a cheaper alternative to Facebook's Libra stablecoin, which could potentially reach 2.7 billion users (35% of the world's population), Russia is taking the lead in issuing a multinational stablecoin backed by commodities.

Russia's cyber initiative connects some of the most promising hydrocarbon-rich economies, stretching across Eurasia, Africa, and South America. Separately, BRICS member states all have plans to issue central bank digital currencies as well. As a result, more than 41% of the world will be using electric-energy-intensive blockchain and smart contract technology. This initiative will potentially further boost science and technology development, create new jobs, improve trade efficiency among member states by replacing other fiat currencies used in trade settlements, and create a technologically resourceful trade block. However, if such technology is fueled by hydrocarbon energy produced and heavily subsidized by member states, temperatures are expected to rise 3.2 degrees Celsius above preindustrial levels by the end of the century, according to the latest emissions gap report, particularly in light of the fact that Russia, Brazil, China, and South Africa are not on track for a 1.5-degree world.[8]

A decisive role could be played by BRICS in finding innovative solutions to the functioning of the current global framework, particularly in transitioning to green economies. Russia's Ministry of Economic Development recently published an action plan to mitigate risks associated with present and future climate change, citing, among other things, the government's calculation of the risk of Russian products becoming unable to compete if they fail to meet new climate-related standards. Ending subsidies for fossil fuels could reduce global emissions by between 1 and 11% by 2030, the UN has found. Eliminating greenhouse gases over the next 20 years could help Earth avoid between 0.3 and 0.8 degrees of warming by 2050, as research suggests.[8]

Russia's Cryptocurrency Laws

The central bank and the FSB imposed a ban on using cryptocurrencies as a payment method. The regulation allows for cryptocurrency-to-ruble exchanges at financial institutions.[10]

Russia is making steps toward digital economic development. The government has formed a working committee in the Duma, the Russian Parliament, which held its first meeting with Bank of Russia financial experts and lawmakers to start working on a crypto regulation proposal to be presented in front of Parliament for voting during 2022.[11] Ahead of this meeting, in a report titled "Cryptocurrencies: Trends, Risks, Measures," the Central Bank of Russia called for a blanket ban on domestic cryptocurrency trading and mining, citing its negative financial and environmental impact.[12]

Regulation	Regulator	Yes	No
Crypto regulation		Proposed	
Sustainability			X
Advertising			X
ICO	Central Bank & Finance Ministry	X	
AML/CFT	Central Bank	X	
Crypto bribes		X	
NFT		Proposed[13]	X
Capital gains tax		X	

Robby Houben, a professor at the University of Antwerp who co-authored a study for the European Parliament about the illicit use of cryptocurrencies and blockchain, published an article on March 1, 2022 titled "Crypto-Assets as a Blind Spot in Sanctions against Russia?" in which he urges crypto sanctions to be implemented to further dry up funding for Russia's invasion of Ukraine.[14]

"Numbers show that crypto-assets are already quite widely adopted in the region, and the scenario is therefore definitely not utopian," Houben emphasizes in his article. The Russian government has estimated that at least $200 billion worth of crypto, or 12% of the overall market, is held by Russians. Blockchain analytics platform Elliptic has identified more than 400 virtual asset service providers where rubles can be used to purchase cryptocurrencies, hundreds of thousands of crypto addresses linked to sanctioned Russia-based individuals or entities, and 15 million Russian crypto addresses involved with illicit transactions. Adam Zarazinski, CEO of Inca Digital—which provides digital asset data and analytics technology to the United States Commodity Futures Trading Commission and Department of Defense—explained, "Since the Ukrainian invasion by Russia on Feb. 24, on Binance, BTC/RUB trades increased about tenfold, and USDT/RUB trades increased about sevenfold and then begin to drop on March 7 when Visa and Mastercard pulled out of Russia. Similarly, Russian Google searches for how to convert rubles to Tether increased fivefold during the same period."

With the Swiss government taking the lead on March 4, 2022, a wave of synchronized sanctions that extend to crypto began falling on Russia since it invaded Ukraine. On March 5, Singapore followed suit. Then came the European Union on March 9. And on March 11, the Group of Seven (G7) countries—including Canada, France, Germany, Italy, Japan, the United Kingdom, and the United States—instituted sanctions "to hold Putin accountable for his continued assault on Ukraine and further isolate Russia from the global financial system."[15]

Notes

1. https://www.bbc.com/news/technology-50902496
2. https://cointelegraph.com/news/russia-leads-multinational-stablecoin-initiative
3. Ibid.
4. Ibid.
5. https://cointelegraph.com/news/2021-ends-with-a-question-are-nfts-here-to-stay
6. https://coinmarketcap.com/alexandria/article/prominent-nft-movements-and-projects-in-russia
7. https://link.springer.com/article/10.1007/s41825-019-00016-8
8. https://www.unep.org/interactive/emissions-gap-report/2019/
9. https://cointelegraph.com/news/russia-leads-multinational-stablecoin-initiative
10. Ibid.
11. https://www.notebookcheck.net/Russia-forms-a-working-group-on-cryptocurrency-regulation.589262.0.html; https://cointelegraph.com/news/russian-parliament-working-group-there-should-be-mechanisms-to-control-crypto-transactions
12. https://cointelegraph.com/news/russian-central-bank-proposes-blanket-ban-on-crypto-mining-and-trading
13. https://news.bitcoin.com/draft-law-about-nfts-submitted-to-russian-parliament/
14. https://verfassungsblog.de/crypto-sanctions/
15. https://cointelegraph.com/news/the-world-has-synchronized-on-russian-crypto-sanctions

Chapter 42

Africa's Solarized Digitalization Agenda in the Time of Coronavirus

The COVID-19 pandemic has highlighted the necessity for the digitalization and sustainable development of African economies.

The seventh session of the Africa Regional Forum on Sustainable Development convened in March 2021 with the theme "Building forward better: Towards a resilient and green Africa to achieve the 2030 Agenda and Agenda 2063" and to promote the economic, social, and environmental dimensions of sustainable development.

Amina Mohammed, deputy secretary-general of the United Nations, pointed out that developing a just, fair economic model that embraces green and renewable energy, resilient infrastructure, and digitalization—while protecting natural resources by broadening partnerships for science, technology, and innovation—could unleash the region's green potential and fuel economic transformation.

UNECA's Digital Agenda

According to a paper titled "Harnessing Emerging Technologies: The Cases of Artificial Intelligence and Nanotechnology," which was provided by Victor Konde, scientific affairs officer at the United Nations, "The global pandemic caused by [COVID-19] has highlighted the importance of technology and innovation in developed countries. [. . .] Digital technologies have transformed how people work, interact, and access services." It also highlights the "interest in the role of emerging technologies in driving Africa's transformation" and in achieving the UN's Sustainable Development Goals.

As the document states, the United Nations Economic Commission for Africa, or UNECA, conducted profound policy research and "provided policy advice to member States on several emerging technologies, such as blockchain, artificial intelligence, and nanotechnology." The author continues:

> The digital economy is unpinned by several key technologies, some of which include artificial intelligence (AI), cloud computing, blockchain, Internet of Things (IoT), virtual reality, and augmented reality. However, as UNCTAD noted, China and the United States currently own 75% of patents on blockchain, account for half of global spending on IoT, and their firms accounts for three quarters of the global market of commercial cloud computing. As a result, China and the United States account for 90% of the 70 largest digital platforms while Africa and Latin America account for a combined share of about one percent (1%).[1]

The internet and tech giants, such as Google and Facebook, spend billions of dollars in an attempt to get more people online in Africa despite a backlash from governments that are trying to shut down access to these services. At the same time, Vera Songwe, UN under-secretary-general and executive secretary of the Economic Commission for Africa, pointed out that "Africa could expand its economy by a staggering $1.5 trillion, by capturing just 10% of the speedily growing artificial intelligence (AI) market, set to reach $15.7 trillion by 2030."[2]

Digital Currencies in Africa

Africa is the second-largest continent in the world in terms of both territory and population (roughly 1.3 billion people), and cryptocurrency is in high demand for the following reasons:

- Countries' national fiat currencies are vulnerable to double-digit hyperinflation, according to the UN.
- Africa has a high unbanked population, a high penetration of smartphone usage, and an increasingly young, migrating population.

During 2020, monthly cryptocurrency transfers under $10,000 in value to and from Africa—often traded person-to-person across the 816 million mobile phones in sub-Saharan Africa alone—skyrocketed 55%, "reaching a peak of $316 million in June." They traded with a large margin that reached up to 70% due to the small number of cryptocurrency retailers. Individual citizens and small businesses located in Nigeria, South Africa, and Kenya accounted for most of this trading activity.

China is the largest trading partner of many African countries. It has been investing ($45 billion in 2019, according to the United Nations Conference on Trade and Development)[3] since the mid-2000s to Africa's technology, communications, and finance infrastructure and blockchain technology education. Already, Egypt, Kenya, Rwanda, and Eswatini have been researching central bank digital currencies (CBDCs). As a BRICS nation, South Africa is piloting a CBDC as part of Russia's multinational digital currency initiative that will be linked with China's mobile Digital Currency Electronic Payment system supported by its Blockchain-based Service Network.

Nigeria Is the World's Second-Largest Bitcoin Market

In its "Nigeria Digital Economy Diagnostic Report" of 2019, the World Bank laid out the country's digital economy potential. Only a year later, amid the COVID-19 pandemic, Nigeria surpassed China and currently ranks second in the world in Bitcoin (BTC) trading, even though it lacks the regulatory framework to support the digital asset business activity.

Bitcoin trading provides a source of income for an increasing number of unemployed young people in addition to being a means of sending and receiving cross-border payments. For example, BTC funded the 2020 #EndSARS protests against police brutality, which were carried out by young people nationwide and spread beyond Nigerian borders, parallel to solidarity protests in different parts of the world.

Recently, the Central Bank of Nigeria banned banks from servicing crypto exchanges and was incentivizing citizens until May 8, 2021, to use licensed international money transfer operators for cross-border payments. Nigeria's securities regulator followed suit by suspending its planned regulatory framework for digital assets. This ban is expected to be in place until a well-devised concrete regulatory framework for the $1.8 trillion cryptocurrency market is developed, perhaps one that incorporates the Nigerian Technology Industry Group's core policy suggestions of instituting Know Your Customer, Anti-Money Laundering, and Combating the Financing of Terrorism regulations. As the chairman of the Economic and Financial Crimes Commission, Abdulrasheed Bawa, explained:

> We are going to digitalize our processes and we are going to create a new full-pledged directorate of intelligence to enable us to gather intelligence so that we will be proactive in our fight against economic and financial crimes and by so doing we will also provide the government with necessary quality advice that will lead to good governance.[4]

Nonfungible Tokens

Severus[5] launched on popular NFT marketplace OpenSea a limited edition NFT collection called "African Hero," to commemorate Africans who have shaped history and to inspire young Africans to build a brighter future.[6]

The Solar Energy Potential of Africa

Africa has abundant energy resources, including solar energy, as it receives more hours of bright sunshine during the course of the year than any other continent. But it lacks reliable access to modern energy, which is needed for digitalization.

The continent is determined to green-energize and solarize its digitalization, as it is most vulnerable to the impacts of climate change, even though it contributes minimally to CO_2 emissions. With the exception of Eritrea and Libya, African countries have ratified the Paris Agreement with ambitious nationally determined contributions.

According to forecasts by the International Renewable Energy Agency, "With the right policies, regulation, governance, and access to financial markets, sub-Saharan Africa could

meet up to 67% of its energy needs [from renewables] by 2030."
And as pointed out by Songwe, it can "provide access to energy
to over 70% of Africans who are without access currently."[7]

Egypt is leading regional efforts to transition to green/solar
energy, with the continent experiencing a surge of growth in
new solar installations, mainly driven by nine countries. In
a first-of-its-kind project, Egypt recently entered into a joint
venture with a Chinese company to locally manufacture sand-
to-cell photovoltaic solar panels, with China having ramped up
its overseas green investment to 57% under the Belt and Road
Initiative, according to research from the International Institute
of Green Finance.[8]

The national lockdowns and international travel bans
imposed as a result of the COVID-19 pandemic have accelerated
green digitalization efforts across African markets, which have
promoted democracy and cryptocurrencies and broken down
geographic barriers to collaboration and distribution. Nigerian
songwriter and singer Burna Boy, with his music, and Ghanaian
artist Amoako Boafo, with his paintings, conquered the world
during 2020.

Accordingly, the UN dedicated the whole year of 2021 to the
creative economy, as it plays a critical role in promoting sustainable development for a green recovery from the COVID-19
pandemic. A sustainable green recovery plan necessitates understanding the links between climate change, health, and inequality, and it requires implementing ambitious climate change
policies that align with the Paris Agreement. More important
than ever, these goals provide a critical framework for a green
COVID-19 recovery. My 12 art shows exhibited at the seventh
session of the Africa Regional Forum on Sustainable Development conference reflected these themes.[9]

Notes

1. https://s3.cointelegraph.com/storage/uploads/view/8939190c6114c6
   6ea59c5d304e10afea.pdf?_ga=2.149664310.1477760826.1654692403-
   519914260.1639274018
2. https://www.uneca.org/stories/un-forum-unveils-the-wonders-of-
   artificial-intelligence-and-other-stis-for-africa
3. https://unctad.org/news/investment-flows-africa-set-drop-25-40-
   2020
4. https://cointelegraph.com/news/africa-s-solarized-digitalization-
   agenda-in-the-time-of-coronavirus
5. www.Severus.finance
6. https://african.business/2022/01/apo-newsfeed/severus-drives-
   african-leadership-with-the-launch-of-limited-edition-african-hero-
   nft-collection/
7. https://www.un.org/africarenewal/magazine/january-2021/push-
   renewables-how-africa-building-different-energy-pathway
8. https://green-bri.org/china-belt-and-road-initiative-bri-investment-
   report-2020/
9. https://cointelegraph.com/news/africa-s-solarized-digitalization-
   agenda-in-the-time-of-coronavirus

Chapter 43

The Need to Report Carbon Emissions Amid the Coronavirus Pandemic

C limate change caused by carbon emissions might be one reason for such a terrible global COVID-19 pandemic scenario.

JPMorgan Chase, the first American bank to create and successfully test a digital coin representing a fiat currency, also provided the most fossil fuel financing out of any bank in the world, according to a 2019 report titled "Banking on Climate Change."[1] The bank recently joined a chorus of other financial institutions and endowments that have declared that they will, going forward, be reluctant to provide funding to the fossil fuel industry—which energizes emerging digital technologies and companies—in order to mitigate the effects of climate change.

In a hard-hitting report released to clients on the same day the World Health Organization published its 32nd coronavirus update, economists at JPMorgan Chase warned that human life "as we know it" could be threatened by climate change. Without action being taken, there could be "catastrophic outcomes."

Carbon pollution defies national borders and is inescapable. The true cost of climate change is felt when it penetrates deep into our respiratory and circulatory systems and damages our lungs, which are highly vulnerable to the coronavirus, according to a report prepared by the WHO. The economists at JPMorgan Chase state that "climate change could affect economic growth, shares, health and how long people live."

In order to mitigate the effects of climate change, there needs to be a global tax on carbon, the report added. This stance echoes that of the Organisation for Economic Co-operation and Development (OECD), which has said that greater reliance on environmental taxation is needed to strengthen global efforts to tackle the principal source of both greenhouse-gas emissions and air pollution, particularly since society is now witnessing the implementation of digital currencies, artificial intelligence, and blockchain technology worldwide. These new digital technologies require very high consumptions of electricity, which is currently produced with coal and fossil fuels that have adverse environmental impacts.

Global Environmental Tax Policy

Environmental taxation is used as an economic instrument to address environmental problems by taxing activities that burden the environment—like a direct carbon tax—or by providing incentives to lessen environmental burdens and preserve environmental activities—like tax credits or subsidies. It's used as part of a market-based climate policy that was pioneered in the United States, which also includes cap-and-trade programs that attempt to limit emissions by putting a cap and price on them.

Environmental taxes are designed to internalize environmental costs and provide economic incentives for people and businesses to promote ecologically sustainable activities, such as reducing carbon emissions, promoting green growth, and fighting climate change through innovation. Some governments make use of them to integrate climate and environmental costs into prices to reduce excessive emissions while also raising revenue to fund vital government services.

The top six global carbon emitters are China, the States, the European Union, India, Russia, and Japan. Their taxes on carbon emissions and subsidies for fossil fuels are as follows:

Carbon emission	Fossil fuel consumption			Fossil fuel reserves			Carbon subsidies	Carbon tax on emissions
	Coal	Oil	Gas	Coal	Oil	Gas		
China	#1	#2	#3	#3	#13	#10	8%	$1.4T
United States	#2	#1	#1	#1	#11	#4	None	$649B
European Union	#4	#2	#2	#16	#21	#20	Various	$289B
India	#3	#3	#14	#4	#24	#23	$5.73 per ton	$209B
Russia	#5	#6	#2	#2	#8	#1	13%	$551B
Japan	Japan does not provide national reports on fiscal support for fossil fuel production, consumption, and subsidies						$3 per ton	Japan has not participated in the G20 fossil fuel subsidy peer review process

cointelegraph.com

Global environmental tax policy
SOURCE: *Cointelegraph.*

Carbon Tax

Under a carbon tax regime, the government sets a price that carbon emitters must pay for each ton of greenhouse gases they emit. This encourages businesses and consumers to take the necessary steps, such as switching fuels or adopting new technologies, to reduce their emissions and avoid paying the tax. These taxes are favored because assigning a fee to carbon pollution is administratively simple when compared to addressing climate change by setting, monitoring, and enforcing caps on greenhouse gas emissions and regulating emissions of the energy-generation sector. Environmental taxes include energy taxes, transport taxes, pollution taxes, and resources taxes.

According to the OECD, outside of road transport, 81% of carbon emissions are untaxed, and tax rates are below the low-end estimate of climate costs for 97% of emissions. Coal, which is characterized by high levels of harmful emissions and accounts for almost half of carbon emissions from energy use in the 42 countries examined by the OECD, is taxed at the lowest rates or goes untaxed. Only 40 out of the 197 governments that have signed on to the first legally binding climate change agreement—the United Nations Framework Convention on Climate Change's 2015 Paris Agreement—have adopted some sort of price on hydrocarbons, either through direct taxes on fossil fuels or through cap-and-trade programs.

Carbon taxes have been implemented in 29 of the jurisdictions that have signed on to the Paris Agreement. A Scandinavian wave starting in the early 1990s saw carbon taxes legislated in Denmark, Finland, Norway, and Sweden, among other countries. A second wave in the mid-2000s saw carbon taxes put in place in Switzerland, Iceland, Ireland, Japan, Mexico, Portugal, and the United Kingdom. In 2019, Canada, Argentina, South

Africa, and Singapore implemented a carbon tax. These tax rates range from $1–139 per ton.

According to the World Bank's "Report of the High-Level Commission of Carbon Prices," a carbon price/tax of between $50 and $100 per ton of carbon emissions would need to be implemented by signatories to deliver on Paris-Agreement commitments by 2030.

Tax Credits

Through tax credits, subsidies, and other business incentives, governments can encourage companies to engage in behaviors and develop technologies, including blockchain, that can reduce carbon emissions. These credits could combat the use of fossil fuels. For example, a new study by the Overseas Development Institute titled "G20 Coal Subsidies: Tracking Government Support to a Fading Industry" (2019) suggests that coal subsidies have increased threefold since the Paris Agreement, even though it commits its signatories to hold global warming to well below two degrees Celsius through significant greenhouse emission cuts.

According to the International Monetary Fund, as well as the International Energy Agency, the elimination of fossil fuel subsidies worldwide would be one of the most effective ways of reducing greenhouse gases and battling global warming.

For example, Saudi Arabia has the world's second-largest oil reserves that sustain 90% of its total public revenues, and is the primary swing oil producer in the Organization of the Petroleum Exporting Countries. According to a study on the country, its energy subsidies in 2012 were $80 billion, representing 11% of the country's gross domestic product. Saudi Arabia has undertaken blockchain-oriented national projects aimed at diversifying and modernizing its economy by backing numerous financial-technology initiatives, including the world's first state-backed bilateral cryptocurrency with the United Arab Emirates, called "Aber," which is Arabic for passing by, crossing, or traveling on a road.[2]

Paris Agreement Climate Change Advocates

The urgency to wean off fossil fuels as a major energy source, given their negative consequences to the world's climate and human life—which has recently been forced into a digital quarantine lifestyle—wasn't only written about in the reports by the OECD and JPMorgan Chase, however. There have been many other climate change advocates penning action.

An op-ed jointly written by the heads of the Bank of England, which is seriously weighing the pros and cons of issuing a central bank digital currency denominated in pounds sterling, and of France's central bank, which plans to test a central bank digital currency for financial institutions during 2020, said that any company that does not change strategically to the new energy reality "will fail to exist."

In an open letter, the founder and CEO of investment giant BlackRock—which is setting up a working group to evaluate its potential involvement in the Bitcoin (BTC) market, including investments in Bitcoin futures—said that "climate change has become a defining factor in companies' long-term prospects." And, investment advisors who manage nearly half the world's invested capital, amounting to more than $34 trillion in assets, urged G20 countries to comply with the Paris Agreement to save the global economy $160 trillion. They pointed to the alternative, which is that noncompliance would result in damages of $54 trillion.

In a landmark German class-action lawsuit, hundreds of thousands of diesel car owners sought compensation over emissions test cheating from Volkswagen, a company in which digitalization impacts all areas of business: development, vehicle production, and the entire work environment, on the shop floor and in the office.

In the biggest settlement of its kind, Brazilian oil company Petróleo Brasileiro—commonly referred to as Petrobras—settled a US class-action lawsuit for $2.95 billion that resulted from the "Operation Car Wash" money-laundering investigation.[3] A memo from the settlement stated that the company made materially false, misleading statements to US investors about climate-related bribery, branding, and lobbying payments—potentially also using cryptocurrencies—to politicians that were designed to control, delay, or block binding climate-motivated policies in various countries, hindering the implementation of green-energy policies in the wake of the Paris Agreement.

In another class-action lawsuit, 17,000 Dutch citizens tried to stop Royal Dutch Shell from extracting oil and gas and force it to reduce its greenhouse-gas emissions to zero by 2050. The company is in talks with a subsidiary of the Chinese oil and chemical giant Sinochem Group and Australian financial-services firm Macquarie Group to develop a blockchain platform, with the goal of reducing trade and settlement inefficiencies, improving transparency, and reducing the risk of fraud in the oil industry.

A landmark legal opinion from the Dutch Supreme Court stated that the Dutch government, which has an upbeat blockchain and crypto action agenda, has explicit duties to protect citizens' human rights in the face of climate change and must reduce emissions by at least 25% of 1990 levels by the end of 2020.

A pioneering proteomics scientist said in an article that "The need to dramatically reduce global emissions is a black swan moment that investors need to pay attention to" because of the significant near-term threat from climate change activism toward the top four global fossil fuel businesses—Exxon Mobil, Chevron, British Petroleum, and Royal Dutch Shell, all of which recently formed a global blockchain consortium—that are behind more than 10% of the world's carbon emissions since 1965, according to a recent report.[4]

The writing has been on the wall for the oil markets for quite some time, given that fossil fuel energy was the worst-performing sector on the S&P 500 index in 2019. In 1980, the energy industry represented 28% of the index's value, according to the Institute for Energy Economics and Financial Analysis. In 2019, it represented less than 5%. The shift away from oil loomed so large that Moody's warned in 2018 that the energy transition represented "significant business and credit risk" for oil companies. Accordingly, on March 8, 2020, Saudi Arabia announced oil price cuts and plans to increase oil production after expanding its downstream oil operations by acquiring Royal Dutch Shell's 50% stake in their refining joint venture, Saudi Aramco Shell Refinery Company, referred to as SASREF, for $631 million.

This kick-started a global oil price war, sending prices, along with world stock market prices and crypto prices—which showed a minute-by-minute correlation with the stock market, negating its status as an uncorrelated investment asset—into a free fall that spiraled into a bear market at the fastest rate in history. The resulting global economic downturn has been unprecedented. The Dow Jones Industrial Average, which is seen as the benchmark index to gauge the health of the global economy, declined by 38% during mid-March of 2020 before seeing a moderate recovery. This was its worst month in 90 years and was emblematic of those incurred during major recessions.

The magnitude of the stock and bond value losses that major corporations—100 of which have been identified as being accountable for more than 70% of the world's greenhouse gas emissions—have sustained as a result of the ongoing global economic decline have been extraordinary, as they have occurred concurrently with the rapid, global spread of the lethal coronavirus in a border-blind fashion. This has led to lockdowns of countries and shutdowns of businesses, sending millions of out-of-work people to the unemployment lines, cut off from health care plans, and with a severe loss of pension and retirement plan assets.

Corporate Internal Carbon Pricing

Public companies are generally required to disclose material information in their financial filings, including climate and related bribery, branding, and lobbying payments. Directors of these public companies are generally required to act in the best interests of the company and its shareholders, and to consider and manage material risks to a company's business.

Shareholders are allowed to challenge companies and/or boards of directors for failure to do so under Rule 10b-5 of the Securities Exchange Act, which gives shareholders the right to file a lawsuit to recover economic losses sustained as a result of fraud related to the trading of their investments in stocks, bonds, tokens, or initial coin offerings. As the US Securities and Exchange Commission has stated, tokens and ICOs that feature and market the potential for profits based on the entrepreneurial or managerial efforts of others contain the hallmarks of a security under US law.

Fraud can come in many forms: corporate misgovernance through tax evasion; a lack of effective internal controls over corruption prevention involving bribery, lobbying, bid-rigging, and money laundering; or poor financial recordkeeping, including statements regarding future environmental liabilities and climate change impacts.

Companies are coming under growing pressure from shareholders, activists, and investment advisors who want companies to be transparent about how the physical impacts of a changing climate will affect their business. They are bringing class-action lawsuits based on climate change.

Originally a uniquely American undertaking, and historically prohibited in most other countries, class-action lawsuits have ramped up and spread across 33 countries. As of January 2020 the total number of climate change cases filed had reached approximately 1,444, with some success.

The threat of multijurisdictional class-action lawsuits stemming from environmental liabilities motivated nearly 1,400 public- and private-sector organizations—including global financial firms responsible for assets in excess of $118 trillion—to support the work of the Task Force on Climate-related Financial Disclosures, which has aligned with the Business Leadership Criteria on Carbon Pricing issued by the United Nations Global Compact's Caring for Climate initiative. Internal carbon pricing has emerged as an important tool to help companies manage climate risks and identify opportunities in the low-carbon economy transition.

During 2018 and 2019, there was a particularly strong increase in corporate internal carbon-pricing initiatives in China, Japan, Mexico, and the United States. Studies estimate that the financial value at risk could be up to 17% of global financial assets, if not more. Digital companies, including crypto mining companies, that haven't yet adopted an internal price/tax will soon have to do so as investors demand more and more insight into the risks of climate disruption, according to a report prepared by the Center for Climate and Energy Solutions.[5]

Country-by-Country Reporting Scheme

Multinational enterprises in 90 countries, which include crypto exchanges and crypto mining companies, also adhere to country-by-country reporting policies as a part of a tax-transparency initiative included in OECD's "Inclusive Framework on BEPS"— BEPS being an acronym for "base erosion and profit shifting."

Country-by-country reporting (CBCR) requires tax administrations to collect and share with other tax administrations information about multinational enterprises that operate in their countries, including multinational enterprise (MNE) group revenue, profit before tax, and tax accrued. The American Institute of Certified Public Accountants issued further nonbinding guidance in a practice aid on how to account for cryptocurrencies.

The goal is to give tax offices the information needed to assess whether there is a risk that an MNE group is avoiding taxes through inappropriate transfer pricing or other means.

In the OECD's March 6 CBCR-related public consultation, 21 of the 78 respondents requested that the OECD revise the BEPS framework to adopt the first global standard on public tax disclosure, published in December 2019 by the Global Reporting Initiative (GRI), that brings tax transparency to thousands of MNEs by making CBCR disclosures publicly available.

One notable submission, signed by 33 US Congresspeople, endorsed the GRI's new CBCR standard by calling on the OECD to ensure that CBCR reporting is "aligned with the GRI." Meanwhile, members of the US House of Representatives have introduced a tax-transparency bill that would require MNEs to publicly disclose key tax and financial information on a country-by-country basis.

The OECD's scheduled second CBCR public consultation on March 17, 2020 was postponed due to the coronavirus pandemic.

One-third of the world's population was locked down during 2020 in order to mitigate the global spread of the coronavirus pandemic, which brought in its wake great losses in health and finance. This has led to a new quarantine lifestyle that necessitates increased digital social and business interaction. Even climate change protesters—who have swarmed the World Economic Forum's annual meeting in Davos, the United Nations Climate Conference, and the headquarters of Royal Dutch Shell—are holding digital climate change protest meetings via Twitter.

Digital technologies require a high consumption of electricity, which is currently mostly produced with fossil fuels that adversely impact the environment. A global shift toward green energy to meet Paris Agreement requirements is likely going to compel changes to the environmental tax policies and tax transparency reporting standards of digital companies, affecting their financing, technology, infrastructure, and regulation. Because human life "as we know it" is threatened by climate change, catastrophic outcomes will only get worse if no action is taken. Carbon pollution, which heightens the coronavirus's lethal impact, is border-blind and inescapable.

Notes

1. https://www.theguardian.com/business/2020/feb/25/jp-morgan-chase-loans-fossil-fuels-arctic-oil-coal
2. https://www.sciencedirect.com/science/article/pii/S2211467X20300195
3. https://cointelegraph.com/news/brazils-operacao-lava-jato-paves-the-way-to-blockchain-implementation-expert-take
4. https://www.theguardian.com/environment/2019/oct/09/revealed-20-firms-third-carbon-emissions
5. https://www.c2es.org/content/internal-carbon-pricing/

Chapter 44

The Pandemic Year Ends with a Tokenized Carbon Cap-and-Trade Solution

Lowering CO_2 emissions and lessening carbon-intensive approaches are the essential goals in global efforts to fight climate change. It was a blazing start to a new decade, with 13% more large, uncontrolled wildfires around the world in 2020 compared with 2019. This spelled dire consequences for CO_2 levels, which made worse a terrible COVID-19 pandemic that led to unprecedented worldwide lockdowns that rapidly pushed the economy toward digitization.

As a result of the COVID-19 pandemic, governments around the world were forced to focus on integrating blockchain technology into their financial services. At the 75th anniversary of the United Nations General Assembly, Sky Guo, a founding member of the Official Monetary and Financial Institutions Forum and co-founder of Cypherium—an enterprise-focused platform facilitating interoperability between blockchains and central bank digital currencies (CBDCs)—discussed how the next generation of foreign policy leaders can leverage emerging digital technologies to solve the world's most pressing challenges, given that 80% of world central banks were evaluating adopting CBDCs.

Switching to CBCDs and a world financial infrastructure that heavily relies on blockchain technology can nevertheless have a formidable impact on CO_2 levels all over the world if the electricity used for energy is produced from coal or other fossil fuels that cause the highest levels of CO_2 and other greenhouse gas pollution.

According to the study "The Carbon Footprint of Bitcoin," conducted by researchers from the Technical University of Munich and MIT, Bitcoin (BTC) mining alone generates between 23.6 and 28.8 megatons in CO_2 emissions each year, which contributes to climate change.[1] The world's CO_2 levels hit new highs in 2019, a trend that repeated itself in 2020 despite coronavirus-related lockdowns that forced a global industrial slowdown, according to a report published by the World Meteorological Organization.[2]

In the time of the global pandemic, the economy will continue to digitize. So, the best way to avoid climate change is by adopting a climate policy that limits emissions and puts a price on them, according to the Environmental Defense Fund.

Carbon credits and markets are frequently incorporated into national and international efforts to mitigate increased concentrations of greenhouse gases in the atmosphere by putting a price on them. Experts often debate the pros and cons of them:

- A carbon tax directly establishes a price on greenhouse gas emissions, so companies are charged fees that accumulate for every ton of emissions they produce.
- A cap-and-trade/energy-trading system issues a set number of emissions "allowances" each year that can be auctioned

to the highest bidder as well as traded on secondary markets, thereby creating a carbon price.

Blockchain technology can be used to track "carbon credits"—a generic term for any tradable certificate or permit representing the right to emit one ton of CO_2—to reduce environmental pollution and carbon emissions, according to the report "Blockchain of Carbon Trading for UN Sustainable Development Goals."[3]

World's First Tradable Carbon Token

The Universal Protocol Alliance, a coalition of leading blockchain companies and crypto firms, launched the world's first tradable carbon token on a public blockchain, dubbed Universal Carbon (UPCO2). It can be bought and held as an investment or burned to offset an individual's carbon footprint. Each token represents one year-ton of CO_2 emissions that have been prevented by a certified REDD+ project preventing rainforest loss or degradation. It is backed by a Voluntary Carbon Unit, a digital certificate issued by Verra—an international standards agency—that enables projects to turn their greenhouse gas reductions into carbon credits that can be traded.

As Juan Pablo Thieriot, co-founder of the UPA and CEO of Uphold, explained[4]:

> This year may go down as the key inflection point for climate change. The year it went from a far-off issue enshrined in distant accords like Kyoto and Paris, to an existential threat affecting the lives of tens of millions of people. In recent months, we've seen Australia and California on fire, ever more powerful hurricanes, the U.S. president-elect Joe Biden announcing a Climate Administration, and companies such as Apple, Microsoft, and Nike voluntarily committing to carbon neutrality.

He also added that "Combating climate change is likely to become the dominant economic issue of the next 20 years."

The UPCO2 token could lead to the establishment of a global clearing price for tokenized carbon credits by allowing market mechanisms to drive industrial and commercial processes in the direction of low emissions or less carbon-intensive approaches, as the supply of carbon credits in 2020 has only represented 22% of global greenhouse gas emissions, according to the World Bank.[5]

Cap-and-Trade Programs of the Top Six CO_2-Emitting Countries/Regions of the World

Cap-and-trade programs use market forces to reduce emissions cost-effectively. This stands in contrast to "command-and-control" approaches in which the government determines performance standards or technology choices for individual facilities. It also differs from a carbon tax in that it provides a high level of certainty about future emissions but not about the price of those emissions (carbon taxes do the inverse).

With cap-and-trade programs, the market determines a price on carbon, which drives investment and market innovation. It is the preferable policy when a jurisdiction has a specified emissions target, such as set by the Paris Agreement. There are a number of studies that have reviewed the success of cap-and-trade programs by identifying some key issues from the top six CO_2-emitting countries/regions in the world.

China

China launched the initial phase of a national carbon market in 2017 with help from the Environmental Defense Fund to limit and reduce CO_2 emissions from factories and other industries in a cost-effective manner. In 2021, China's Ministry of Ecology and Environment moved closer to completing the launch of the market, releasing draft rules—in addition to registry and settlement regulations—for its national energy trading system.[6]

The emissions trading scheme, or ETS, will initially cover coal- and gas-fired power plants.

Based on the plant's power generation output, it will allocate allowances, or permits, and each fuel and technology will have different benchmarks. The ETS is expected to be the world's largest and expand to seven additional sectors, covering one-seventh of worldwide CO_2 emissions from fossil fuels. A report by the International Energy Agency dubbed "China's Emissions Trading Scheme: Designing Efficient Allowance Allocation" makes policy recommendations for China's ETS.[7]

United States

Efforts in the United States to create a nationwide cap-and-trade system in 2009 proved unsuccessful.[8] Instead, 10 states now participate in the Regional Greenhouse Gas Initiative, a cap-and-trade program established in 2009, while California has operated a cap-and-trade program since 2013 that is linked with a program in Quebec, Canada.

A study published by the Harvard Project on Climate Agreements dubbed "Carbon Taxes vs. Cap and Trade: Theory and Practice" argues that an economy-wide carbon pricing system is essential for any U.S. national policy that seeks to achieve meaningful, cost-effective reductions in CO_2 emissions.[9] Another study by the World Resources Institute titled "Putting a Price on Carbon: Reducing Emissions" finds that a well-designed carbon tax or cap-and-trade program could be the centerpiece of U.S. efforts to reduce greenhouse gas emissions.[10]

European Union

The European Union has the world's first, and its largest, major carbon market.[11] Its ETS is at the core of its policy for fighting climate change, and it is one of the most important tools at its disposal for the cost-effective reduction of greenhouse gas emissions.

A study titled "Personal Carbon Trading: A Review of Research Evidence and Real-World Experience of a Radical Idea" points out that personal carbon trading, a catch-all term for multiple downstream cap-and-trade policies, is an innovative CO_2 mitigation approach.[12] It seeks to limit a society's carbon emissions by engaging individuals in the process, and it is able to cover over 40% of national carbon emissions by combining various mechanisms to drive socioeconomic and psychological behavioral change.

Another study, "The European Union Emissions Trading System Reduced CO_2 Emissions Despite Low Prices," points out that the prices produced by carbon markets are often considered too low relative to the social cost associated with carbon, but nevertheless, the EU's ETS resulted in a 3.8% reduction of total EU-wide emissions.[13]

India

In 2019, the Indian state of Gujarat launched the first-ever emissions trading system for particulate pollution.[14] It serves as a pilot for the rest of India, as well as the world, and a means of reducing air pollution and facilitating economic growth. Additionally, leading companies in India set up their own carbon pricing mechanisms in a three-phase process.[15] India's emissions trading systems were reviewed in a report prepared by the Environment Defense Fund titled "India: An Emissions Trading Case Study."[16]

Russia

Currently, there is no cap-and-trade carbon pricing mechanism in Russia. A study dubbed "Carbon Tax or Cap-and-Trade for Russia? Evidence from RICE Model and Other Considerations" states that Russia should select a carbon tax over a cap-and-trade system due to political, economic, and historical factors, but it concludes that Russia is unlikely to take decisive action to tackle climate change in the near future.[17]

Japan

Japan has had a cap-and-trade program in place for Tokyo since 2010.[18] A study titled "The Impact of the Tokyo Emissions Trading Scheme (ETS) on Office Buildings: What Factor Contributed to the Emission Reduction?" evaluates Tokyo's ETS, which was the first emissions trading program for greenhouse gas emissions from office buildings.[19]

While the government of Tokyo called the ETS successful, not everyone believes that it was the driving force behind the nation's emission reductions. Some have argued that it was actually due to the Great East Japan Earthquake in 2011, which resulted in increased electricity prices. In the aforementioned study, researchers conducted an econometric analysis using a facility-level data set for Japanese office buildings, finding that half of the emission reduction resulted from the ETS, while the other half was a result of the electricity price increases.

As Patricia Espinosa, executive secretary of the United Nations Framework Convention on Climate Change, pointed out: "COVID-19 hasn't put climate change on hold."[20]

And as Alexandre Gellert Paris of the UNFCCC explained:

As countries, regions, cities and businesses work to rapidly implement the Paris Climate Change Agreement, they need to make use of all innovative and cutting-edge technologies available. Blockchain could contribute to greater stakeholder involvement, transparency and engagement and help bring trust and further innovative solutions in the fight against climate change, leading to enhanced climate actions.[21]

Notes

1. https://www.researchgate.net/publication/331407183_The_Carbon_Footprint_of_Bitcoin
2. https://public.wmo.int/en/media/press-release/carbon-dioxide-levels-continue-record-levels-despite-covid-19-lockdown
3. https://www.mdpi.com/2071-1050/12/10/4021
4. https://www.prnewswire.com/news-releases/worlds-first-tradable-carbon-token-is-set-to-democratize-access-to-the-most-important-new-asset-class-for-generations-301182669.html
5. https://openknowledge.worldbank.org/bitstream/handle/10986/33809/9781464815867.pdf
6. https://carbon-pulse.com/113565/
7. https://www.iea.org/reports/chinas-emissions-trading-scheme
8. https://www.c2es.org/content/cap-and-trade-basics/
9. https://www.belfercenter.org/publication/carbon-taxes-vs-cap-and-trade-theory-and-practice
10. https://www.wri.org/research/putting-price-carbon-reducing-emissions
11. https://ec.europa.eu/clima/eu-action/eu-emissions-trading-system-eu-ets_en
12. https://www.researchgate.net/publication/267324287_Personal_carbon_trading_a_review_of_research_evidence_and_real-world_experience_of_a_radical_idea
13. https://www.pnas.org/doi/10.1073/pnas.1918128117

14. https://epod.cid.harvard.edu/news/india-launches-worlds-first-particulate-emission-trading
15. https://www.climatescorecard.org/2020/03/indian-businesses-take-the-lead-on-carbon-pricing/
16. https://www.edf.org/sites/default/files/india-case-study-may2015.pdf
17. https://www.climatescorecard.org/2020/03/an-absence-of-carbon-pricing-in-russia/
18. https://icapcarbonaction.com/en?option=com_etsmap&task=export&format=pdf&layout=list&systems%5B%5D=51
19. https://www.researchgate.net/publication/340002895_The_impact_of_the_Tokyo_emissions_trading_scheme_on_office_buildings_what_factor_contributed_to_the_emission_reduction
20. https://www.aljazeera.com/news/2020/11/23/gas-emissions-expected-to-stay-steady-despite-covid-19-lockdowns
21. https://unfccc.int/news/how-blockchain-technology-could-boost-climate-action

Chapter 45
The UN's COP26 Climate Change Goals Include Emerging Tech and Carbon Taxes

New global carbon market rules with an NFT cap-and-trade platform emerge from the UN's COP26 conference.

The 2021 United Nations Climate Change Conference (COP26), where I exhibited my art, took place in Glasgow, Scotland and ended with the adoption of the Glasgow Climate Pact, bringing nearly 200 countries closer to keeping global temperature rise by 2100 under 1.5 degrees Celsius.[1]

The conference remained more focused on emission reductions than on developed countries' provisions of support to developing countries, as outlined in UN-Energy's summary of the Ministerial Thematic Forums, which highlighted key recommendations and milestones toward the achievement of Sustainable Development Goal 7[2] and net-zero emissions. Key elements of the global roadmap include:

- **Close the energy access gap:** Provide access to electricity for the globe's 760 million people who lack it. Ensure clean-energy cooking solutions for the 2.6 billion people who rely on harmful fuels.
- **Rapidly transition to clean energy:** Abandon all coal plants in the pipeline and reduce coal power capacity by 50% by 2030. Rapidly scale up energy transition solutions to reach 8,000 gigawatts of renewable energy by 2030 by increasing the annual rate of energy efficiency from 0.8–3.0%.
- **Leave no one behind:** Integrate equity and equality in energy-sector policy by planning and financing, creating green energy jobs, and mainstreaming energy-sector policies and strategies into ones that ensure just energy transitions.
- **Mobilize adequate and well-directed finance:** Triple clean-energy investment globally by 2030 to accelerate access to finance. Phase out inefficient subsidies for fossil fuels to support market-based transitions to clean energy. Create enabling policy and regulatory frameworks to leverage private-sector investment in clean energy.
- **Harness innovation, technology, and data:** Expand the supply of energy innovation that addresses key gaps and increases demand for clean, sustainable energy technologies and innovation through market-oriented policies, harmonized international standards, and carbon pricing mechanisms.

The COP26 conference made history for being the first climate summit to explicitly include a "phasedown of coal" in its decision, and it laid out new rules for carbon market mechanisms, commonly referred to as Article 6. A recent research paper estimated that putting a global carbon market in place would save the world around $300 billion annually by 2030.[3]

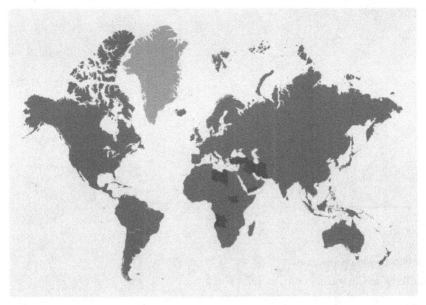

cointelegraph.com

The state of the Paris Agreement
SOURCE: UNFCC, *Cointelegraph*.

Article 6 of the Paris Agreement,[4] which covers international cooperation—including carbon markets—established new rules for trading carbon credits representing a metric ton of carbon that has been reduced or removed from the atmosphere. The new rules create an accounting system that is intended to prevent the double-counting of emissions reductions and is made up of two parts: a centralized system open to the public and private sectors, and a separate bilateral system that will allow countries to trade credits that they can use to help meet their decarbonization targets.

Emissions and expected warming based
on pledges and current policies

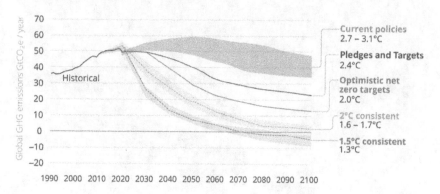

2100 warming projections
SOURCE: Climate Action Tracker, *Cointelegraph*.

Joseph Pallant, climate innovation director at Ecotrust Canada and founder and executive director of Blockchain for Climate Foundation, explained: "Emissions reductions outcomes are the most important, and soon to be the most valuable, assets of the world."[5]

He continued: "The BITMO Platform, built on Ethereum, enables cross-border collaboration on emissions reductions, distributing the benefits of clean energy, natural climate solutions, and better infrastructure to all corners of the globe."

The BITMO Platform is a project of Blockchain for Climate Foundation, which created it to advance Article 6 of the Paris Agreement and use blockchain technology to bring forward a more effective, efficient global carbon market. It allows for the issuance and exchange of "blockchain internationally transferred mitigation outcomes" (BITMOs) on the Ethereum blockchain as ERC-1155 nonfungible tokens (NFTs). Each token represents one metric ton of CO_2, and the relevant carbon credit data is embedded in the NFT.

Article 6 intends to connect worldwide opportunities for emissions reductions to the needed capital and demand. For a global carbon market to reflect real emissions reductions, the accounting infrastructure needs to ensure integrity and cooperation and avoid double-counting emissions reductions. The BITMO Platform acts as a secure record for the issuance, transfer, and retirement of each country's internationally transferred mitigation outcomes that can be integrated or reconciled with national carbon registries and future UN Framework Convention on Climate Change requirements. BITMOs help achieve global climate goals by making any relevant data easily visible, available to the public, and settled immediately when exchanged, avoiding the double-counting of emissions reductions.

Carbon Tax

Another one of the major points of discussion among world leaders at the COP26 conference in Glasgow included implementing a carbon tax, which shifts the liability for the consequences of climate change to the polluters responsible, according to the World Bank. Currently, there are 69 countries with carbon taxes, ranging from $1–139 per metric ton.

Carbon tax rates per metric ton of CO_2e, April 2021

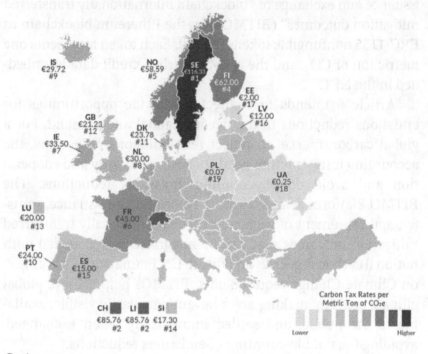

Carbon taxes in Europe
SOURCE: Tax Foundation, *Cointelegraph*.

The administration of US President Joe Biden has outlined $555 billion in spending to confront climate change as a part of the Build Back Better Act, which includes a proposed methane fee[6] designed to incentivize oil and gas companies to reduce their methane emissions.

Notes

1. https://unfccc.int/sites/default/files/resource/cma2021_L16_adv.pdf
2. https://sdgs.un.org/goals
3. https://www.worldscientific.com/doi/full/10.1142/S2010007821 50007X
4. https://www.carbonbrief.org/in-depth-q-and-a-how-article-6-carbon-markets-could-make-or-break-the-paris-agreement/
5. Interview
6. https://www.cnbc.com/2021/11/02/-biden-epa-gets-tough-on-methane-leaks-from-oil-and-gas-sector-.html

Index

Page numbers followed by *f* and *t* refer to figures and tables, respectively.

Aber, 5, 56, 211–212, 320
Abu Dhabi, 246
Africa, 307–312. *See also specific countries*
  Bitcoin market in, 310–311
  digital currencies in, 309–311
  digitalization, 307–309
  nonfungible tokens in, 311
  solar energy potential of, 311–312
  sustainable economic development in, 307
"African Hero" NFT collection, 311
Africrypt, 167, 167*t*
Airbus Defense and Space, 261
Air pollution, 262, 281, 288, 332
Akoin, 55

AlphaBay, x–xi, 1–2, 82–85
Altcoins, 51–56. *See also* Central bank issued digital currency (CBDC); Stablecoins
  central bank digital currency, 53–56
  in COVID-19 pandemic, 53–56
  global interest in, 54–56
  stablecoins, 51–52
  utility settlement coins, 52–53
Alternative investments, *see* Cryptocurrency-based new financial alternatives
American Institute of Certified Public Accountants (AICPA), 98–99
American Seafoods, 127

Anadol, Refik, 219
Antigua and Barbuda, x, 83
Anti-Money Laundering and
    Counter-Terrorism Financing
    Act (2006), 62, 89, 113
Anti-money laundering standards,
    of Financial Action Task
    Force, 78, 81–84
Applied Blockchain, 176–177
Argentina, 127
Art museums, 140–143, 143*f*
Asia Digital Exchange, 224
Atomic Energy Act, 107–108
Australia, 45, 48, 62, 93,
    119–120, 250
Australian Transaction Report and
    Analysis Centre
    (AUSTRAC), 62
Avalanche, 216, 219

Banks, digital asset management
    services of, 35
Bank Secrecy Act (BSA), 87–88
Behavioral economics, 46–49
Belgium, x, 48, 83
Belt and Road Initiative (BRI), 5–6,
    55, 274, 275*f*, 312
Bike-sharing programs, 264–266
Binance, 212, 231, 283,
    295, 305–306
Binary Bitcoin options, 34, 48–49
Bitcoin (BTC), 9–18
    about, 9–10
    in Brazil, 187
    BTC-e exchange, xi, 1–2, 84–88
    Chinese ban on, 15–17
    in corruption cases, 101–102
    FinCEN regulations on, 69–70
    global adoption of, 5, 217, 230

hedge funds invested in,
    39–43, 41*f*
hedging investments in, 37–43
in Japan, 251–252
mining of, 14–15, 279
money laundering involving,
    82–83, 102
Nigerian market for, 310–311
and Paris Agreement, 320
rebuilding after Hurricane Irma
    with, 17–18
valuation of, ix, 1 (*See also*
    Volatility of cryptocurrency)
wallets for, 11–14
Bitcoin exchange-traded funds
    (ETFs), 35, 182, 192
Bitcoin Market, 251
Bitcoin Spreads, 47–49
Bitfinex, 94
BitMEX, 89
BITMO Platform, 340–341
Bitstamp, 82, 94
BlackRock, 320
Blockchain adoption. *See also*
    specific platforms
    in Brazil, 186
    in Canada, 191
    of Ethereum, 22–23
    in Germany, 201–202
    in Hong Kong, 275–277
    in India, 287–288
    in Israel, 175–177
    in Japan, 245–251
    in Malta, 197
    in the Netherlands, 159–160
    in Portugal, 155–156
    in Puerto Rico, 230–231
    in Singapore, 223
    in South Africa, 165–166

in South Korea, 181–182
in Switzerland, 170
in Turkey, 215–217
in United Arab
   Emirates, 210–211
in United States, 111–115, 237
Blockchain applications:
carbon emission tracking,
   327–329
charity art auction for
   COVID-19 victims, 145–146
government transparency and
   efficiency, 111–115
for meatpacking industry,
   117, 119–124
mobile payments, 4, 56,
   271–274, 282, 288–289
for seafood industry,
   124–133
solar technology, 248–249
supply chain manage-
   ment, 117–133
tracking corruption in government funds and
   grants, 123–124
trust and, xii, 2
Blockchain-Based Service Network
   (BSN), 277–278
Blockchain Research Institute
   (BRI), 193
Blue Agave, Operation, 72–73
BNDES Token, 123
"Bored Ape #9449" (NFT),
   137–138, 138f
Brazil:
central bank digital currencies
   in, 303–304
digital asset use and regulation
   in, 185–188

digitalization of energy sector
   in, 298
meatpacking industry
   in, 120–123
Operation Car Wash in, 321
in Russia's stablecoin initiative,
   6, 56, 166, 187, 295–296
solar power satellites of, 301
Bribes, 97–99, 121–123
Brockman, Bob, 103
BTC-e Bitcoin exchange, xi,
   1–2, 84–88
Build Back Better Act, 342
Bulgaria, xi, 84–88
Business incentives to reduce
   emissions, 243–244,
   316, 319–320
Buterin, Vitalik, 21, 22, 24, 28, 295
Bycatch, 125

Canada, x, 48, 82, 83, 93, 191–195
Carawan, Phillip, 130
Carbon cap-and-trade programs
   and tokens, 327–334
blockchain to track, 327–329
carbon tax regimes vs., 328–330
in China, 330–331
and COP26 goals, 339–340
in European Union, 332
in India, 332
in Japan, 333–334
in Russia, 333
in United States, 331
Universal Carbon
   token, 329–330
Carbon emissions, 315–326
blockchain to track, 327–329
in BRICS countries, 303–304
carbon tax regime, 318–319

Carbon emissions (*Continued*)
climate change advocates
on, 320–323
country-by-country reporting
of, 325–326
and environmental tax policy,
316–317, 317*t*
in European Union, 260
incentives to reduce, 319–320
internal carbon pricing, 323–324
and severity of COVID-19
pandemic, 315–316
UN COP26 goals for,
337–341, 340*f*
"Carbon Offset vIRL" NFTs, 148
Carbon tax, 316, 318–319
cap-and-trade programs
vs., 328–330
in European Union, 267
in India, 292
in Japan, 254
and UN COP26 goals,
341–342, 342*f*
in United States, 242–243
Caribbean, 17–18
Carne Fraca, Operation, 120–123
Cartel de Jalisco Nueva
Generación (CJNG), 70–73
Car Wash, Operation, 185–186, 321
Celestial Hermitage
museum, 142, 301
Centers for Disease Control and
Prevention (CDC), 64,
118, 119, 129
Central African Republic, 5
Central bank issued digital
currency (CBDC), 53
in Africa, 309–310
in Brazil, 187

in BRICS countries, 303–304
in Canada, 193
in China, 272
during COVID-19 pan-
demic, 53–56
in Germany, 203
global interest in, 4–5,
54–56
in Israel, 177
in Japan, 252
in Malta, 198
in the Netherlands, 161
in Portugal, 156
in Singapore, 225
in South Africa, 166
in South Korea, 182
switching to, 327–328
in Switzerland, 171
in Turkey, 218–219
in United Arab
Emirates, 211–212
Charitable giving:
blockchain-assisted, 145–146
NFTs for, 142–143, 143*f*,
146–148
rebuilding after
Hurricane Irma, 18
China, 271–283
Bitcoin ban in, 15–17
Bitcoin-invested hedge
funds in, 41
blockchain-based mobile
payment system, 4, 56,
271–274, 282
carbon cap and-trade program
in, 330–331
carbon emissions by, 317*t*
central bank digital currencies
in, 272, 303–304

cryptocurrency mining in, 14, 274, 275f, 278–281

digitalization of energy sector in, 298

digital yuan in, 5–6, 55

energy tax policies of, 282–283

fintech in Hong Kong, 275–277

intellectual property espionage in, 108

internal carbon pricing in, 324

in multinational stablecoin initiative, 6, 56, 166, 187, 295–296

NFTs and metaverse in, 277–278

regulation of digital assets in, 283

seafood trade in, 125, 126

solar power satellites of, 301

space power satellites of, 281–282

stablecoins in, 4, 55, 272–273

theft in, 93, 94

China National Space Agency, 281–282

Climate change advocates, on fossil fuels, 320–323

Climate change-based class-action lawsuits, 283, 321, 324

CoaliChain, 175–176

Coghlan, Giles, 53–54

Coinbase Analytics tool, 73–74

Coinbase Inc., 38, 43

Coincheck, 251–252

Cold wallets, 12

Collusion, 131–133

Commodity Futures Trading Commission (CFTC), 30, 40, 42, 89, 97

Common Reporting Standard (CRS), 35

Contracts, smart, 22

Coronavirus pandemic, see COVID-19 pandemic

Corruption, 114

in Brazil, 120–123, 185–186

and government funds/grants, 123–124

in Puerto Rico, 230

in United States, 101–102, 123–124

Jeffrey Wertkin case, 101–102

Costa Rica, 82

Country-by-country reporting (CbCR), 31, 121, 325–326

COVID-19 pandemic:

altcoins debuting in, 53–56

art auction for victims of, 145–146

blockchain for tracking, 119

carbon emissions and, 315–316, 326, 327

and cryptocurrency adoption, 217–218

and digitalization agenda in Africa, 307–308

illicit use of cryptocurrency in, 70

impact of, on museums, 140–141

nonfungible tokens in, 3–4

and opioid epidemic, 63–64, 67

supply chain management during, 117–118, 124–127

sustainable recovery from, 312

US deficit and, 103

Credit crisis, in Japan, 245–246

Crypto Assets Fund, 42

Cryptocurrencies:
   described, 9, 10
   illicit use of (*see* Illicit use of
      cryptocurrency)
   regulatory classification of, 97
   volatility of (*see* Volatility of
      cryptocurrency)
Cryptocurrency adoption, 3*f. See
   also specific types*
   in Africa, 309–311
   in Brazil, 187
   in Canada, 191–192
   in Germany, 201, 202
   in Israel, 177
   in Japan, 251–252
   in Malta, 197
   in the Netherlands, 160
   in Portugal, 156
   in Puerto Rico, 231
   in Singapore, 223–224
   in South Africa, 165, 166
   in South Korea, 181, 182
   in Switzerland, 170
   in Turkey, 217–218
   in United Arab Emirates, 211
Cryptocurrency-based new financial alternatives, 33–35, 47–49
Cryptocurrency Enforcement
   Framework, 76–78
Cryptocurrency ETFs, 35,
   182, 187, 192
Cryptocurrency exchanges, 34. *See
   also* BTC-e Bitcoin exchange
Cryptocurrency Intelligence
   Program, 75
Cryptocurrency investment
   funds, 191–192
Cryptocurrency tumblers and
   mixing services, 59–62

in Australia, 62
in European Union, 60–61
Helix, 89–90
in Japan, 62
money laundering
   with, 12–13, 90
prevalence of, 59–60, 60*f*
in United States, 61
Cryptograph, 148
"CryptoPunk #5293"
   (NFT), 142, 143*f*
CryptoVerses, 177
Cryptsy, 82, 94
Customs and Border
   Protection (CBP), 64
Cybercrime task forces and
   policies, 75–80
   Cryptocurrency Enforcement
      Framework, 76–78
   Cryptocurrency Intelligence
      Program, 75
   EU Digital Finance Strategy, 80
   Joint Cybercrime Action
      Taskforce, 78–79, 79*t*
   and monitoring of cryptocur-
      rency tumblers/mixing
      services, 60–62
   in United States, 69–79, 79*t*
Cyber Fraud Task Force (CFTF), 76
Cyprus, x, 61, 83, 86
Czech Republic, 93

Darknet, 63–67. *See also specific
   markets*
   drug-trafficking via, 64–66, 70
   in Germany, 204–205, 205*t*
   money laundering on, 82, 89–90
   and opioid epidemic, 63–64
   Tor browser to access, 66–67, 90

DarkSide, 95
Dash, 202
DCash, 231
DCEP (currency), 272
Decentralized Digital Certificate
   (DDC), 278
Decker, Julie, 144
Denmark, 262
Department of Defense (DoD),
   64, 114–115
Department of Homeland Security
   (DHS), 115
Digital assets, defined, 4
Digital asset management services,
   from banks, 35
Digital currencies, *see* Central
   bank issued digital currency
   (CBDC); Cryptocurrencies
Digital Economy state program,
   297–298
Digital Euro, 6, 56, 156,
   161, 198, 203
Digital Finance Strategy,
   European Union, 80
Digital India initiative, 287–289
Digital Innovation Authority Bill,
   Malta, 198–199
Digitalization:
   in Africa, 307–309
   of museums, 140–141
   in Russia, 296–298
   in Turkey, 215
   in UAE, 210–211
Digital Turkish Lira Research and
   Development Project, 218–219
Digital yuan, 5–6, 55
DisrupTor, Operation, 67
DNBcoin, 161
Dogecoin, 182

DoinGud, 147
Drones, 176–177, 291–292, 300
Drug-trafficking, 64–66,
   70–73, 83–84

Egypt, 312
Electric transportation, 249,
   263–266, 291
El Salvador, 5
Endowment effect, 47
Energy efficiency, of
   Ethereum, 23–24
"Energy from the Desert"
   project, 249
Enterprise Ethereum Alliance, 193
Environmental education, 143–145
Environmental impact:
   of Bitcoin mining, 14–15
   of blockchain development,
   238–239
   of nonfungible tokens, 136–137
Environmental Protection
   Agency, 23
Environmental tax policy:
   of China, 282–283
   in European Union, 267
   global, 316–317, 317t
   in India, 292
   in Japan, 253–256
   in Russia, 302–304, 304t
   of stablecoin initiative participants, 302–304, 304t
   of United States, 241–244
Equality, in COP26 goals, 338
Espionage, intellectual property,
   107–108
Ether (ETH), 21, 37, 97–99,
   192–193, 217
"Ethereal Aether" exhibition, 135,
   141–142, 141f, 301

Ethereum, 21–24
  adoption of, 22–23
  in Canada, 191
  energy efficiency of, 23–24
  fee structure of, 24
  initial coin offerings on, 28
  NFT platforms using,
    140, 219, 220
  for smart contracts, 22
  and valuation of Ether, 21
Eurasian Economic Union
    (EAEU), 6, 56, 166, 295–296,
    298. *See also specific countries*
Euro, digital, 6, 56, 156,
    161, 198, 203
European Securities and Markets
    Authority (ESMA), 48
European Space Agency
    (ESA), 260–261
European Union (EU), 259–269.
    See also specific countries
  carbon cap-and-trade
    programs in, 332
  carbon emissions by, 317t
  cybercrime task forces and
    policies, 78–80, 79t
  electric transportation
    in, 263–266
  investigation of cryptocurrency
    tumblers/mixing services,
    60–61
  regulatory and tax policies in,
    266–268, 269t
  smart cities in, 261–263
  solarization in, 259–260,
    263–266
  space power satellites
    of, 260–261
Europol, x, 64, 79, 82–84

Evolution, 82
Exchange-traded funds (ETFs), 35,
    182, 187, 192
Executive Order on Ensuring
    Responsible Development of
    Digital Assets, 4

Facebook, 238, 303
Fairness, 47–48
FamousSparrow group, 108
Federal Bureau of Investigation
    (FBI), x, xi, 10, 48, 64, 65, 69,
    74, 94, 95, 101
Federal Deposit Insurance
    Corporation (FDIC), xi, 85
Fee structure, Ethereum, 24
Fidelity Investments, 43
Financial Action Task
    Force, 77, 81–84
Financial Crimes Enforcement
    Network (FinCEN), xi, 30–31,
    42, 61, 69–70, 73,
    84–88, 97, 102
Financial Market Supervisory
    Authority (FINMA), 13, 35, 52
Financial Services Agency
    (FSA), Japan, 62
Financial Services Commission,
    South Korea, 183
Fintech Blockchain Group,
    41–42
Fishing, illegal, 125
Food safety issues, 118–123,
    128–129
Foreign Account Tax Compliance
    Act (FATCA), 31, 35
Foreign Corrupt Practices Act
    (FCPA), ix, 1, 98, 121–122
Forget Finance, 203

Fossil fuel use and industry. *See also* Carbon emissions
  in China, 279–280, 282, 331
  climate change advocates on, 320–323
  in EU, 262
  funding for, 315–316
  in India, 292–293
  in Japan, 255–256
  market share for, 322–323
  in Russia, 302, 302*t*
France, x, 6, 56, 83, 261, 265
Fraud:
  in Brazil, 188*t*
  in Canada, 194*t*
  and climate-change-related class-action lawsuits, 323–324
  with initial coin offerings, 29
  in Israel, 177*t*
  in seafood industry, 129–131
Fukushima nuclear crisis, 248, 254, 256
Fuller, Richard Buckminster, 225

G20 countries, xii, 2, 255
General Services Administration (GSA), 112
Germany:
  climate-change-based class action lawsuit, 321
  digital asset use and regulation in, 201–206
  electric transportation in, 264, 265
  illicit use of cryptocurrency in, x, 83
  smart cities in, 262
  tax rebates on solar power, 267
GiveDirectly, 146

Gold tokens, 170
Gosselin, Viviane, 144
Government agencies with blockchain programs, 111–119
  Centers for Disease Control and Prevention, 118–119
  Department of Agriculture, 118–119
  Department of Defense, 114–115
  Department of Homeland Security, 115
  General Services Administration, 112
  National Aeronautics and Space Administration, 115
  State Department, 113–114
  Treasury Department, 112–113
Government funds and grants, 114, 123–124
Greece, xi, 85
Green energy, *see* Renewable energy
Greenhouse gas emissions, UN COP26 goals for, 337–341
Grid-connected rooftop solar power, 290–291
Grid-connected solar programs, 289–290
Griffith, Virgil, 107
Gross domestic product, of India, 288
Ground X, 182

Hamilton, Patrick, 144
Hansa, x–xi, 1–2, 83–85
Hedge funds, Bitcoin-invested, 39–43, 41*f*
Hedging Bitcoin investments, 37–43, 41*f*

Helix, 89–90
Helvet, Project, 171
Hic et Nunc marketplace, 135–136,
    139–140, 187–188
Hong Kong, 275–277
Hot wallets, 11–12
Huobi, 283
Hurricane Irma, 15, 17–18,
    229–230, 232
Hurricane Maria, 229–230, 232
Hydra, 66, 67, 204–205

Illicit use of cryptocur-
    rency, 59–116
  in the Netherlands,
    161–162, 162t
  in Brazil, 185–186, 188t
  bribes, 97–99
  in Canada, 194t
  in China, 273–274
  corruption, 101–102
  cryptocurrency tumblers and
    mixing services for, 59–62
  on darknet, 63–67
  in Germany, 204–205, 205t
  intellectual property espio-
    nage, 107–108
  in Israel, 177t
  in Japan, 251–252
  in Malta, 198t
  money laundering, 81–90
  in Portugal, 157t
  prevention of, 216–217
  in Puerto Rico, 232t
  ransom payments, 94–95
  in Singapore, 226t
  in South Africa, 167, 167t
  in South Korea, 183, 183t
  in Switzerland, 171t

  task forces and policies to
    prevent, 75–80
  tax evasion, 103–105
  theft hacking, 93–94
  in Turkey, 220t
  in United Arab Emirates, 212t
  US investigations of, 69–74
Implementation Act,
    Netherlands, 162
India, 287–293
  blockchain-based mobile
    payments in, 288–289
  carbon cap-and-trade
    program in, 332
  carbon emissions by, 317t
  central bank digital currencies
    in, 303–304
  Digital India initiative,
    287–288
  digitalization of energy sector
    in, 298
  drones and solar power satellite
    systems in, 291–292
  electric vehicles in, 291
  environmental tax policy in,
    292
  in multinational stablecoin
    initiative, 6, 56, 166,
    187, 295–296
  seafood market in, 125
  smart, solar cities in, 289–291
  solar power satellites of, 301
Initial coin offerings (ICOs),
    27–31, 160–161
Innovation (startups):
  in Brazil, 187
  in Canada, 193
  in China, 275–277
  and COP26 goals, 338

in Germany, 203
in Israel, 177
in Malta, 198
in the Netherlands, 160–161
in Portugal, 156
in Puerto Rico, 231
in Singapore, 224–225
in South Africa, 166
in South Korea, 182
in Switzerland, 171
in Turkey, 218
in United Arab Emirates, 211
Innovative Technology
    Arrangements Bill, 199
Intellectual property espionage,
    107–108
Internal carbon pricing,
    323–324
Internal Revenue Service (IRS), 31,
    38, 73, 97, 98
Internal Revenue Service Criminal
    Investigations Division
    (IRS-CI), x, xi, 61, 85, 169
International Emergency
    Economic Powers Act, 107
International Monetary Fund
    (IMF), xii, 2, 243–244
Investment tax credit, 243
Investors:
    behavioral economics for,
        46–49
    effects of failing to hedge
        Bitcoin portfolios, 38
    reactions of, to Bitcoin price
        volatility, 45–49
    successful hedging of Bitcoin
        investments by, 37–38
Israel, 48, 175–178
Italy, 61

Japan, 245–256
    Bitcoin trading in, 45
    carbon cap-and-trade program
        in, 333–334
    carbon emissions by, 317t
    central bank issued digital
        currency in, 252
    credit crisis in, 245–246
    cryptocurrency adoption
        in, 251–252
    environmental, regulatory, and
        tax policy in, 253–256, 256t
    illicit use of cryptocurrency in,
        82, 85, 93, 251
    internal carbon pricing in, 324
    monitoring of cryptocurrency
        tumblers/mixing services
        by, 62
    nonfungible tokens in, 252–253
    solarized blockchain adoption
        in, 245–251
Japanese Space Agency
    (JAXA), 250–251
JBS S.A., 119–123
Joint Criminal Opioid and Darknet
    Enforcement (J-CODE),
    64, 65, 67
Joint Cybercrime Action Taskforce
    (J-CAT), 204
JPMorgan Chase, 52–53,
    238, 315–316

Karma, 9, 216
Keys, digital wallet, 13
Kovner, Bruce, 40

LaCollection platform, 143
Lanez, Tory, 193–194

Liberty Reserve, 82
Libra stablecoin, 303
Liechtenstein, x
Lightspark, 4
Li Jiadong, 89
Litecoin, 47
Lithuania, x, 5, 55, 83

Ma, George, 144
McAfee, John, 104–105
MalKamak (code name), 108
Malta, 61, 197–199, 262
Meatpacking industry,
    117, 119–124
Mental accounting, theory
    of, 46–47
Messi, Leo, 198
Metaverse, 4, 202–204, 277–278
Metaverso NFT summit, 231
Mexico, 324
Microsoft Exchange Server
    attacks, 108
Mining of cryptocurrency:
    Bitcoin, 14–15
    in Brazil, 187
    in Canada, 192–193
    carbon footprint of, 328
    in China, 274, 275f, 278–281
    environmental impact of, 23–24
    in Germany, 202
    in Israel, 177
    in Malta, 198
    in the Netherlands, 160
    in Portugal, 156
    in Puerto Rico, 231
    in Singapore, 224
    in South Africa, 166
    in South Korea, 182
    in Switzerland, 170

    in Turkey, 218
    in United Arab Emirates, 211
    Ministry of Economy, Trade, and
        Industry (METI), 246, 247
    Ministry of New Renewable
        Energy, India, 289–291
Mirror International Trading, 167
Mixing services, see
    Cryptocurrency tumblers and
        mixing services
Mobile phones:
    African cryptocurrency trans-
        fers via, 309
    blockchain-based payment
        system, 4, 56, 217–277,
        282, 288–289
    cryptocurrency mining
        via, 274, 275f
MonarxNFT series, 139
Monero, 60, 79, 82, 90
Monetary Authority of Singapore,
    223, 226–227
Money laundering, 81–90
    BitMEX settlement for, 89
    in Brazil, 185–186, 188t
    in Canada, 194t
    charges against Tian Yinyin and
        Li Jiadong, 89
    crypto tumblers/mixers
        for, 12–13, 59
    Financial Action Task Force's
        AML standards, 81–84
    Hansa and AlphaBay cases, x–xi
    Helix indictment, 89–90
    shuttering of BTC-e
        for, xi, 84–88
    in South Korea, 183t
    Suex case, 88–89
Mt. Gox, 82, 85, 93, 251

MSeafood, 131
Multinational enterprises (MNEs), emission reporting by, 325–326
Multinational stablecoin initiative of Russia, 6, 56
  Brazil in, 187
  environmental tax policy of participants, 302–304, 302t
  Vladimir Putin's involvement in, 295–296
  South Africa in, 166, 309–310
Musk, Elon, 14–15, 54

Nakamoto, Satoshi, 9–10
National Aeronautics and Space Administration (NASA), 115
National Bank for Economic and Social Development (BNDES), 122–123, 187
National Cryptocurrency Enforcement Team (NCET), 78
National Defense Authorization Act, 114–115
National Oceanic and Atmospheric Administration, 128–129
Netherlands, x, 83, 159–162, 263–264, 321
Nextera, 241
Nigeria, 45, 310–311
Noncustodial wallets, 11–13
Nonfungible tokens (NFTs), 135–148. See also specific exhibitions and NFTs
  in Africa, 311
  on BITMO Platform, 341
  in Brazil, 187–188
  in Canada, 193–194
  at charity art auction, 145–146
  in China, 277–278
  in COVID-19 pandemic, 3–4, 145–146
  digitalization of museums, 140–141
  for environmental education, 143–145
  environmental impact, valuation, and regulation of, 136–138, 137f, 138f
  in Germany, 203–204
  in Israel, 177
  in Japan, 252–253
  in Malta, 198
  for museum fundraising, 142–143, 143f
  in the Netherlands, 161
  in Portugal, 156–157
  in Puerto Rico, 231
  in Russia, 301
  in Singapore, 225
  in South Africa, 167
  in South Korea, 182–183
  sustainable, 138–140, 146–148
  in Switzerland, 171
  in Turkey, 219–220
  in United Arab Emirates, 212
  and UN SDGs, 146–148, 147f
North Korea, 93, 94

Ocean warming, 297
Office of Foreign Assets Control (OFAC), 73, 88–89, 97
Office of the Inspector General, xi, 85
Onymous, Operation, 82
OpenSea platform, 140, 146, 219, 220

Opioid epidemic, 63–64, 67
Options:
  binary Bitcoin, 34, 48–49
  hedging investments with,
    39–43, 41*f*
Organisation for Economic Co-
  operation and Development
  (OECD), xii, 2, 121,
  242, 316, 325
Oseguera Gonzalez, Jessica
  Johanna (La Negra), 71
Overfishing, 125

Pacific Seafood, 127–128
Pak (artist), 137, 137*f*
Paris Agreement, 14–17
  and Bitcoin ban in China,
    16–17
  Bitcoin mining and, 14–15, 279
  blockchain to realize goals of,
    318, 334, 340–341
  carbon emission goals of, 243,
    244, 320–323
  and COP26 goals, 339–340, 339*f*
  and green recovery from
    COVID-19 pandemic, 312
  solar energy goals, 260, 290
Paycer, 203
Petro, 5, 55
Photovoltaic (PV) technology,
  247–248, 259–260, 263, 312
"The Pixel" (NFT), 137, 137*f*
Planner-doer model, 48–49
Polygon Web3, 203–204
Ponzi schemes, 167
Portugal, 61, 155–157
Postal Inspection Service
  (USPIS), 64
Post-feed-in tariff (FIT) solar
  power, 250, 254
Price fixing, 131–133

Public-private partnerships
  (PPPs), 113–114
Puerto Rico, 229–232
Putin, Vladimir, 295–296
Pyramid schemes, 188*t*, 194*t*
Python, Project, 70–73

Quebec, crypto mining in, 192–193

Rafael, Carlos, 131
Ransom payments, 94–95
"Recovery Roses" (NFT), 147*f*
Regulation of digital assets:
  and Bitcoin price volatility,
    45–49
  in Brazil, 188, 188*t*
  in Canada, 194, 195*t*
  in China, 283
  in European Union,
    266–268, 269*t*
  by FinCEN, 69–70
  in Germany, 205–206, 206*t*
  and ICOs, 29–31
  in Israel, 178, 178*t*
  in Japan, 251, 256*t*
  in Malta, 198–199, 199*t*
  in the Netherlands, 162, 162*t*
  in Nigeria, 310–311
  nonfungible tokens, 136–138
  in Portugal, 155, 157, 157*t*
  in Puerto Rico, 232
  in Russia, 304–306, 305*t*
  in Singapore, 226–227, 227*t*
  in South Africa, 165, 167, 167*t*
  in South Korea, 183, 183*t*
  in Switzerland, 172, 172*t*
  in Turkey, 220, 221*t*
  in United Arab Emirates,
    212, 213*t*
  in United States, 151–152, 152*t*

Renewable energy. *See also*
    Solarization (solar energy)
    in China, 280–281
    COP26 goals for, 338
    in India, 293
    in Puerto Rico, 229–230, 232
    in Russia, 298–299
    in United States, 239
Renewable Energy Directive,
    EU, 266–267
Renewable energy tokens, 186
Royal Dutch Shell, 321
Russia, 295–306
    carbon cap-and-trade
        program in, 333
    carbon emissions by, 317*t*
    central bank digital currencies
        in, 303–304
    digitalization of energy sector,
        296–298
    environmental tax policy in,
        302–304, 304*t*
    multinational stablecoin
        initiative of, 6, 166, 187,
        295–296, 302–304, 304*t*
    nonfungible tokens in, 301
    regulation of digital assets in,
        304–306, 305*t*
    sanctions against, 4, 151–152,
        194, 306
    solar energy and water pollution
        in, 298–300
    solar power satellite systems
        of, 300–301
Russian Association of
    Cryptocurrency and
    Blockchain, 298

St. John, 18
Samsung Group, 181–182

Saudi Arabia, 5, 56, 246, 319–320
Seafood industry, 124–133
Securities Exchange Act, 323
Self-control problems, planner-
    doer model for, 48–49
Senegal, 55
Services and Virtual Financial
    Asset Bill, 199
Shaw, David, 40
Silk Road (marketplace), 10, 73, 82,
    83, 85, 94
Singapore, 223–227
Six Digital Exchange (SDX), 171
Small Business Innovation
    Research (SBIR) grants, 115
Smart cities, 211, 261–263, 289–291
Smart contracts, 22
SoftBank Vision Fund, 246, 247
Solar Cities program, 290
Solarization (solar energy):
    in Africa, 311–312
    in China, 280–283
    of electric transportation,
        263–266
    in European Union, 259–260,
        263–266
    in India, 287–293
    in Japan, 245–251
    in Russia, 298–301
    in United Arab
        Emirates, 210–211
    in United States, 238–239
SolaRoad, 266
Solar power satellite (SPS) systems,
    239–241, 292, 300–301
Son, Masayoshi, 246
Soren Brothers, 144
Soros, George, 39–40, 53
South Africa, 309–310
    central bank digital currencies
        in, 303–304

South Africa (*Continued*)
  digital asset use and regulation
    in, 165–167
  digitalization of energy
    sector, 298
  Russia's stablecoin initiative, 6,
    56, 166, 187, 295–296
  solar power satellites of, 301
South Korea, 46, 181–183
Space power satellites,
  260–261, 281–282
Spain, 262
Special Economic Measures
  (Russia) Regulations,
  Canada, 194
Spreads, Bitcoin, 47–49
Stablecoins. *See also* Multinational
  stablecoin initiative of Russia
  in China, 4, 55, 272–273
  described, 51–52
  in Venezuela, 5, 55
State aid, in European
  Union, 267–268
Steinhardt, Michael, 39
Sub-Saharan Africa, 311–312
Subsidies, 243–244, 292–293,
  316, 319–320
Suex, 88–89
Supply chain management, 117–133
  in Australia, 119–120
  in Brazil, 120–123
  during COVID-19 pandemic,
    117–118, 124–127
  for meatpacking industry,
    117, 119–124
  price fixing and collusion,
    131–133
  for seafood industry, 124–133
  in United States, 118–119,
    123–124, 128–131

Sustainable blockchain development, xii, 2, 5–6, 237–342
  in Africa, 307–312
  carbon cap-and-trade programs
    and tokens for, 327–334
  and carbon emission report-
    ing, 315–326
  in China, 271–283
  in European Union, 259–269
  in Germany, 203
  in India, 287–293
  in Japan, 245–256
  in Russia, 295–306
  and UN COP26 goals, 337–342
  in United Arab Emirates, 209
  in United States, 237–244
Sustainable economic development, in Africa, 307
Sustainable nonfungible tokens,
  138–140, 146–148
SustVest, 210
Switzerland, 169–172

Tax credits, 243–244, 316, 319–320
Taxe 3, 60–61
Tax evasion, in United States,
  103–105, 130–131, 169
Tax policy, 60–61, 232, 254. *See also*
  Environmental tax policy
TeamLab, 252–253
Terror financing, 177*t*
Tether, 295
Tezos, 29, 139–140
Thailand, x, 83
Thaler, Richard H, 46–48
Theft hacking, 12–13, 93–94
  in Brazil, 188*t*
  in Canada, 194*t*
  in Germany, 205*t*
  in Japan, 251–252

in Malta, 198*t*
in the Netherlands,
  161–162, 162*t*
in Portugal, 157*t*
prosecution of, 82
in Puerto Rico, 232*t*
in Singapore, 226*t*
in South Africa, 167, 167*t*
in South Korea, 183*t*
in Switzerland, 171*t*
in Turkey, 220*t*
in United Arab Emirates, 212*t*
Theory of mental accounting,
  46–47
Tian Yinyin, 89
Toebbe, Jonathan, 107–108
Tokyo, Japan, 333
Tor (The Onion Router)
  browser, 66–67, 90
Tornado Crash, 12
TradeLens, 238
Transfer of Fund Regulation, EU,
  205–206
Tribe Accelerator, 224–225
Tuccillo, Roy, Sr. and Roy, Jr., 131
Tumblers, *see* Cryptocurrency
  tumblers and mixing
  services
Turkey, 45, 215–221

Ubin, Project, 225
Ukraine, 4
United Arab Emirates (UAE), 5,
  56, 209–213, 320
United Kingdom, x, 61, 83, 265
United Nations Climate Change
  Conference (COP26), 337–342
United Nations Economic
  Commission for Africa
  (UNECA), 308–309

United Nations Food and
  Agriculture
  Organization, 126, 132
United Nations Framework
  Convention on Climate
  Change (UNFCCC), 268. *See
  also* Paris Agreement
United Nations Sustainable
  Development Goals,
  146–148, 147*f*, 338
United States. *See also specific
  agencies*
  blockchain adoption in,
    111–115, 118–119, 237
  carbon cap-and-trade
    program in, 331
  carbon emissions by, 317*t*
  COVID-19 and seafood industry
    in, 127–128
  cybercrime task forces and
    policies, 69–79, 79*t*
  digital asset use in (*see specific
    types of assets and uses*)
  environmental tax policy
    of, 241–244
  ICO regulations in, 29–31
  internal carbon pricing in, 324
  investigations of illicit
    use of cryptocurrency
    in, 69–74
  monitoring of crypto tumblers/
    mixing services in, 61
  opioid and COVID-19 epidem-
    ics in, 63–64
  regulation of digital assets in,
    151–152, 152*t*
  solarization in, 238–239
  solar power satellites of, 239–241
  supply chain management in,
    118–119, 123–124, 128–131

United States (*Continued*)
sustainable blockchain development in, 237–244
tax evasion in, 103–105, 130–131, 169
tracking government funds and grants in, 123–124
US Department of Agriculture (USDA), 118–119, 128
US Department of Justice (DOJ), ix–xi, 1–2, 64, 76–78, 85, 88, 89, 94, 95, 101–104, 169
US Drug Enforcement Agency (DEA), x, 64, 65, 70–74
US Food and Drug Administration (FDA), 123–124, 128, 129
US Immigration and Customs Enforcement (ICE), xi, 61, 64, 75, 85
US Seafood Import Monitoring Program, 129
US Secret Service, xi, 76, 85
US Securities and Exchange Commission (SEC), 29–30, 42, 97, 104
US State Department, 113–114
US Treasury Department, 112–113. *See also* Financial Crimes Enforcement Network (FinCEN); Office of Foreign Assets Control (OFAC)
Universal Carbon (UPCO2) token, 329–330
Unmanned aerial vehicles (UAVs), 176–177, 291–292
Utherverse.io, 204
Utility settlement coins, 52–53

Valuation:
of Bitcoin, ix, 1, 37

of Ether, 21, 37
for initial coin offerings, 28
of nonfungible tokens, 137–138, 137*f*, 138*f*
VeChain, 282–283
Venezuela, 5, 45, 55
Vinnik, Alexander, xi, 85–86, 88
Virtual currency prediction markets, 33
Volatility of cryptocurrency:
and adoption in Turkey, 215, 217–218
altcoins, 51–56
and China's Bitcoin ban, 16
hedging Bitcoin investments, 37–43
initial coin offerings, 27–31
investors' and regulators' reactions to, 45–49
and new financial alternatives, 27–31

Wallets, Bitcoin, 11–14
Water pollution, 299–301
WePower, 249
Wertkin, Jeffrey, 101–102
Whitepapers, ICO, 27
World Economic Forum, xii, 2
Worldwide asset eXchange (WAX) platform, 147–148
Xapo, 13
XBT Provider, 42–43

Yard (NFT artist), 156–157
Yuan, digital, 5–6, 55

Zimbabwe, 45
ZKM Centre for Art and Media, 203
Znamya project, 300–301

\